_p_

THE PATH

A JOURNEY THROUGH THE BIBLE

D0063035

Library of Congress Cataloging-In-Publication Data

Names: Wilson Shobe, Melody, commentator. | Creech, David, commentator.

Title: The path : a journey through the Bible / edited by Melody Wilson Shobe and David Creech ; iIllustrations by Roger Speer.

Description: First edition. | Cincinnati : Forward Movement, 2016.

Identifiers: LCCN 2016024172 (print) | LCCN 2016024492 (ebook) | ISBN 9780880284356 (book : alk. paper) | ISBN 9780880284356 ()

Subjects: LCSH: Bible--Criticism, interpretation, etc.

Classification: LCC BS191.5.A1 2016 .C56 2016 (print) | LCC BS191.5.A1 2016 (ebook) | DDC 220.5/20436--dc23

LC record available at https://lccn.loc.gov/2016024172

ISBN: 9780880284356

Printed in USA

Praise for *The Path: A Journey through the Bible*

This accessible journey through the Good Book reclaims the Bible as a grand story, from God's creation to Christ's return, and returns us again and again to its central questions of love, sin, and redemption. *The Path* is a perfect entry point for people who want to know more about the Bible but don't know where to start.

—Jana Riess
Author of *Flunking Sainthood* and
*The Twible: All the Chapters of the Bible
in 140 Characters or Less,
Now with 68% More Humor!*

For those of us who are hungry for the Bible, editors Melody Wilson Shobe and David Creech not only give us meat, but they also cut it up for us. Simplified, yes. Dumbed down, not at all. *The Path* is practical and accessible—a terrific resource in an attention-challenged world.

—Chris Yaw
Founder, Church*Next*

Taking its cue from the world of hiking, *The Path* is a wonderful resource for those who want to explore—or re-explore—the overarching story of the Bible. The selected passages offer a perfect overview of the Bible's contents, without becoming overwhelming. The notes provide helpful information, without taking away from the story.

The book is perfect for a lone traveler into the text of the Bible or for a small-group expedition. *The Path* is one of the best ways to familiarize yourself with the rich and life-changing message of the Bible that I've ever seen.

—Roy L. Heller
Perkins School of Theology,
Southern Methodist University

—THE—
PATH

A JOURNEY THROUGH THE BIBLE

Melody Wilson Shobe, Editor

David Creech, New Testament Editor

Forward Movement
Cincinnati, Ohio

Table of Contents

About this Book

The Bible is everywhere.

Many of us learned about it first as children, hunched over desks, decorating coloring pages in our Sunday School classrooms. The stories we heard were mostly the ones with animals—Noah and the ark; Daniel in the lions' den; Mary, pregnant with Jesus, making the journey to Bethlehem on a donkey. We colored the pages and soaked in the stories, and they settled somewhere deep inside us.

But, of course, the Bible isn't only for children. In churches of every stripe, people gather each Sunday to hear sections of scripture read aloud. We welcome the verses with singing or silence or incense. We bow our heads or raise our hands. We proclaim after hearing the passages that they are "The Word of the Lord." These bits of the Bible, read and sung and preached, also find their way into our hearts and minds.

And we don't only have exposure to Bibles in church. The Bible is the greatest-selling book of all time. In fact, the American Bible Society reports that 88 percent of households in the United States own at least one Bible—and the average household has not one, not two, but four Bibles.

Even if you have never set foot in a church, and even if you don't have a Bible in your house, you still know about the Bible.

The Bible is the subject of much of the greatest art of all time: The stories of the Bible are painted in glory and splendor across the vast expanse of the Sistine Chapel, captured in light and shadow by the deft hand of Rembrandt, told by bits of jewel-colored glass in synagogue and church windows constructed across hundreds of years and around the world.

We find the Bible nestled in the pages of literature. It is explicit in the works of the great masters: Dante's *Divine Comedy*, Milton's *Paradise Lost*, Steinbeck's *East of Eden*, Faulkner's *The Sound and the Fury*, and many more. But the Bible's themes and references run much deeper than that. You can find them in Lewis's *Chronicles of Narnia*, L'Engle's *A Wrinkle in Time*, in Rowling's *Harry Potter* series, in the works of Stephen King and in dozens upon dozens of other books, from high literature to bestselling page-turners.

The Bible also finds its way onto the silver screen. You can see it in biblical epics like *The Ten Commandments*, *The Passion of the Christ*, or *Noah*. And you can hear its words in much more unlikely places: *Pulp Fiction*, *Saving Private Ryan*, *The Shawshank Redemption*, *Wedding Crashers*, *Life of Brian*, and hundreds of other famous movies all reference and explore parts of the Bible.

Yes, the Bible is everywhere.

Yet in spite of (or maybe because of) its prevalence, most of us don't really know the Bible. Although we have a lot of Bibles in our houses, and we've read and watched and heard a lot of things *about* the Bible, most of us have never read the Bible.

The truth is, we are intimidated. Opening the Bible and trying to read it feels like being dropped off without a map in the middle of a remote wilderness. We know certain major landmarks: Moses and the Ten Commandments, Jonah and the whale, Jesus walking on water, but when we are down in the weeds, we can't see how the stories connect to one another. We want to read the Bible, but we aren't quite sure how to navigate its pages. We search for God in the midst of the Bible, but we aren't sure which direction to turn. We yearn to follow Jesus more closely, but we don't know where to start that journey or how to get to the trailhead.

The Path: A Journey through the Bible is an opportunity to walk through the Bible in an easy and accessible format. *The Path* is the story of the Bible, excerpted and condensed so that it is easier to read. In the pages of this book, we have laid out a clear trail, an easy-to-follow pathway, so that you can journey from one Bible story to the next and see how they connect to each other. As you read through *The Path*, you will see all of the major landmarks of the Bible's story—and you will walk in the footsteps of faithful men and women who have done their best to follow God's call. By reading *The Path*, you will journey through the Bible step-by-step, experiencing an amazing 360-degree overview of the vast, sweeping story of God's extraordinary love for ordinary people.

Inside the gilded-edge pages of the Bible, underneath that intimidating cover, between and through those lists of hard-to-pronounce names, in the midst of that wilderness of words is an incredible, epic story. It is the story of God's extraordinary love that overflowed into the creation of the world, the earth, and all that is in it, including humanity. It is the story of God's relentless, unwavering, unstoppable love for his people, people who are flawed and funny and ordinary, just like you and me. It is the story of the journey of all-too-ordinary people who have tried, sometimes with glorious success and sometimes with abject failure, to respond to God's love. It's the story of how God keeps trying to call us back to him, even when we have wandered and strayed from the path. It's the story of how, in the fullness of time, God came among us, love incarnate, in the person of Jesus Christ, to show us how to walk through this world with love and compassion. It's the story of Jesus' life, of his death, and of his resurrection. The Bible is the story of the founding of the Church, the followers of Jesus in the world, the people of the Way, proclaiming Christ's word and continuing his work. It's the story of you and me, the descendants of these flawed, broken, and beautiful characters, the inheritors of the promise of God.

The Path is an invitation to journey through the Bible, to walk through this wilderness of words and see God revealed in them and hear God speaking through them. So let's get started on this epic adventure: a journey through the Bible to grow closer to God!

FORMAT OF THE BOOK

Although it looks like a regular book, *The Path* is the Bible. All of the regular text in this book is directly from the New Revised Standard Version of the Bible. It is not a summary of the Bible, our interpretation of the Bible, or a story about the Bible. It is the Bible. On very rare occasions, we substituted a noun for a pronoun for the sake of clarity; these are noted in brackets. Other than that, the biblical text has not been edited or amended in any way, so that most of what you are reading in *The Path* is the Bible itself.

But, of course, *The Path* is not the entire Bible. Instead, it is *excerpts* from the Bible, selected texts that cover most of the "great landmarks" from the Bible's story. This is intended to give you an idea of the overarching narrative, the sweeping story of God's great love for us. As you read this book, you will be walking, in roughly chronological order, through most of the major moments of the biblical narrative. This journey gives you a sense of how the smaller stories of the Bible, some that are familiar and some that might be surprising, fit together to tell a bigger story. You might notice another difference between *The Path* and the Bible: There are no verse numbers. We wanted you to read the *The Path* excerpts in a narrative form, as stories without interruption. At the end of each chapter, there is a list of citations, so that you will know exactly which parts of the Bible you have been reading

In between the long selections of the Bible, you will see small paragraphs that are written in italics. The italicized text in this book is summary, written by the editors. We use these paragraphs to give you an overview of what is happening in the biblical text that was omitted. Think of these paragraphs as a kind of "shortcut;" they enable us to bypass some of the more lengthy sections of the Bible, so we can keep walking to the important landmarks. These brief paragraphs of explanation help connect the individual components of the narrative. In writing these summaries, we have tried to stick as closely as possible to the words of the Bible itself, without adding a lot of interpretation or our own ideas. Of course, any excerpt or summary is an interpretation, but we have tried to be as unbiased as possible.

In addition to the summaries, text boxes with notes offer additional information. "Point of Interest" boxes explain a word or a term that might be confusing or highlight an important element that might be easy to miss. "Scenic View" boxes give a bit of history or background, so that you can better see the big picture of the Bible's story. "You Are Here" boxes invite readers to find themselves in the story, to connect the ancient scripture to modern life. "Trail Crossing" boxes point out connections to other parts of the biblical story. These notes are not meant to be exhaustive but are simply a chance to learn more as you read along. These text boxes function like a trail map, giving you a bit more information about the things that you are passing as you journey through the Bible.

At the end of each chapter, a list of questions presents an opportunity to wrestle with the biblical text and see what it is saying to you. If you are reading this book as part of a class or small group, you can use the questions for group discussion. If you are reading this book on your own, you can use them as a starting point for prayer, reflection, or journaling. Each chapter also includes suggestions for next steps. These prompts provide even more ways for you to engage the story from the chapter. Some involve reading parts of the Bible that were skipped;

others give ideas for prayer or action. The questions and next steps are an important part of continuing your journey of faith beyond the pages of the Bible, so that you can follow Jesus more closely in your daily life.

HOW TO USE THIS BOOK

The Path is yours, to read, to study, and (hopefully) to enjoy. This is a chance to walk with and through the scriptures on your journey of faith. It is an opportunity to explore the path that leads us into deeper relationship with Jesus Christ. There is no wrong way to read this book. However, we do have some ideas for how you might get the most out of reading this incredible story.

If you are reading *The Path* on your own, you might choose to sit down and read it straight through, as you would any regular book. The Bible is just as exciting as any soap opera or bestselling novel; it's full of suspense, drama, love, and even humor! Reading *The Path* as you would any ordinary book can give you an opportunity to be swept up in the story and to hear how all the pieces of the story fit together like a puzzle to give us an even bigger picture of God's love.

Alternatively, you might want to take time to savor and study this story, to take a stroll, rather than hike all day. If so, you might decide to read *The Path* one chapter a day or one chapter a week until you have finished. If you choose this approach, utilize the reflection questions at the end of each chapter, taking time to think, pray, or write about them.

The Path is also designed for group use. Companions make every journey more fun, and this journey is no exception. *The Path* would make an ideal small-group study. Your group could read a chapter at a time and gather weekly to talk about the questions for the journey together. A group study is a wonderful way to explore this story in companionship with others and learn together what God might be saying to you, both as individuals and as a community, through this epic adventure.

Finally, *The Path* can be used as a companion to a curriculum offered by Forward Movement called *Living Discipleship: Exploring the Bible*. This course is a year-long exploration of the Bible, with twenty-six sessions that tell the overarching biblical narrative, from Genesis to Revelation. Designed for use in weekly formation time, each session is approximately an hour long. With twenty-six sessions, this means that *Exploring the Bible* is intended to function as the formation curriculum in a church for an entire program year—either on Sundays or another day of the week. There is a companion book for children, *The Path: Family Storybook*, so that children, youth, and adults can hear the same stories and walk together through the narrative of God's great love. And *Pathways of Faith* is an all-ages coloring book with original illustrations for each of the chapters, creating an opportunity to engage scripture with your creative mind.

However you choose to use *The Path*, we pray that you hear God speaking to you through this story—and as you journey, discover that it is God's story of love for you.

WHAT WAS INCLUDED IN THIS BOOK (AND WHAT WAS LEFT OUT!)

Excerpting the Bible is no easy task, and it was incredibly difficult to decide which parts of the Bible would be included in *The Path* and what would be left out. As you read through this book, you will likely notice some familiar (and important) stories that are missing. We had to leave many of our favorite stories and verses on the cutting room floor! That does not mean those stories aren't important, but simply that we did not have space for them in this book. Here are the guidelines we used in deciding what to keep in and what to cut out.

- Our most important goal in this book was to tell the overarching story of the Bible: from God's creation of the world, to God's relationship with Abraham and his descendants, through God's incarnation in Jesus Christ, and in God's presence in the spread of the Church. In order to make that story comprehensible, we had to emphasize parts of the Bible that are narrative, or story based, and sometimes leave out parts of the Bible that are more teaching or instruction based. Those teachings are still important, but if we had included all of the laws of Leviticus or all of the minute instructions of Paul, we wouldn't have been able to keep *The Path* short and readable!

- We felt it was important to include most of the highlights and best-known Bible stories. We asked a wide variety of people for input on what they thought were the "landmark" stories of salvation history. Those lists typically included things like: Creation, Noah, the Exodus, David and Goliath, prophecies from Isaiah, Jesus' birth, death, and resurrection, and Paul's conversion. We also looked at the Revised Common Lectionary, the assigned readings for the year read aloud in many churches, and especially at the stories that are included as part of the Easter Vigil's stories of salvation. We used those texts as a starting point for the key stories that needed to be included in this book so that readers would get a sense of the main parts of the Bible and how they fit together.

- We wanted to capture the Bible in all of its beauty, complexity, and difficulty. We did *not* want to omit things simply because they are hard to read or challenge us. For example, the stories of Joshua, with violence that can be difficult to read and understand, is an important part of the story of God and God's people.

The notes and questions aim to help you engage those difficult texts.

Our hope is that *The Path* is just a starting point: this is an introductory foray into the story of God's great love for you. And after you have walked this path and learned the terrain, we hope that you will want to return to this beautiful landscape again and again. We hope that this guided hike along *The Path* will ignite your passion and give you the confidence to journey on new and different trails, through the entire Bible, so that you will explore and discover anew the extraordinary story of God's love for you.

1

God Saw That It Was Good

CREATION

In the beginning when God created the heavens and the earth, the earth was a formless void and darkness covered the face of the deep, while a wind from God swept over the face of the waters. Then God said, "Let there be light;" and there was light. And God saw that the light was good; and God separated the light from the darkness. God called the light Day, and the darkness he called Night. And there was evening and there was morning, the first day.

And God said, "Let there be a dome in the midst of the waters, and let it separate the waters from the waters." So God made the dome and separated the waters that were under the dome from the waters that were above the dome. And it was so. God called the dome Sky. And there was evening and there was morning, the second day.

And God said, "Let the waters under the sky be gathered together into one place, and let the dry land appear." And it was so. God called the dry land Earth, and the waters that were gathered together he called Seas. And God saw that it was good. Then God said, "Let the earth put forth vegetation: plants yielding seed, and fruit trees of every kind on earth that bear fruit with the seed in it." And it was so. The earth brought forth vegetation: plants yielding seed of every kind, and trees of every kind bearing fruit with the seed in it. And God saw that it was good. And there was evening and there was morning, the third day.

And God said, "Let there be lights in the dome of the sky to separate the day from the night; and let them be for signs and for seasons and for days and years, and let them be lights in the dome of the sky to give light upon the earth." And it was so. God made the two great lights—the greater light to rule the day and the lesser light to rule the night—and the stars. God set them in the dome of the sky to give light upon the earth, to rule over the day and over the night, and to separate the light from the darkness. And God saw that it was good. And there was evening and there was morning, the fourth day.

And God said, "Let the waters bring forth swarms of living creatures, and let birds fly above the earth across the dome of the sky." So God created the great sea monsters and every living creature that moves, of every kind, with which the waters swarm, and every winged bird of every kind. And God saw that it was good. God blessed them, saying, "Be fruitful and multiply and fill the waters in the seas, and let birds multiply on the earth." And there was evening and there was morning, the fifth day.

And God said, "Let the earth bring forth living creatures of every kind: cattle and creeping things and wild animals of the earth of every kind." And it was so. God made the wild animals of the earth of every kind, and the cattle of every kind, and everything that creeps upon the ground of every kind. And God saw that it was good.

Then God said, "Let us make humankind in our image, according to our likeness; and let them have dominion over the fish of the sea, and over the birds of the air, and over the cattle, and over all the wild animals of the earth, and over every creeping thing that creeps upon the earth."

So God created humankind in his image,
  in the image of God he created them;
  male and female he created them.

God blessed them, and God said to them, "Be fruitful and multiply, and fill the earth and subdue it; and have dominion over the fish of the sea and over the birds of the air and over every living thing that moves upon the earth." God said, "See, I have given you every plant yielding seed that is upon the face of all the earth, and every tree with seed in its fruit; you shall have them for food. And to every beast of the earth, and to every bird of the air, and to everything that creeps on the earth, everything that has the breath of life, I have given every green plant for food." And it was so. God saw everything that he had made, and indeed, it was very good. And there was evening and there was morning, the sixth day.

> **POINT OF INTEREST**
> On the sixth day of creation, things are described as "very good." What makes this day different?

Thus the heavens and the earth were finished, and all their multitude. And on the seventh day God finished the work that he had done, and he rested on the seventh day from all the work that he had done. So God blessed the seventh day and hallowed it, because on it God rested from all the work that he had done in creation.

These are the generations of the heavens and the earth when they were created.

THE GARDEN OF EDEN

In the day that the Lord God made the earth and the heavens, when no plant of the field was yet in the earth and no herb of the field had yet sprung up—for the Lord God had not caused it to rain upon the earth, and there was no one to till the ground; but a stream would rise from the earth, and water the whole face of the ground— then the Lord God formed man from the dust of the ground, and breathed into his nostrils the breath of life; and the man became a living being. And the Lord God planted a garden in Eden, in the east; and there he put the man whom he had formed. Out of the ground the Lord God made to grow every tree that is pleasant to the sight and good for food, the tree of life also in the midst of the garden, and the tree of the knowledge of good and evil.

SCENIC VIEW

Genesis 2 offers a slightly different version of the story of creation. Read carefully and try to notice the differences in emphasis and order.

The Lord God took the man and put him in the garden of Eden to till it and keep it. And the Lord God commanded the man, "You may freely eat of every tree of the garden; but of the tree of the knowledge of good and evil you shall not eat, for in the day that you eat of it you shall die." Then the Lord God said, "It is not good that the man should be alone; I will make him a helper as his partner." So out of the ground the Lord God formed every animal of the field and every bird of the air, and brought them to the man to see what he would call them; and whatever the man called every living creature, that was its name. The man gave names to all cattle, and to the birds of the air, and to every animal of the field; but for the man there was not found a helper as his partner. So the Lord God caused a deep sleep to fall upon the man, and he slept; then he took one of his ribs and closed up its place with flesh. And the rib that the Lord God had taken from the man he made into a woman and brought her to the man. Then the man said,

"This at last is bone of my bones
and flesh of my flesh;
this one shall be called Woman,
for out of Man this one was taken."

Therefore a man leaves his father and his mother and clings to his wife, and they become one flesh. And the man and his wife were both naked, and were not ashamed.

THE PEOPLE'S DISOBEDIENCE

Now the serpent was more crafty than any other wild animal that the Lord God had made. He said to the woman, "Did God say, 'You shall not eat from any tree in the garden'?" The woman said to the serpent, "We may eat of the fruit of the trees in the garden; but God said, 'You shall not eat of the fruit of the tree that is in the middle of the garden, nor shall you touch it, or you shall die.'" But the serpent said to the woman, "You will not die; for God knows that when you eat of it your eyes will be opened, and you will be like God, knowing good and evil." So when the woman saw that the tree was good for food, and that it was a delight to the eyes, and that the tree was to be desired to make one wise, she took of its fruit and ate; and she also gave some to her husband, who was with her, and he ate. Then the eyes of both were opened, and they knew that they were naked; and they sewed fig leaves together and made loincloths for themselves.

> **YOU ARE HERE**
> The serpent changes the words of God just a bit. Look back at the previous page to see exactly what God says about the tree. How do the serpent's words compare with what God says to the man? What might this say to us about listening carefully to God?

They heard the sound of the Lord God walking in the garden at the time of the evening breeze, and the man and his wife hid themselves from the presence of the Lord God among the trees of the garden. But the Lord God called to the man, and said to him, "Where are you?" He said, "I heard the sound of you in the garden, and I was afraid, because I was naked; and I hid myself." He said, "Who told you that you were naked? Have you eaten from the tree of which I commanded you not to eat?" The man said, "The woman whom you gave to be with me, she gave me fruit from the tree, and I ate." Then the Lord God said to the woman, "What is this that you have done?" The woman said, "The serpent tricked me, and I ate."

The Lord God said to the serpent,
"Because you have done this,
    cursed are you among all animals
    and among all wild creatures;
upon your belly you shall go,
    and dust you shall eat
    all the days of your life.

I will put enmity between you and the woman,
    and between your offspring and hers;
he will strike your head,
    and you will strike his heel."

To the woman [God] said,
"I will greatly increase your pangs in childbearing;
    in pain you shall bring forth children,
yet your desire shall be for your husband,
    and he shall rule over you."

And to the man [God] said,
"Because you have listened to the voice of your wife,
    and have eaten of the tree
about which I commanded you,
    'You shall not eat of it,'
cursed is the ground because of you;
    in toil you shall eat of it all the days of your life;

thorns and thistles it shall bring forth for you;
  and you shall eat the plants of the field.
By the sweat of your face
  you shall eat bread
until you return to the ground,
  for out of it you were taken;
you are dust,
  and to dust you shall return."

The man named his wife Eve, because she was the mother of all living. And the Lord God made garments of skins for the man and for his wife, and clothed them.

Then the Lord God said, "See, the man has become like one of us, knowing good and evil; and now, he might reach out his hand and take also from the tree of life, and eat, and live forever"—therefore the Lord God sent him forth from the garden of Eden, to till the ground from which he was taken. He drove out the man; and at the east of the garden of Eden he placed the cherubim, and a sword flaming and turning to guard the way to the tree of life.

> **YOU ARE HERE**
> When God asks the man and the woman about their behavior, the first thing they do is try to shift responsibility by blaming others. Does this resonate with your life?

SCRIPTURE CITATIONS
GENESIS 1:1-2:9 | 2:15—3:24

QUESTIONS FOR THE JOURNEY

1. The Bible tells the story of creation in two different ways. What might this tell us about the nature of creation? What might it tell us about the Bible?

2. According to Genesis 2, the human is put in the garden with a purpose: to till it and keep it. What does this suggest about the relationship between humans and the earth? What does this passage suggest about the relationship between humans and animals?

3. Before God sends the people out of the garden, he makes clothes for them. How does this act of tenderness relate to the punishment immediately preceding? What might we learn about God from this action?

4. Sin is often defined as "separation from God." Although the word sin doesn't appear in the Bible until later, Adam and Eve's actions in this story are traditionally seen as the entrance of sin into the world. What does this story reveal about the nature and impact of sin?

5. In this chapter, we hear the Bible's story of how the world began. How might this story complement and enhance scientific explanations for the origin of the universe?

NEXT STEPS

- We have another account of creation in the Bible: It's in the Gospel of John. Read John 1 in the Bible. What connections do you see between John 1 and Genesis 1?

- Look at the two stories in this chapter about the creation of humans, and pay careful attention to the words used. What does each story tell us about what humans are like? What is their relationship to God? What is their relationship to one another?

2

The Sign of the Covenant

CAIN AND ABEL

Now the man knew his wife Eve, and she conceived and bore Cain, saying, "I have produced a man with the help of the Lord." Next she bore his brother Abel. Now Abel was a keeper of sheep, and Cain a tiller of the ground. In the course of time Cain brought to the Lord an offering of the fruit of the ground, and Abel for his part brought of the firstlings of his flock, their fat portions. And the Lord had regard for Abel and his offering, but for Cain and his offering he had no regard. So Cain was very angry, and his countenance fell. The Lord said to Cain, "Why are you angry, and why has your countenance fallen? If you do well, will you not be accepted? And if you do not do well, sin is lurking at the door; its desire is for you, but you must master it."

> **SCENIC VIEW**
> The story doesn't tell us why God didn't regard Cain's offering, though scholars have all sorts of different ideas. Instead, God focuses on Cain's response to what has happened, rather than the reason for it.

Cain said to his brother Abel, "Let us go out to the field." And when they were in the field, Cain rose up against his brother

Abel, and killed him. Then the Lord said to Cain, "Where is your brother Abel?" He said, "I do not know; am I my brother's keeper?" And the Lord said, "What have you done? Listen; your brother's blood is crying out to me from the ground! And now you are cursed from the ground, which has opened its mouth to receive your brother's blood from your hand. When you till the ground, it will no longer yield to you its strength; you will be a fugitive and a wanderer on the earth." Cain said to the Lord, "My punishment is greater than I can bear! Today you have driven me away from the soil, and I shall be hidden from your face; I shall be a fugitive and a wanderer on the earth, and anyone who meets me may kill me." Then the Lord said to him, "Not so! Whoever kills Cain will suffer a sevenfold vengeance." And the Lord put a mark on Cain, so that no one who came upon him would kill him. Then Cain went away from the presence of the Lord, and settled in the land of Nod, east of Eden.

So Cain and his wife had children and their children had children, and their descendants spread, raising livestock, playing music, and developing tools: forming the basis of civilization. And Adam and Eve had another child, whom they named Seth, and Seth had children, and his children had children, and his descendants spread over the earth. When God created humankind, he made them in the likeness of God. Male and female he created them, and he blessed them and named them "Humankind" when they were created. But people failed to live as though they were created in the image of God. Instead of living lives of love and goodness and mercy, they engaged in violence and wickedness and evil.

NOAH AND THE ARK

The Lord saw that the wickedness of humankind was great in the earth, and that every inclination of the thoughts of their hearts was only evil continually. And the Lord was sorry that he had made humankind on the earth, and it grieved him to his heart. So the Lord said, "I will blot out from the earth the human beings I have created—people together with animals and creeping things and birds of the air, for I am sorry that I have made them." But Noah found favor in the sight of the Lord.

YOU ARE HERE
Wickedness and evil grieve God "to his heart." What are some of the things in the world today that you think might grieve the heart of God? Spend some time in prayer about those things.

And God said to Noah, "I have determined to make an end of all flesh, for the earth is filled with violence because of them; now I am going to destroy them along with the earth. Make yourself an ark of cypress wood; make rooms in the ark, and cover it inside and out with pitch. This is how you are to make it: the length of the ark three hundred cubits, its width fifty cubits, and its height thirty cubits. Make a roof for the ark, and finish it to a cubit above; and put the door of the ark in its side; make it with lower, second, and third decks. For my part, I am going to bring a flood of waters on the earth, to destroy from under heaven all flesh in which is the breath of life; everything that is on the earth shall die. But I will establish my covenant with you; and you shall come into the ark, you, your sons, your wife, and your sons' wives with you. And of every living thing, of all flesh, you shall bring two of every kind into the ark, to keep them alive with you; they shall be male and female. Of the birds according to their kinds, and of the animals according to their kinds, of every creeping thing of the ground according to its kind, two of every kind shall come in to you, to keep them alive. Also take with you every kind of food that is eaten, and store it up; and it shall serve as food for you and for them." Noah did this; he did all that God commanded him.

And Noah with his sons and his wife and his sons' wives went into the ark to escape the waters of the flood. Of clean animals, and of animals that are not clean, and of birds, and of everything that creeps on the ground, two and two, male and female, went into the ark with Noah, as God had commanded Noah. And after seven days the waters of the flood came on the earth. The flood continued forty days on the earth; and the waters increased, and bore up the ark, and it rose high above the earth. The waters swelled and increased greatly on the earth; and the ark floated on the face of the waters. The waters swelled so mightily on the earth that all the high mountains under the whole heaven were covered; the waters swelled above the mountains, covering them fifteen cubits deep. And all flesh died that moved on the earth, birds, domestic animals, wild animals, all swarming creatures that swarm on the earth, and all human beings; everything on dry land in whose nostrils was the breath of life died.

But God remembered Noah and all the wild animals and all the domestic animals that were with him in the ark. And God made a wind blow over the earth, and the waters subsided; the fountains of the deep and the windows of the heavens were closed, the rain from the heavens was restrained, and the waters gradually receded from the earth. At the end of forty days Noah opened the window of the ark that he had made and sent out the raven; and it went to and fro until the waters were dried up from the earth. Then he sent out the dove from him, to see if the waters had subsided from the face of the ground; but the dove found no place to set its foot, and it returned to him to the ark, for the waters were still on the face of the whole earth. So he put out his hand and took it and brought it into the ark with him. He waited another seven days, and again he sent out the dove from the ark; and the dove came back to him in the evening, and there in its beak was a freshly plucked olive leaf; so Noah knew that the waters had subsided from the earth. Then he waited another seven days, and sent out the dove; and it did not return to him any more.

In the six hundred first year, in the first month, on the first day of the month, the waters were dried up from the earth; and

Noah removed the covering of the ark, and looked, and saw that the face of the ground was drying. In the second month, on the twenty-seventh day of the month, the earth was dry. Then God said to Noah, "Go out of the ark, you and your wife, and your sons and your sons' wives with you. Bring out with you every living thing that is with you of all flesh—birds and animals and every creeping thing that creeps on the earth—so that they may abound on the earth, and be fruitful and multiply on the earth." So Noah went out with his sons and his wife and his sons' wives. And every animal, every creeping thing, and every bird, everything that moves on the earth, went out of the ark by families.

AFTER THE FLOOD

Then Noah built an altar to the Lord, and took of every clean animal and of every clean bird, and offered burnt offerings on the altar. And when the Lord smelled the pleasing odor, the Lord said in his heart, "I will never again curse the ground because of humankind, for the inclination of the human heart is evil from youth; nor will I ever again destroy every living creature as I have done.

> **YOU ARE HERE**
> The first thing that Noah does when he leaves the ark is to build an altar and make an offering to God. What might Noah's response teach us?

As long as the earth endures,
>> seedtime and harvest, cold and heat,
> summer and winter, day and night,
>>> shall not cease."

God blessed Noah and his sons, and said to them, "Be fruitful and multiply, and fill the earth. As for me, I am establishing my covenant with you and your descendants after you, and with every living creature that is with you, the birds, the domestic animals, and every animal of the earth with you, as many as came out of the ark. I establish my covenant with you, that never again shall all flesh be cut off by the waters of a flood,

POINT OF INTEREST

A covenant is a binding legal agreement between two parties, where each one makes promises to the other. This is the first of the covenants God makes in the Bible, often called the Noahic covenant. In addition to Noah, who does God make this covenant with?

and never again shall there be a flood to destroy the earth." God said, "This is the sign of the covenant that I make between me and you and every living creature that is with you, for all future generations: I have set my bow in the clouds, and it shall be a sign of the covenant between me and the earth. When I bring clouds over the earth and the bow is seen in the clouds, I will remember my covenant that is between me and you and every living creature of all flesh; and the waters shall never again become a flood to destroy all flesh. When the bow is in the clouds, I will see it and remember the everlasting covenant between God and every living creature of all flesh that is on the earth." God said to Noah, "This is the sign of the covenant that I have established between me and all flesh that is on the earth." The sons of Noah who went out of the ark were Shem, Ham, and Japheth. Ham was the father of Canaan. These three were the sons of Noah; and from these the whole earth was peopled.

THE TOWER OF BABEL

Now the whole earth had one language and the same words. And as they migrated from the east, they came upon a plain in the land of Shinar and settled there. And they said to one another, "Come, let us make bricks, and burn them thoroughly." And they had brick for stone, and bitumen for mortar. Then they said, "Come, let us build ourselves a city, and a tower with its top in the heavens, and let us make a name for ourselves; otherwise we shall be scattered abroad upon the face of the whole earth." The Lord came down to see the city and the tower, which mortals had built. And the Lord said, "Look, they are one people, and they have all one language; and this is only the beginning of what they will do; nothing that they propose to do will now be impossible for them. Come, let us go down, and confuse their language there, so that they will not understand one another's speech." So the Lord scattered them abroad from there over the face of all the earth, and they left off building the city. Therefore it was called Babel, because there the Lord confused the language of all the earth; and from there the Lord scattered them abroad over the face of all the earth.

So Noah's sons and their wives had children, and once again people spread over the face of the earth. From Noah's descendants came a variety of nations, people who founded cities and civilizations and from whom arose different languages and customs. And one of Noah's descendants, the great-great-great-great-great-great-great-great grandson of Shem, was a man named Terah.

Now these are the descendants of Terah. Terah was the father of Abram, Nahor, and Haran; and Haran was the father of Lot. Haran died before his father Terah in the land of his birth, in Ur of the Chaldeans. Abram and Nahor took wives; the name of Abram's wife was Sarai, and the name of Nahor's wife was Milcah. She was the daughter of Haran the father of Milcah and Iscah. Now Sarai was barren; she had no child.

Terah took his son Abram and his grandson Lot son of Haran, and his daughter-in-law Sarai, his son Abram's wife, and they went out together from Ur of the Chaldeans to go into the land of Canaan; but when they came to Haran, they settled there. The days of Terah were two hundred five years; and Terah died in Haran.

And Terah's son Abram survived him, living on in Haran.

Scripture Citations
GENESIS 4:1-16 | 5:1b-2 | 6:5-8, 13-22 | 7:7-10, 17-22 |
8:1-3a, 6-22 | 9:1, 9-19 | 11:1-9, 27-32

QUESTIONS FOR THE JOURNEY

1. Cain and Abel is the first of many stories in the Bible of sibling conflict. Why do you think this might be?

2. The story of Noah is often told as a children's story, yet it has some difficult parts. What do you notice about this story, reading it again? Which parts are difficult for you? Which parts sound like good news?

3. These stories balance God's punishment with God's mercy: God punishes Cain yet also protects him; God destroys nearly all living creatures but saves Noah and a pair of each species of animal. What do these things tell us about God? How do you understand the relationship between God's judgment and God's mercy?

4. In this story, God's anger at humanity has implications for the animals and all of creation; the animals die alongside the wicked people. God's final covenant is also with "every living creature." What might these things tell us about the relationship between God, humanity, and creation?

NEXT STEPS

- When Noah and his family finally return to dry land, the first thing they do is build an altar and make offerings to God. Sit down and make a list of blessings that you have received from God and times when God has been especially present with you. Spend some time in prayer, reflecting on what kind of offering you might be called to make to God in thanksgiving for all that you have received.

- The story of the Tower of Babel is usually read on the feast of Pentecost. Read the story of Pentecost in Acts 2:1-13. How is that story related to the Tower of Babel?

3

The Ancestor of a Multitude

GOD CALLS ABRAM

Now the Lord said to Abram, "Go from your country and your kindred and your father's house to the land that I will show you. I will make of you a great nation, and I will bless you, and make your name great, so that you will be a blessing. I will bless those who bless you, and the one who curses you I will curse; and in you all the families of the earth shall be blessed." So Abram went, as the Lord had told him; and Lot went with him. Abram was seventy-five years old when he departed from Haran. Abram took his wife Sarai and his brother's son Lot, and all the possessions that they had gathered, and the persons whom they had acquired in Haran; and they set forth to go to the land of Canaan.

Abram continued on, journeying as God had commanded. Along the way, Abram and Lot separated—Lot chose to head eastward, toward the Jordan river, near Sodom and Gomorrah, and Abram settled in the land of Canaan. Now, Abram was usually faithful, but even he had doubts. Twice he doubted the protection of God, and pretended that Sarai was his sister, instead of his wife, in order to protect her. And more than once he questioned God's promise. How could he and his descendants live in a land that was already occupied by others? How could he and Sarai even have descendants, when Sarai was barren and they were both growing old? But again and again, in spite of the hardships they faced, the Lord reiterated his promise to Abram, saying:

"Raise your eyes now, and look from the place where you are, northward and southward and eastward and westward; for all the land that you see I will give to you and to your offspring forever. I will make your offspring like the dust of the earth; so that if one can count the dust of the earth, your offspring also can be counted. Rise up, walk through the length and the breadth of the land, for I will give it to you."

And

"Do not be afraid, Abram, I am your shield; your reward shall be very great."

And

"Look toward heaven and count the stars, if you are able to count them." Then [God] said to [Abram], "So shall your descendants be." And Abraham believed the Lord; and the Lord reckoned it to him as righteousness.

Still, Abram and Sarai worried that the promises of God were impossible and took matters into their own hands.

THE BIRTH OF ISHMAEL

So, after Abram had lived ten years in the land of Canaan, Sarai, Abram's wife, took Hagar the Egyptian, her slave-girl, and gave her to her husband Abram as a wife. He went in to Hagar, and she conceived. Hagar bore Abram a son; and Abram named his son, whom Hagar bore, Ishmael. Abram was eighty-six years old when Hagar bore him Ishmael.

GOD RENAMES ABRAHAM AND SARAH

When Abram was ninety-nine years old, the Lord appeared to Abram, and said to him, "I am God Almighty; walk before me, and be blameless. And I will make my covenant between me and you, and will make you exceedingly numerous." Then Abram fell on his face; and God said to him, "As for me, this is my covenant with you: You shall be the ancestor of a multitude of nations. No longer shall your name be Abram, but your name shall be Abraham; for I have made you the ancestor of a multitude of nations. I will make you exceedingly fruitful; and I will make nations of you, and kings shall come from you. I will establish my covenant between me and you, and your offspring after you throughout their generations, for an everlasting covenant, to be God to you and to your offspring after you. And I will give to you, and to your offspring after you, the land where you are now an alien, all the land of Canaan, for a perpetual holding; and I will be their God."

> **SCENIC VIEW**
> This is the second covenant God explicitly makes with people, the Abrahamic covenant. Look back at the Noahic covenant in Genesis 9:8-17. How does this covenant compare to that one?

God said to Abraham, "As for you, you shall keep my covenant, you and your offspring after you throughout their generations. This is my covenant, which you shall keep, between me and you and your offspring after you: Every male among you shall be circumcised. You shall circumcise the flesh of your foreskins, and it shall be a sign of the covenant between me and you. Throughout your generations every male among you shall be circumcised when he is eight days old, including the slave born in your house and the one bought with your money from any foreigner who is not of your offspring. Both the slave born in your house and the one bought with your money must be circumcised. So shall my covenant be in your flesh an everlasting covenant. Any uncircumcised male who is not circumcised in the flesh of his foreskin shall be cut off from his people; he has broken my covenant."

God said to Abraham, "As for Sarai your wife, you shall not call her Sarai, but Sarah shall be her name. I will bless her, and moreover I will give you a son by her. I will bless her, and she shall give rise to nations; kings of peoples shall come from her." Then Abraham fell on his face and laughed, and said to himself, "Can a child be born to a man who is a hundred years old? Can Sarah, who is ninety years old, bear a child?" And Abraham said to God, "O that Ishmael might live in your sight!" God said, "No, but your wife Sarah shall bear you a son, and you shall name him Isaac. I will establish my covenant with him as an everlasting covenant for his offspring after him. As for Ishmael, I have heard you; I will bless him and make him fruitful and exceedingly numerous; he shall be the father of twelve princes, and I will make him a great nation. But my covenant I will establish with Isaac, whom Sarah shall bear to you at this season next year." And when he had finished talking with him, God went up from Abraham. That very day Abraham and his son Ishmael were circumcised; and all the men of his house, slaves born in the house and those bought with money from a foreigner, were circumcised with him.

> **TRAIL CROSSING**
>
> Names in the Bible are very important; when God gives someone a new name, it usually signifies a major transformation. Check out some of the other important name-change stories: Jacob (Genesis 32:22-32) and Simon (Matthew 16:13-20).

Now the people of Sodom and Gomorrah, where Abraham's cousin, Lot, and Lot's family lived, were wicked in the sight of the Lord. They violated the laws of hospitality, accosting and abusing strangers and visitors to their city. So God told Abraham that he was going to destroy the cities of Sodom and Gomorrah and all the people in them.

ABRAHAM BARGAINS FOR SODOM

Then Abraham came near and said, "Will you indeed sweep away the righteous with the wicked? Suppose there are fifty righteous within the city; will you then sweep away the place and not forgive it for the fifty righteous who are in it? Far be it from you to do such a thing, to slay the righteous with the wicked, so that the righteous fare as the wicked! Far be that from you! Shall not the Judge of all the earth do what is just?" And the Lord said, "If I find at Sodom fifty righteous in the city, I will forgive the whole place for their sake." Abraham answered, "Let me take it upon myself to speak to the Lord, I who am but dust and ashes. Suppose five of the fifty righteous are lacking? Will you destroy the whole city for lack of five?" And he said, "I will not destroy it if I find forty-five there." Again he spoke to him, "Suppose forty are found there." He answered, "For the sake of forty I will not do it." Then he said, "Oh do not let the Lord be angry if I speak. Suppose thirty are found there." He answered, "I will not do it, if I find thirty there." He said, "Let me take it upon myself to speak to the Lord. Suppose twenty are found there." He answered, "For the sake of twenty I will not destroy it." Then he said, "Oh do not let the Lord be angry if I speak just once more. Suppose ten are found there." He answered, "For the sake of ten I will not destroy it." And the Lord went his way, when he had finished speaking to Abraham; and Abraham returned to his place.

Yet the Lord was unable to find even ten righteous people in the cities, and God destroyed Sodom and Gomorrah, raining down sulfur and fire, sparing only Lot, Lot's wife, and their two daughters, instructing them not to look back or stop as they left the city. But Lot's wife looked back, and she became a pillar of salt.

THE BIRTH OF ISAAC

The Lord dealt with Sarah as he had said, and the Lord did for Sarah as he had promised. Sarah conceived and bore Abraham a son in his old age, at the time of which God had spoken to him. Abraham gave the name Isaac to his son whom Sarah bore him. And Abraham circumcised his son Isaac when he was eight days old, as God had commanded him. Abraham was a hundred years old when his son Isaac was born to him. Now Sarah said, "God has brought laughter for me; everyone who hears will laugh with me." And she said, "Who would ever have said to Abraham that Sarah would nurse children? Yet I have borne him a son in his old age."

> **SCENIC VIEW**
>
> Isaac's name means "laughter"—because Sarah laughed when God told her she would have a son in her old age. Read that story in Genesis 18:1-22.

HAGAR AND ISHMAEL ARE SENT AWAY

The child grew, and was weaned; and Abraham made a great feast on the day that Isaac was weaned. But Sarah saw the son of Hagar the Egyptian, whom she had borne to Abraham, playing with her son Isaac. So she said to Abraham, "Cast out this slave woman with her son; for the son of this slave woman shall not inherit along with my son Isaac." The matter was very distressing to Abraham on account of his son. But God said to Abraham, "Do not be distressed because of the boy and because of your slave woman; whatever Sarah says to you, do as she tells you, for it is through Isaac that offspring shall be named for you. As for the son of the slave woman, I will make a nation of him also, because he is your offspring."

So Abraham rose early in the morning, and took bread and a skin of water, and gave it to Hagar, putting it on her shoulder, along with the child, and sent her away. And she departed, and wandered about in the wilderness of Beer-sheba.

When the water in the skin was gone, she cast the child under one of the bushes. Then she went and sat down opposite him a good way off, about the distance of a bowshot; for she said, "Do not let me look on the death of the child." And as she sat opposite him, she lifted up her voice and wept. And God heard the voice of the boy; and the angel of God called to Hagar from heaven, and said to her, "What troubles you, Hagar? Do not be afraid; for God has heard the voice of the boy where he is. Come, lift up the boy and hold him fast with your hand, for I will make a great nation of him." Then God opened her eyes and she saw a well of water. She went, and filled the skin with water, and gave the boy a drink.

POINT OF INTEREST

God was faithful to his promise to Ishmael, who also had many descendants. Muslims trace their ancestry through Ishmael, just as Jews and Christians trace theirs through Isaac. Thus all three religions, Islam, Judaism, and Christianity, are offspring of Abraham and brothers in faith.

God was with the boy, and he grew up; he lived in the wilderness, and became an expert with the bow. He lived in the wilderness of Paran; and his mother got a wife for him from the land of Egypt.

THE BINDING OF ISAAC

After these things God tested Abraham. He said to him, "Abraham!" And he said, "Here I am." He said, "Take your son, your only son Isaac, whom you love, and go to the land of Moriah, and offer him there as a burnt offering on one of the mountains that I shall show you." So Abraham rose early in the morning, saddled his donkey, and took two of his young men with him, and his son Isaac; he cut the wood for the burnt offering, and set out and went to the place in the distance that God had shown him. On the third day Abraham looked up and saw the place far away. Then Abraham said to his young men, "Stay here with the donkey; the boy and I will go over there; we will worship, and then we will come back to you." Abraham took the wood of the burnt offering and laid it on his son Isaac, and he himself carried the fire and the knife. So the two of them walked on together. Isaac said to his father Abraham, "Father!" And he said, "Here I am, my son." He said, "The fire and the wood are here, but where is the lamb for a burnt offering?" Abraham said, "God himself will provide the lamb for a burnt offering, my son." So the two of them walked on together.

When they came to the place that God had shown him, Abraham built an altar there and laid the wood in order. He bound his son Isaac, and laid him on the altar, on top of the wood. Then

POINT OF INTEREST
In the pagan religions of this time, human sacrifice was not uncommon. In this story we learn that our God is different from the other gods and does not require human sacrifice.

Abraham reached out his hand and took the knife to kill his son. But the angel of the Lord called to him from heaven, and said, "Abraham, Abraham!" And he said, "Here I am." He said, "Do not lay your hand on the boy or do anything to him; for now I know that you fear God, since you have not withheld your son, your only son, from me." And Abraham looked up and saw a ram, caught in a thicket by its horns. Abraham went and took the ram and offered it up as a burnt offering instead of his son. So Abraham called that place "The Lord will provide"; as it is said to this day, "On the mount of the Lord it shall be provided."

The angel of the Lord called to Abraham a second time from heaven, and said, "By myself I have sworn, says the Lord: Because you have done this, and have not withheld your son, your only son, I will indeed bless you, and I will make your offspring as numerous as the stars of heaven and as the sand that is on the seashore. And your offspring shall possess the gate of their enemies, and by your offspring shall all the nations of the earth gain blessing for themselves, because you have obeyed my voice." So Abraham returned to his young men, and they arose and went together to Beer-sheba; and Abraham lived at Beer-sheba.

Sarah died and was buried. Abraham was growing very old and didn't want his son, Isaac, to marry a Canaanite, so Abraham sent his servant to find a wife for Isaac back in the land of Abraham's birth. There the servant met Rebekah, a distant relative of Abraham, and God gave him a sign that Rebekah was the woman who should be Isaac's wife. Rebekah's brother, Laban, agreed, and Rebekah journeyed with the servant to meet Isaac.

Isaac took Rebekah, and she became his wife; and he loved her. So Isaac was comforted after his mother's death.

SCRIPTURE CITATIONS

GENESIS 12:1-5 | 13:14a-17 | 15:1b, 5b-6 |
16:3-4a, 15-16 | 17:1-22, 26-27 | 18:23-33 | 21:1-21 |
22:1-19 | 24:67b

QUESTIONS FOR THE JOURNEY

1. Abraham's journey with God involves leaving behind his home and everything he has ever known. What might you have to leave behind or let go of in order to follow God's call?

2. When Abraham begins his journey with God, he doesn't know where the path will lead or what his destination will be like. How does Abraham's example challenge you in your journey with God? How does it comfort you?

3. Abraham encounters God in some very different or unusual ways: He hears God command him to leave his home and sacrifice his son; he argues with God at Sodom and Gomorrah; he has visions from God about his future. Does this seem

different from the way that we are used to thinking about humanity's encounters with God? When have you encountered God in an unusual or different way than you expected?

4. Abraham argues and bargains with God, calling on God to show mercy to the people of Sodom and Gomorrah. In fact, many of the faithful people in the Bible argue with God. What might that teach us about faith? Have you ever argued or bargained with God? Why or why not?

5. The story of Abraham's near sacrifice of Isaac is painful to read and defies simple explanations. How do you wrestle with this story?

NEXT STEPS

- Read some stories from the life of Abraham that are not included in this chapter (Genesis 18:1-22 and Genesis 20:1-18 are two interesting ones). What do you notice in these stories? How do they add to your understanding of Abraham?

- Abraham's faith is lauded in the New Testament in Hebrews 11:1-22. Read that account of the faith of Abraham. How does this selection from Hebrews portray Abraham's story? What is missing? What might we learn from it? How does Abraham's story speak to you most clearly about what faith means?

- Isaac's part in the biblical narrative is brief; the story mostly skips from Abraham to Jacob. Read Genesis 24 to learn about Isaac meeting his wife, Rebekah.

4

Joseph Had a Dream

Isaac and Rebekah wanted to have children, but Rebekah was barren. So Isaac prayed to the Lord, and the Lord granted his prayer. Rebekah conceived twin boys: Esau and Jacob. From the beginning, the boys were at odds. They struggled together so much in Rebekah's womb that she cried out to God, and God told her that they were two nations, divided, that one would be stronger than the other and the elder would serve the younger. It wasn't a smooth start. And it didn't help that, as they grew, their parents played favorites; Isaac loved Esau, but Rebekah loved Jacob. As the oldest son, Esau should inherit his father's birthright and blessing. But Jacob was a bit of a trickster.

> **TRAIL CROSSING**
> Like Isaac's mother Sarah, Rebekah is at first unable to have children. Barren women and unlikely children play an important part in the Bible. Check out the stories of Hannah (1 Samuel 1:2), the Shunammite woman (2 Kings 4:8-37) and Elizabeth (Luke 1:5-15).

Once when Jacob was cooking a stew, Esau came in from the field, and he was famished. Esau said to Jacob, "Let me eat some of that red stuff, for I am famished!" (Therefore he was called Edom.) Jacob said, "First sell me your birthright."

Esau said, "I am about to die; of what use is a birthright to me?" Jacob said, "Swear to me first." So he swore to him, and sold his birthright to Jacob. Then Jacob gave Esau bread and lentil stew, and he ate and drank, and rose and went his way. Thus Esau despised his birthright.

When Isaac was old and his eyes were dim so that he could not see, he called his elder son Esau and said to him, "My son"; and he answered, "Here I am." He said, "See, I am old; I do not know the day of my death. Now then, take your weapons, your quiver and your bow, and go out to the field, and hunt game for me. Then prepare for me savory food, such as I like, and bring it to me to eat, so that I may bless you before I die."

Rebekah was listening when Isaac spoke to his son Esau. So she called Jacob in and told him to bring her two tender kid goats, and she prepared Isaac's favorite stew. She wrapped the skins of the goats around Jacob's hands and neck, so that he would feel hairy like his brother Esau. Then Rebekah handed the savory food and bread to her son Jacob, and he went in, pretending to be his brother Esau.

So [Jacob] went in to his father, and said, "My father"; and he said, "Here I am; who are you, my son?" Jacob said to his father, "I am Esau your firstborn. I have done as you told me; now sit up and eat of my game, so that you may bless me." But Isaac said to his son, "How is it that you have found it so quickly, my son?" He answered, "Because the Lord your God granted me success." Then Isaac said to Jacob, "Come near, that I may feel you, my son, to know whether you are really my son Esau or not." So Jacob went up to his father Isaac, who felt him and said, "The voice is Jacob's voice, but the hands are the hands of Esau." He did not recognize him, because his hands were hairy like his brother Esau's hands; so he blessed him. He said, "Are you really my son Esau?" He answered, "I am." Then he said, "Bring it to me, that I may eat of my son's game and bless you." So he brought it to him, and he ate; and he brought him wine, and he drank. Then his father Isaac said to him, "Come near and kiss me, my son." So he came near and kissed him; and he smelled the smell of his garments, and blessed him, and said,

> "Ah, the smell of my son
>> is like the smell of a field that the Lord has blessed.
> May God give you of the dew of heaven,
>> and of the fatness of the earth,
>> and plenty of grain and wine.
> Let peoples serve you,
>> and nations bow down to you.
> Be lord over your brothers,
>> and may your mother's sons bow down to you.
> Cursed be everyone who curses you,
>> and blessed be everyone who blesses you!"

As soon as Isaac had finished blessing Jacob, when Jacob had scarcely gone out from the presence of his father Isaac, his brother Esau came in from his hunting. He also prepared savory food, and brought it to his father. And he said to his father, "Let my father sit up and eat of his son's game, so that you may bless me." His father Isaac said to him, "Who are you?" He answered, "I am your firstborn son, Esau." Then Isaac trembled violently, and said, "Who was it then that hunted game and brought it to me, and I ate it all before you came, and I have blessed him?— yes, and blessed he shall be!"

When Esau heard his father's words, he cried out with an exceedingly great and bitter cry, and said to his father, "Bless me, me also, father!" But he said, "Your brother came deceitfully, and he has taken away your blessing." Esau said, "Is he not rightly named Jacob? For he has supplanted me these two times. He took away my birthright; and look, now he has taken away my blessing." Then he said, "Have you not reserved a blessing for me?" Isaac answered Esau, "I have already made him your lord, and I have given him all his brothers as servants, and with grain and wine I have sustained him. What then can I do for you, my son?" Esau said to his father, "Have you only one blessing, father? Bless me, me also, father!" And Esau lifted up his voice and wept.

Then his father Isaac answered him:

"See, away from the fatness of the earth
shall your home be,
and away from the dew of heaven
on high.
By your sword you shall live,
and you shall serve your brother;
but when you break loose,
you shall break his yoke from
your neck."

Esau hated Jacob for stealing his blessing and plotted to kill him. So Rebekah sent Jacob to her brother, Laban, so that he could stay safe until Esau calmed down. One night on his journey, Jacob lay down to sleep, resting his head on a stone.

JACOB'S DREAM AT BETHEL

And [Jacob] dreamed that there was a ladder set up on the earth, the top of it reaching to heaven; and the angels of God were ascending and descending on it. And the Lord stood beside him and said, "I am the Lord, the God of Abraham your father and the God of Isaac; the land on which you lie I will give to you and to your offspring; and your offspring shall be like the dust of the earth, and you shall spread abroad to the west and to the east and to the north and to the south; and all the families of the earth shall be blessed in you and in your offspring. Know that I am with you and will keep you wherever you go, and will bring you back to this land; for I will not leave you until I have done what I have promised you." Then Jacob woke from his sleep and said, "Surely the Lord is in this place—and I did not know it!" And he was afraid, and said,

"How awesome is this place! This is none other than the house of God, and this is the gate of heaven." So Jacob rose early in the morning, and he took the stone that he had put under his head and set it up for a pillar and poured oil on the top of it. He called that place Bethel; but the name of the city was Luz at the first. Then Jacob made a vow, saying, "If God will be with me, and will keep me in this way that I go, and will give me bread to eat and clothing to wear, so that I come again to my father's house in peace, then the Lord shall be my God, and this stone, which I have set up for a pillar, shall be God's house; and of all that you give me I will surely give one-tenth to you."

POINT OF INTEREST

Giving one-tenth to God is called a tithe. Jacob isn't the first person to do this, Abram tithes in Genesis 14:19-20. In Leviticus 27:30-34, tithing will be established as biblical law. While 10 percent might seem like a lot, tithing is actually the lowest biblical standard of giving. John the Baptist will encourage giving away half of everything we have (Luke 3:11), and Jesus will call for giving away everything (Matthew 19:21).

Jacob journeyed until he came to the home of Laban, his mother's brother. Laban had two daughters: Leah and Rachel. Jacob fell deeply in love with the younger daughter, Rachel, and promised to serve Laban seven years if he could marry her. But Laban gave Jacob a taste of his own medicine, tricking him into marrying Leah first. Jacob served another seven years, so that he could marry Rachel as well. Jacob had children with both of his wives, Rachel and Leah, and his wives' maids, Zilpah and Bilhah. In all, Jacob had thirteen children: twelve sons and one daughter. Jacob worked hard, but he also resorted to trickery, fooling Laban out of the best of his flocks. Jacob grew exceedingly rich; he had large flocks, male and female slaves, and camels and donkeys. Finally, after many years, Jacob headed home, with his wives and children and riches, to face his brother Esau once again. Unsure of the welcome he would receive, Jacob sent presents ahead of him, in order to appease Esau. The night before he was to see his brother again, Jacob was sleeping alone in camp, when something surprising happened.

Jacob was left alone; and a man wrestled with him until daybreak. When the man saw that he did not prevail against Jacob, he struck him on the hip socket; and Jacob's hip was put out of joint as he wrestled with him. Then he said, "Let me go, for the day is breaking." But Jacob said, "I will not let you go, unless you bless me." So he said to him, "What is your name?" And he said, "Jacob." Then the man said, "You shall no longer be called Jacob, but Israel, for you have striven with God and with humans, and have prevailed." Then Jacob asked him, "Please tell me your name." But he said, "Why is it that you ask my name?" And there he blessed him. So Jacob called the place Peniel, saying, "For I have seen God face to face, and yet my life is preserved." The sun rose upon him as he passed Penuel, limping because of his hip.

Jacob and Esau reconciled, and Jacob settled in the land where he had grown up, the land of Canaan. There Jacob and his wives grew old, and they raised their children. In addition to his daughter, Dinah, Jacob had twelve sons: Reuben, Simeon, Levi, Judah, Zebulun, Issachar, Dan, Gad, Asher, Naphtali, Joseph, and Benjamin. But Joseph was Jacob's favorite, and just as with his father before him, playing favorites caused trouble.

POINT OF INTEREST
Early translators made a mistake with the Hebrew and translated this phrase "a coat of many colors." A "long robe with sleeves" is a much more accurate (though less colorful) translation.

Now Israel loved Joseph more than any other of his children, because he was the son of his old age; and he had made him a long robe with sleeves. But when his brothers saw that their father loved him more than all his brothers, they hated him, and could not speak peaceably to him. Once Joseph had a dream, and when he told it to his brothers, they hated him even more. He said to them, "Listen to this dream that I dreamed. There we were, binding sheaves in the field. Suddenly my sheaf rose and stood upright; then your sheaves gathered around it, and bowed down to my sheaf." His brothers said to him, "Are you indeed to reign over us? Are you indeed to have dominion over us?" So they hated him even more because of his dreams and his words.

One day, Joseph's brothers were out in a field, pasturing their father's flock. Jacob sent Joseph out to find them.

So Joseph went after his brothers, and found them at Dothan. They saw him from a distance, and before he came near to them, they conspired to kill him. They said to one another, "Here comes this dreamer. Come now, let us kill him and throw him into one of the pits; then we shall say that a wild animal has devoured him, and we shall see what will become of his dreams." But when Reuben heard it, he delivered him out of their hands, saying, "Let us not take his life." Reuben said to them, "Shed no blood; throw him into this pit here in the wilderness, but lay no hand on him"—that he might rescue him out of their hand and restore him to his father. So when Joseph came to his brothers, they stripped him of his robe, the long robe with sleeves that he wore; and they took him and threw him into a pit. The pit was empty; there was no water in it.

Then they sat down to eat; and looking up they saw a caravan of Ishmaelites coming from Gilead, with their camels carrying gum, balm, and resin, on their way to carry it down to Egypt. Then Judah said to his brothers, "What profit is it if we kill our brother and conceal his blood? Come, let us sell him to the Ishmaelites, and not lay our hands on him, for he is our brother, our own flesh." And his brothers agreed. When some Midianite traders passed by, they drew Joseph up, lifting him out of the pit, and sold him to the Ishmaelites for twenty pieces of silver. And they took Joseph to Egypt.

In Egypt, Joseph went to work for Potiphar, an officer of Pharaoh. God was with Joseph, and he became very successful. Potiphar made Joseph the overseer of his house and put Joseph in charge of everything. Unfortunately, Joseph's good fortune did not last. Potiphar's wife tried to seduce Joseph, and when he refused her advances, she unjustly accused him of assaulting her. As a result,

Potiphar had Joseph thrown into jail. Yet even in jail, God was with Joseph. Joseph was given charge over the other prisoners, and he cared for them. One night, two of the prisoners, Pharaoh's cupbearer and baker, who had been thrown in jail for displeasing Pharaoh, had dreams. Joseph, the dreamer, had also been given the gift of interpreting dreams by God. He correctly interpreted their dreams for them: that the baker would be executed, but the cupbearer would be restored to favor. Joseph asked the cupbearer to remember him and to speak to Pharaoh on his behalf. Yet as soon as he was out of jail, the cupbearer forgot Joseph. For two years, Joseph remained in jail, until Pharaoh began having troubling dreams. Then the cupbearer remembered Joseph and told Pharaoh about him.

Then Pharaoh sent for Joseph, and he was hurriedly brought out of the dungeon. When he had shaved himself and changed his clothes, he came in before Pharaoh. And Pharaoh said to Joseph, "I have had a dream, and there is no one who can interpret it. I have heard it said of you that when you hear a dream you can interpret it." Joseph answered Pharaoh, "It is not I; God will give Pharaoh a favorable answer." Then Pharaoh said to Joseph, "In my dream I was standing on the banks of the Nile; and seven cows, fat and sleek, came up out of the Nile and fed in the reed grass. Then seven other cows came up after them, poor, very ugly, and thin. Never had I seen such ugly ones in all the land of Egypt. The thin and ugly cows ate up the first seven fat cows, but when they had eaten them no one would have known that they had done so, for they were still as ugly as before. Then I awoke. I fell asleep a second time and I saw in my dream seven ears of grain, full and good, growing on one stalk, and seven ears, withered, thin, and blighted by the east wind, sprouting after them; and the thin ears swallowed up

> **TRAIL CROSSING**
> Jacob and Joseph are two of many important dreamers in the Bible, and God often speaks to people through dreams. Compare this story to Daniel's story (Daniel 2). Then read the story of another Joseph who had dreams from God (Matthew 1:18-25, 2:13-15, and 2:19-23).

the seven good ears. But when I told it to the magicians, there was no one who could explain it to me."

Then Joseph said to Pharaoh, "Pharaoh's dreams are one and the same; God has revealed to Pharaoh what he is about to do. The seven good cows are seven years, and the seven good ears are seven years; the dreams are one. The seven lean and ugly cows that came up after them are seven years, as are the seven empty ears blighted by the east wind. They are seven years of famine. It is as I told Pharaoh; God has shown to Pharaoh what he is about to do. There will come seven years of great plenty throughout all the land of Egypt. After them there will arise seven years of famine, and all the plenty will be forgotten in the land of Egypt; the famine will consume the land. The plenty will no longer be known in the land because of the famine that will follow, for it will be very grievous. And the doubling of Pharaoh's dream means that the thing is fixed by God, and God will shortly bring it about. Now therefore let Pharaoh select a man who is discerning and wise, and set him over the land of Egypt. Let Pharaoh proceed to appoint overseers over the land, and take one-fifth of the produce of the land of Egypt during the seven plenteous years. Let them gather all the food of these good years that are coming, and lay up grain under the authority of Pharaoh for food in the cities, and let them keep it. That food shall be a reserve for the land against the seven years of famine that are to befall the land of Egypt, so that the land may not perish through the famine."

JOSEPH'S RISE TO POWER

The proposal pleased Pharaoh and all his servants. Pharaoh said to his servants, "Can we find anyone else like this—one in whom is the spirit of God?" So Pharaoh said to Joseph, "Since God has shown you all this, there is no one so discerning and wise as you. You shall be over my house, and all my people shall order themselves as you command; only with regard to the throne will I be greater than you." And Pharaoh said to Joseph, "See, I have set you over all the land of Egypt." Removing his signet ring from his hand, Pharaoh put it on Joseph's hand; he arrayed him in garments of fine linen, and put a gold chain around his neck. He had him ride in the chariot of his second-in-command; and they cried out in front of him, "Bow the knee!" Thus he set him over all the land of Egypt. Moreover Pharaoh said to Joseph, "I am Pharaoh, and without your consent no one shall lift up hand or foot in all the land of Egypt." Thus Joseph gained authority over the land of Egypt.

Joseph's prediction came true, and a terrible famine spread throughout the world. But Egypt had enough grain, because they had stored extra at Joseph's direction. People came from far and wide to get grain from Egypt, and Joseph was in charge of distribution. One day, Joseph's brothers traveled all the way from the land of Canaan to seek food in Egypt. They had no idea that the governor they were asking for food was the very brother that they had sold into slavery. They bowed down low before him, just as Joseph had imagined in his dream so many years before. Joseph recognized his brothers immediately, but he pretended not to know them. He told his guards that they were spies, and had them thrown into jail. Then, when he finally let them go, he snuck a silver cup into their bags and pretended that they had stolen it. He took his youngest brother, Benjamin, as a prisoner in punishment for stealing. But Judah, the same brother who had sold Joseph into slavery all those years ago, begged and pleaded for Benjamin to be set free.

Then Joseph could no longer control himself before all those who stood by him, and he cried out, "Send everyone away from me." So no one stayed with him when Joseph made himself known to his brothers. And he wept so loudly that the Egyptians heard it, and the household of Pharaoh heard it. Joseph said to his brothers, "I am Joseph. Is my father still alive?" But his brothers could not answer him, so dismayed were they at his presence.

Then Joseph said to his brothers, "Come closer to me." And they came closer. He said, "I am your brother, Joseph, whom you sold into Egypt. And now do not be distressed, or angry with yourselves, because you sold me here; for God sent me before you to preserve life. For the famine has been in the land these two years; and there are five more years in which there will be neither plowing nor harvest. God sent me before you to preserve for you a remnant on earth, and to keep alive for you many survivors. So it was not you who sent me here, but God; he has made me a father to Pharaoh, and lord of all his house and ruler over all the land of Egypt. Hurry and go up to my father and say to him, 'Thus says your son Joseph, God has made me lord of all Egypt; come down to me, do not delay. You shall settle in the land of Goshen, and you shall be near me, you and your children and your children's children, as well as your flocks, your herds, and all that you have. I will provide for you there—since there are five more years of famine to come—so that you and your household, and all that you have, will not come to poverty.' And now your eyes and the eyes of my brother Benjamin see that it is my own mouth that speaks to you. You must tell my father how greatly I am honored in Egypt, and all that you have seen. Hurry and bring my father down here." Then he fell upon his brother Benjamin's neck and wept, while Benjamin wept upon his neck. And he kissed all his brothers and wept upon them; and after that his brothers talked with him.

The brothers did as Joseph asked. They went home and got their father and all of the family and household and everything they owned and brought them back to Egypt. Joseph and Jacob were joyfully reunited. Pharaoh gave homes and land to Joseph's father and all his brothers and their families, and they settled in the land of Egypt. On his deathbed, Jacob blessed his twelve sons, who would become the twelve tribes of Israel. Jacob also blessed Joseph's sons, Ephraim and Manasseh, then he died.

Realizing that their father was dead, Joseph's brothers said, "What if Joseph still bears a grudge against us and pays us back in full for all the wrong that we did to him?" So they approached Joseph, saying, "Your father gave this instruction before he died, 'Say to Joseph: I beg you, forgive the crime of your brothers and the wrong they did in harming you.' Now therefore please forgive the crime of the servants of the God of your father." Joseph wept when they spoke to him. Then his brothers also wept, fell down before him, and said, "We are here as your slaves." But Joseph said to them, "Do not be afraid! Am I in the place of God? Even though you intended to do harm to me, God intended it for good, in order to preserve a numerous people, as he is doing today. So have no fear; I myself will provide for you and your little ones." In this way he reassured them, speaking kindly to them.

JOSEPH'S LAST DAYS AND DEATH

So Joseph remained in Egypt, he and his father's household; and Joseph lived one hundred ten years. Then Joseph said to his brothers, "I am about to die; but God will surely come to you, and bring you up out of this land to the land that he swore to Abraham, to Isaac, and to Jacob." And Joseph died, being one hundred ten years old; he was embalmed and placed in a coffin in Egypt.

Scripture Citations
GENESIS 25:29-34 | 27:1-4, 18-40 | 28:12-22 | 32:24-31 |
   37:3-8 | 37:17b-28 | 41:14-44, 45b | 45:1-15 |
   50:15-22, 24, 26

QUESTIONS FOR THE JOURNEY

1. Jacob, who inherits God's promise to Abraham and becomes Israel, the one after whom God's faithful people is named, is not always an admirable character. A liar and a trickster, Jacob is an unlikely exemplar of faith. What might we learn from his inclusion in God's story?

2. After his dream at Bethel, Jacob says, "Surely the Lord is in this place—and I did not know it!" Where are some of the places that you feel God's presence most clearly? Have you ever experienced God's presence in a particularly unlikely place? What was that like?

3. One of the pivotal moments in Jacob's life is when he wrestles with the man at Penuel. After that moment, Jacob believes that he has seen God face to face. How is wrestling a good metaphor for the life of faith? What other metaphors help describe your relationship with God?

4. Joseph says to his brothers that God used for good what they had intended for harm. What does this tell us about how God works in Joseph's life? What might it say about the presence of God in our lives?

5. Joseph's journey with God involves a lot of ups and downs, but Joseph sees God present with him at all times. What are some of the high points and low points in your journey with God? How do you see God present in those moments?

6. What connections did you hear between Jacob and Joseph's stories and the stories from previous weeks?

NEXT STEPS

- This week we hear two important stories of forgiveness and reconciliation: Jacob and Esau (Genesis 33:1-17) and Joseph and his brothers (Genesis 45:1-15 and 50:15-22). Read these accounts again. What might we learn from them about forgiveness and reconciliation? Where in your life do you need to seek or give forgiveness and be reconciled?

- In today's story, we hear about a variety of ways that God speaks to people. God appears to Jacob in the form of a man who wrestles with him and God speaks to Joseph through dreams. How has God spoken to you in your life?

5

I Am Who I Am

Though Joseph and his extended family lived in Egypt for many years, they knew that it was not their true home. On his deathbed, Jacob made Joseph promise to take his body back to Canaan, and Joseph extracted the same promise from his children. During the famine, all the people of Egypt had sold their land to Pharaoh and given themselves over to be Pharaoh's slaves in return for being fed. So, though the Israelites worked hard and prospered, their land, their livestock, and even their lives did not belong to them but to Pharaoh. This didn't matter during Joseph's lifetime, because Pharaoh trusted and respected Joseph, so the Israelites were treated well. But as time passed, things began to change.

A NEW KING IN TOWN

Now a new king arose over Egypt, who did not know Joseph. He said to his people, "Look, the Israelite people are more numerous and more powerful than we. Come, let us deal shrewdly with them, or they will increase and, in the event of war, join our enemies and fight against us and escape from the land." The Egyptians became ruthless in imposing tasks on the Israelites, and made their lives bitter with hard service in mortar and brick and in every kind of field labor. They were ruthless in all the tasks that they imposed on them.

The king of Egypt said to the Hebrew midwives, one of whom was named Shiphrah and the other Puah, "When you act as midwives to the Hebrew women, and see them on the birthstool, if it is a boy, kill him; but if it is a girl, she shall live." But the midwives feared God; they did not do as the king of Egypt commanded them, but they let the boys live. So the king of Egypt summoned the midwives and said to them, "Why have you done this, and allowed the boys to live?" The midwives said to Pharaoh, "Because the Hebrew women are not like the Egyptian women; for they are vigorous and give birth before the midwife comes to them." So God dealt well with the midwives; and the people multiplied and became very strong. And because the midwives feared God, he gave them families. Then Pharaoh commanded all his people, "Every boy that is born to the Hebrews you shall throw into the Nile, but you shall let every girl live."

> **SCENIC VIEW**
>
> Shiphrah and Puah are so important to the story that we are given their names to remember through the centuries—an honor not accorded to many. Women play an important role in the story of Moses; his life is saved in turn by Shiprah and Puah, by his unnamed mother, his sister Miriam, Pharaoh's daughter, and later his wife, Zipporah.

THE BIRTH OF MOSES

Now a man from the house of Levi went and married a Levite woman. The woman conceived and bore a son; and when she saw that he was a fine baby, she hid him three months. When she could hide him no longer she got a papyrus basket for him, and plastered it with bitumen and pitch; she put the child in it and placed it among the reeds on the bank of the river. His sister stood at a distance, to see what would happen to him.

The daughter of Pharaoh came down to bathe at the river, while her attendants walked beside the river. She saw the basket among the reeds and sent her maid to bring it. When she opened it, she saw the child. He was crying, and she took pity on him. "This must be one of the Hebrews' children," she said. Then his sister said to Pharaoh's daughter, "Shall I go and get you a nurse from the Hebrew women to nurse the child for you?" Pharaoh's daughter said to her, "Yes." So the girl went and called the child's mother. Pharaoh's daughter said to her, "Take this child and nurse it for me, and I will give you your wages." So the woman took the child and nursed it. When the child grew up, she brought him to Pharaoh's daughter, and she took him as her son. She named him Moses, "because," she said, "I drew him out of the water."

MOSES FLEES TO MIDIAN

One day, after Moses had grown up, he went out to his people and saw their forced labor. He saw an Egyptian beating a Hebrew, one of his kinsfolk. He looked this way and that, and seeing no one he killed the Egyptian and hid him in the sand. When he went out the next day, he saw two Hebrews fighting; and he said to the one who was in the wrong, "Why do you strike your fellow Hebrew?" He answered, "Who made you a ruler and judge over us? Do you mean to kill me as you killed the Egyptian?" Then Moses was afraid and thought, "Surely the thing is known." When Pharaoh heard of it, he sought to kill Moses.

Moses fled Egypt and went out into the desert. While drawing water from a well, Moses met Zipporah, who would become his wife; they married and eventually had children. Moses was safe in exile, working as a shepherd for his father-in-law, Jethro. And then, one day, everything changed.

GOD CALLS MOSES

Moses was keeping the flock of his father-in-law Jethro, the priest of Midian; he led his flock beyond the wilderness, and came to Horeb, the mountain of God. There the angel of the Lord appeared to him in a flame of fire out of a bush; he looked, and the bush was blazing, yet it was not consumed. Then Moses said, "I must turn aside and look at this great sight, and see why the bush is not burned up." When the Lord saw that he had turned aside to see, God called to him out of the bush, "Moses, Moses!" And he said, "Here I am." Then he said, "Come no closer! Remove the sandals from your feet, for the place on which you are standing is holy ground." He said further, "I am the God of your father, the God of Abraham, the God of Isaac, and the God of Jacob." And Moses hid his face, for he was afraid to look at God.

> **POINT OF INTEREST**
> Most of the time, when people in the Bible encounter God or God's angels, they are afraid and hide their faces. God's glory, holiness, and majesty are so overwhelming that they inspire awe and even fear. This response is not a fear of punishment but is based in an older understanding of fear as a mixture of dread and reverence.

Then the Lord said, "I have observed the misery of my people who are in Egypt; I have heard their cry on account of their taskmasters. Indeed, I know their sufferings, and I have come down to deliver them from the Egyptians, and to bring them up out of that land to a good and broad land, a land flowing with milk and honey, to the country of the Canaanites, the Hittites, the Amorites, the Perizzites, the Hivites, and the Jebusites. The cry of the Israelites has now come to me; I have also seen how the Egyptians oppress them. So come, I will send you to Pharaoh to bring my people, the Israelites, out of Egypt."

But Moses said to God, "Who am I that I should go to Pharaoh, and bring the Israelites out of Egypt?" God said, "I will be with you; and this shall be the sign for you that it is I who sent you: when you have brought the people out of Egypt, you shall worship God on this mountain."

But Moses said to God, "If I come to the Israelites and say to them, 'The God of your ancestors has sent me to you,' and they ask me, 'What is his name?' what shall I say to them?" God said to Moses, "I AM WHO I AM." He said further, "Thus you shall say to the Israelites, 'I AM has sent me to you.'" God also said to Moses, "Thus you shall say to the Israelites, 'The Lord, the God of your ancestors, the God of Abraham, the God of Isaac, and the God of Jacob, has sent me to you':

> This is my name forever,
>   and this my title for all
>   generations.

Go and assemble the elders of Israel, and say to them, 'The Lord, the God of your ancestors, the God of Abraham, of Isaac, and of Jacob, has appeared to me, saying: I have given heed to you and to what has been done to you in Egypt. I declare that I will bring you up out of the misery of Egypt, to the land of the Canaanites, the Hittites, the Amorites, the Perizzites, the Hivites, and the Jebusites, a land flowing with milk and honey.' They will listen to your voice; and you and the elders of Israel shall go to the king of Egypt and say to him, 'The Lord, the God of the Hebrews, has met with us; let us now go a three days' journey into the wilderness, so that we may sacrifice to the Lord our God.'

I know, however, that the king of Egypt will not let you go unless compelled by a mighty hand. So I will stretch out my hand and strike Egypt with all my wonders that I will perform in it; after that he will let you go.

Then Moses answered, "But suppose they do not believe me or listen to me, but say, 'The Lord did not appear to you.'" The

Lord said to him, "What is that in your hand?" He said, "A staff." And he said, "Throw it on the ground." So he threw the staff on the ground, and it became a snake; and Moses drew back from it. Then the Lord said to Moses, "Reach out your hand, and seize it by the tail"—so he reached out his hand and grasped it, and it became a staff in his hand—"so that they may believe that the Lord, the God of their ancestors, the God of Abraham, the God of Isaac, and the God of Jacob, has appeared to you."

Again, the Lord said to him, "Put your hand inside your cloak." [Moses] put his hand into his cloak; and when he took it out, his hand was leprous, as white as snow. Then God said, "Put your hand back into your cloak"—so he put his hand back into his cloak, and when he took it out, it was restored like the rest of his body— "If they will not believe you or heed the first sign, they may believe the second sign. If they will not believe even these two signs or heed you, you shall take some water from the Nile and pour it on the dry ground; and the water that you shall take from the Nile will become blood on the dry ground."

But Moses said to the Lord, "O my Lord, I have never been eloquent, neither in the past nor even now that you have spoken to your servant; but I am slow of speech and slow of tongue."

> **TRAIL CROSSING**
> Moses is not alone in asking God to send someone else; most of the people God calls think they are not good enough. Check out Isaiah 6:1-6, Jeremiah 1:4-10, and Jonah 1 to learn about some of the other unlikely people whom God called.

Then the Lord said to him, "Who gives speech to mortals? Who makes them mute or deaf, seeing or blind? Is it not I, the Lord? Now go, and I will be with your mouth and teach you what you are to speak."

But Moses said, "O my Lord, please send someone else." Then the anger of the Lord was kindled against Moses and he said, "What of your brother Aaron the Levite? I know that he can speak fluently; even now he is coming out to meet you, and when he sees you his heart will be glad. You shall speak to him and put the words in his mouth; and I will be with your mouth and with his mouth, and will teach you what you shall do. He indeed shall speak for you to the people; he shall serve as a mouth for you, and you shall serve as God for him. Take in your hand this staff, with which you shall perform the signs."

MOSES RETURNS TO EGYPT

So Moses took his wife and his sons, put them on a donkey, and went back to the land of Egypt; and Moses carried the staff of God in his hand. And the Lord said to Moses, "When you go back to Egypt, see that you perform before Pharaoh all the wonders that I have put in your power; but I will harden his heart, so that he will not let the people go. Then you shall say to Pharaoh, 'Thus says the Lord: Israel is my firstborn son. I said to you, "Let my son go that he may worship me." But you refused to let him go; now I will kill your firstborn son.'"

Moses told Aaron all the words of the Lord with which he had sent him, and all the signs with which he had charged him. Then Moses and Aaron went and assembled all the elders of the Israelites. Aaron spoke all the words that the Lord had spoken to Moses, and performed the signs in the sight of the people. The people believed; and when they heard that the Lord had given heed to the Israelites and that he had seen their misery, they bowed down and worshiped.

So Moses and Aaron did as God had asked, going before Pharaoh and demanding that he let God's people go, but Pharaoh didn't listen. In fact, as punishment, Pharaoh made the Israelites work even harder, requiring them to make more bricks with less straw.

THE PLAGUES

Then the Lord said to Moses, "Pharaoh's heart is hardened; he refuses to let the people go. Go to Pharaoh in the morning, as he is going out to the water; stand by at the river bank to meet him, and take in your hand the staff that was turned into a snake. Say to him, 'The Lord, the God of the Hebrews, sent me to you to say, "Let my people go, so that they may worship me in the wilderness." But until now you have not listened. Thus says the Lord, "By this you shall know that I am the Lord." See, with the staff that is in my hand I will strike the water that is in the Nile, and it shall be turned to blood. The fish in the river shall die, the river itself shall stink, and the Egyptians shall be unable to drink water from the Nile.'" The Lord said to Moses, "Say to Aaron, 'Take your staff and stretch out your hand over the waters of Egypt—over its rivers, its canals, and its ponds, and all its pools of water—so that they may become blood; and there shall be blood throughout the whole land of Egypt, even in vessels of wood and in vessels of stone.'"

> **POINT OF INTEREST**
>
> The magicians of Egypt are able to replicate the first two plagues with their magic. They are not, however, able to reverse any of the plagues, so they simply add to their own misery by multiplying the blood and the frogs. When it comes to the third plague, the magicians are no longer able to even copy the actions of God.

Moses and Aaron did just as the Lord commanded. In the sight of Pharaoh and of his officials he lifted up the staff and struck the water in the river, and all the water in the river was turned into blood, and the fish in the river died. The river stank so that the Egyptians could not drink its water, and there was blood throughout the whole land of Egypt. But the magicians of Egypt did the same by their secret arts; so Pharaoh's heart remained hardened, and he would not listen to them, as the Lord had said. Pharaoh turned and went into his house, and he did not take even this to heart. And all the Egyptians had to dig along the Nile for water to drink, for they could not drink the water of the river.

Pharaoh still refused to let the Israelites go. So, seven days later, Moses and Aaron returned to Pharaoh to ask him again. Once again Pharaoh said no, so God sent the second plague, a plague of frogs that covered the whole country. Pharaoh promised that he would let the people go, but as soon as the frogs left, Pharaoh's heart was hardened, and he refused. Again and again Moses and Aaron came before Pharaoh, asking him to let God's people go. God sent one plague after another: first water turned to blood, then frogs covered the land, then gnats filled the air, then flies swarmed all around, then disease killed the livestock, then boils covered the Egyptians, then thunder and hail flattened the crops, then locusts devoured the plants and trees, then darkness descended, so thick it could be felt. With each plague, Pharaoh would relent, promising to let the people go. Yet as soon as the plague had passed, Pharaoh's heart would harden, and he would rescind his promise. At last, God told Moses that he would bring one final plague upon Pharaoh and Egypt.

Moses said, "Thus says the Lord: About midnight I will go out through Egypt. Every firstborn in the land of Egypt shall die, from the firstborn of Pharaoh who sits on his throne to the firstborn of the female slave who is behind the handmill, and all the firstborn of the livestock. Then there will be a loud cry throughout the whole land of Egypt, such as has never been or will ever be again. But not a dog shall growl at any of the Israelites—not at people, not at animals—so that you may know that the Lord makes a distinction between Egypt and Israel. Then all these officials of yours shall come down to me, and bow low to me, saying, 'Leave us, you and all the people who follow you.' After that I will leave." And in hot anger he left Pharaoh. The Lord said to Moses, "Pharaoh will not listen to you, in order that my wonders may be multiplied in the land of Egypt." Moses and Aaron performed all these wonders before Pharaoh; but the Lord hardened Pharaoh's heart, and he did not let the people of Israel go out of his land.

The Lord said to Moses and Aaron in the land of Egypt: This month shall mark for you the beginning of months; it shall be the first month of the year for you. Tell the whole congregation of Israel that on the tenth of this month they are to take a lamb for each family, a lamb for each household. If a household is too small for a whole lamb, it shall join its closest neighbor in obtaining one; the lamb shall be divided in proportion to the number of people who eat of it. Your lamb shall be without blemish, a year-old male; you may take it from the sheep or from the goats. You shall keep it until the fourteenth day of this month; then the whole assembled congregation of Israel shall slaughter it at twilight. They shall take some of the blood and put it on the two doorposts and the lintel of the houses in which they eat it. They shall eat the lamb that same night; they shall eat it roasted over the fire with unleavened bread and bitter herbs. Do not eat any of it raw or boiled in water, but roasted over the fire, with its head, legs, and inner organs. You shall let none of it remain until the morning; anything that remains until the morning you shall burn. This is how you shall eat it: your loins girded, your sandals on your feet, and your staff in your hand; and you shall eat it hurriedly. It is the passover of the Lord. For I will pass through the land of Egypt that night, and I will strike down every firstborn in the land of Egypt, both human beings and animals; on all the gods of Egypt I will execute judgments: I am the Lord. The blood shall be a sign for you on the houses where you live: when I see the blood, I will pass over you, and no plague shall destroy you when I strike the land of Egypt.

This day shall be a day of remembrance for you. You shall celebrate it as a festival to the Lord; throughout your generations you shall observe it as a perpetual ordinance. Seven days you shall eat unleavened bread; on the first day you shall remove

SCENIC VIEW

This story describes the first Passover, when God passed over the houses of the people of Israel and spared them from the plague of the firstborn. From this time onward, Jews will celebrate the Passover each year to remember how God rescued them.

leaven from your houses, for whoever eats leavened bread from the first day until the seventh day shall be cut off from Israel. On the first day you shall hold a solemn assembly, and on the seventh day a solemn assembly; no work shall be done on those days; only what everyone must eat, that alone may be prepared by you. You shall observe the festival of unleavened bread, for on this very day I brought your companies out of the land of Egypt: you shall observe this day throughout your generations as a perpetual ordinance. In the first month, from the evening of the fourteenth day until the evening of the twenty-first day, you shall eat unleavened bread. For seven days no leaven shall be found in your houses; for whoever eats what is leavened shall be cut off from the congregation of Israel, whether an alien or a native of the land. You shall eat nothing leavened; in all your settlements you shall eat unleavened bread.

Then Moses called all the elders of Israel and said to them, "Go, select lambs for your families, and slaughter the passover lamb. Take a bunch of hyssop, dip it in the blood that is in the basin, and touch the lintel and the two doorposts with the blood in the basin. None of you shall go outside the door of your house until morning. For the Lord will pass through to strike down the Egyptians; when he sees the blood on the lintel and on the two doorposts, the Lord will pass over that door and will not allow the destroyer to enter your houses to strike you down. You shall observe this rite as a perpetual ordinance for you and your children. When you come to the land that the Lord will give you, as he has promised, you shall keep this observance. And when your children ask you, 'What do you mean by this observance?' you shall say, 'It is the passover sacrifice to the Lord, for he passed over the houses of the Israelites in Egypt, when he struck down the Egyptians but spared our houses.'" And the people bowed down and worshiped. The Israelites went and did just as the Lord had commanded Moses and Aaron.

THE TENTH PLAGUE:
DEATH OF THE FIRSTBORN

At midnight the Lord struck down all the firstborn in the land of Egypt, from the firstborn of Pharaoh who sat on his throne to the firstborn of the prisoner who was in the dungeon, and all the firstborn of the livestock. Pharaoh arose in the night, he and all his officials and all the Egyptians, and there was a loud cry in Egypt, for there was not a house without someone dead. Then he summoned Moses and Aaron in the night, and said, "Rise up, go away from my people, both you and the Israelites! Go, worship the Lord, as you said. Take your flocks and your herds, as you said, and be gone. And bring a blessing on me too!"

All the Israelites did just as the Lord had commanded Moses and Aaron. That very day the Lord brought the Israelites out of the land of Egypt, company by company.

Scripture Citations
EXODUS 1:8-11, 13-22 | 2:1-15 | 3:1-20 |
  4:1-17, 20-23, 28-31 | 7:14-24 | 11:4-10 | 12:1-32, 50-51

QUESTIONS FOR THE JOURNEY

1. Moses is one of the most important biblical figures, yet one of the first things we learn about Moses is that he killed an Egyptian and hid the body. How does this fit with your childhood image of Moses? What might we learn from this part of Moses' life story?

2. Moses is taking his usual, daily walk with his sheep when God appears to him in the burning bush. The Bible tells us that Moses had to "turn aside" to see and encounter God. What might this say to us about how we see and encounter God? Have you ever

had to step off your normal path in order to experience God more fully? What was that like?

3. Moses has an amazing encounter with God, but he still doesn't feel "good enough" to answer God's call. Moses worries that he isn't eloquent in speech, and he asks God to send someone else. Have you ever felt "not good enough" to serve God? How might God's response to Moses speak to you?

4. Throughout the story of the plagues, the Bible tells us again and again that Pharaoh's "heart was hardened." What do you think that means?

5. Sometimes it is Pharaoh himself who hardens his heart, and sometimes the Bible says that God hardens Pharaoh's heart. What do you think the difference might be between those two descriptions? What are the effects of a hardened heart in the Bible? What effects do you see today of hardened hearts?

6. This chapter tells of the first Passover, and the institution of the Passover meal that Jews observe to this day. You may see some similarities in this story to that of Jesus' final days. The Last Supper that Jesus shared with his disciples was likely a Passover meal (Mark 14:12-25), a branch of hyssop is used to feed Jesus sour wine when he is crucified (John 19:29), and Jesus is referred to in John 1:29 as the Passover Lamb. How might we understand those parts of the life of Jesus in light of this story?

NEXT STEPS

• Moses' encounter with God in the burning bush is called a theophany, a revelation or showing of God. The Bible is full of stories of theopanies. Look at some of the other stories of God showing up to people, like Isaiah 6:1-6, Luke 3:21-22, and Revelation 1:9-19. What do you notice about these stories? How are they similar? What are the differences?

• When God speaks to Moses from the burning bush, he tells Moses two of his names. One is "I am who I am" and the other is "I am the God of Abraham, the God of Isaac, and the God

of Jacob." What might each of those names tell us about God?
Look at some other names of God in the Bible (Genesis 17:7-13,
Judges 6:24, Isaiah 9:6, James 1:17). What might these many
names teach us about God? What names of God have been
important to you?

6

The Waters Were Divided

After the final plague, the death of the firstborn son of every Egyptian family, Pharaoh finally relented and let the Israelites go. They packed up that very evening and started out, just as God had told them. As they traveled, God went in front of them in a pillar of cloud by day, to lead them along the way, and in a pillar of fire by night, to give them light, so that they might travel by day and by night. But their journey was not to be an easy one.

PHAROAH PURSUES THE ISRAELITES

When the king of Egypt was told that the people had fled, the minds of Pharaoh and his officials were changed toward the people, and they said, "What have we done, letting Israel leave our service?" So he had his chariot made ready, and took his army with him; he took six hundred picked chariots and all the other chariots of Egypt with officers over all of them. The Lord hardened the heart of Pharaoh king of Egypt and he pursued the Israelites, who were going out boldly. The Egyptians pursued them, all Pharaoh's horses and chariots, his chariot drivers and his army; they overtook them camped by the sea, by Pi-hahiroth, in front of Baal-zephon.

As Pharaoh drew near, the Israelites looked back, and there were the Egyptians advancing on them. In great fear the Israelites cried out to the Lord. They said to Moses, "Was it because there were no graves in Egypt that you have taken us away to die in the wilderness? What have you done to us, bringing us out of Egypt? Is this not the very thing we told you in Egypt, 'Let us alone and let us serve the Egyptians'? For it would have been better for us to serve the Egyptians than to die in the wilderness." But Moses said to the people, "Do not be afraid, stand firm, and see the deliverance that the Lord will accomplish for you today; for the Egyptians whom you see today you shall never see again. The Lord will fight for you, and you have only to keep still."

CROSSING OF THE RED SEA

Then the Lord said to Moses, "Why do you cry out to me? Tell the Israelites to go forward. But you lift up your staff, and stretch out your hand over the sea and divide it, that the Israelites may go into the sea on dry ground. Then I will harden the hearts of the Egyptians so that they will go in after them; and so I will gain glory for myself over Pharaoh and all his army, his chariots, and his chariot drivers. And the Egyptians shall know that I am the Lord, when I have gained glory for myself over Pharaoh, his chariots, and his chariot drivers."

The angel of God who was going before the Israelite army moved and went behind them; and the pillar of cloud moved from in front of them and took its place behind them. It came between the army of Egypt and the army of Israel. And so the cloud was there with the darkness, and it lit up the night; one did not come near the other all night.

Then Moses stretched out his hand over the sea. The Lord drove the sea back by a strong east wind all night, and turned the sea into dry land; and the waters were divided. The Israelites went into the sea on dry ground, the waters forming a wall for them on their right and on their left. The Egyptians pursued, and went into the sea after them, all of Pharaoh's horses, chariots, and chariot drivers. At the morning watch the Lord in the pillar of fire and cloud looked down upon the Egyptian army, and threw the Egyptian army into panic. He clogged their chariot wheels so that they turned with difficulty. The Egyptians said, "Let us flee from the Israelites, for the Lord is fighting for them against Egypt."

> **TRAIL CROSSING**
> This is the second time that God has appeared to Moses in fire: first in the burning bush and now in a pillar of cloud and fire. Read about some of the other times God shows up in fire: 1 Kings 18:20-39, 2 Kings 2:11, Daniel 3:19-30.

Then the Lord said to Moses, "Stretch out your hand over the sea, so that the water may come back upon the Egyptians, upon their chariots and chariot drivers." So Moses stretched out his hand over the sea, and at dawn the sea returned to its normal depth. As the Egyptians fled before it, the Lord tossed the Egyptians into the sea. The waters returned and covered the chariots and the chariot drivers, the entire army of Pharaoh that had followed them into the sea; not one of them remained. But the Israelites walked on dry ground through the sea, the waters forming a wall for them on their right and on their left. Thus the Lord saved Israel that day from the Egyptians; and Israel saw the Egyptians dead on the seashore. Israel saw the great work that the Lord did against the Egyptians. So the people feared the Lord and believed in the Lord and in his servant Moses.

> **SCENIC VIEW**
> The portions of the Bible that are songs are some of the oldest parts of the text. Here we are told that Miriam leads the people in singing immediately after their deliverance. In fact, singing and dancing is often the biblical response to good news. Check out 2 Samuel 6:5, Psalm 149:3, and Luke 1:45-55.

Then the prophet Miriam, Aaron's sister, took a tambourine in her hand; and all the women went out after her with tambourines and with dancing. And Miriam sang to them:

> "Sing to the Lord, for he has triumphed gloriously;
>   horse and rider he has thrown into the sea."

The Israelites rejoiced and sang, for God had delivered them from Egypt and miraculously led them across the Red Sea. Moses followed God's command and led the Israelites into the wilderness. Their rejoicing soon turned to complaining, as the people realized that life in the wilderness would not always be easy. In spite of all that they had seen and experienced, the people continued to doubt God's love and promise of provision.

The whole congregation of the Israelites complained against Moses and Aaron in the wilderness. The Israelites said to them, "If only we had died by the hand of the Lord in the land of Egypt, when we sat by the fleshpots and ate our fill of bread; for you have brought us out into this wilderness to kill this whole assembly with hunger."

Then the Lord said to Moses, "I am going to rain bread from heaven for you, and each day the people shall go out and gather enough for that day. I have heard the complaining of the Israelites; say to them, 'At twilight you shall eat meat, and in the morning you shall have your fill of bread; then you shall know that I am the Lord your God.'"

In the evening quails came up and covered the camp; and in the morning there was a layer of dew around the camp. When the layer of dew lifted, there on the surface of the wilderness was a fine flaky substance, as fine as frost on the ground. When the Israelites saw it, they said to one another, "What is it?" For they did not know what it was. Moses said to them, "It is the bread that the Lord has given you to eat. This is what the Lord has commanded: 'Gather as much of it as each of you needs, an omer to a person according to the number of persons, all providing for those in their own tents.'" The Israelites did so, some gathering more, some less. But when they measured it with an omer, those who gathered much had nothing over, and those who gathered little had no shortage; they gathered as much as each of them needed. And Moses said to them, "Let no one leave any of it over until morning." But they did not listen to Moses; some left part of it until morning, and it bred worms and became foul. And Moses was angry with them. Morning by morning they gathered it, as much as each needed; but when the sun grew hot, it melted.

On the sixth day they gathered twice as much food, two omers apiece. When all the leaders of the congregation came and told Moses, he said to them, "This is what the Lord has commanded: 'Tomorrow is a day of solemn rest, a holy sabbath to the Lord; bake what you want to bake and boil what you want to boil, and all that is left over put aside to be kept until morning.'" So they put it aside until morning, as Moses commanded them; and it did not become foul, and there were no worms in it. Moses said, "Eat it today, for today is a sabbath to the Lord; today you will not find it in the field. Six days you shall gather it; but on the seventh day, which is a sabbath, there will be none." So the people rested on the seventh day.

The house of Israel called it manna; it was like coriander seed, white, and the taste of it was like wafers made with honey. The Israelites ate manna forty years, until they came to a habitable land; they ate manna, until they came to the border of the land of Canaan.

From the wilderness of Sin the whole congregation of the Israelites journeyed by stages, as the Lord commanded. They camped at Rephidim, but there was no water for the people to drink. The people quarreled with Moses, and said, "Give us water to drink." Moses said to them, "Why do you quarrel with me? Why do you test the Lord?" But the people thirsted there for water; and the people complained against Moses and said, "Why did you bring us out of Egypt, to kill us and our children and livestock with thirst?" So Moses cried out to the Lord, "What shall I do with this people? They are almost ready to stone me." The Lord said to Moses, "Go on ahead of the people, and take some of the elders of Israel with you; take in your hand the staff with which you struck the Nile, and go. I will be standing there in front of you on the rock at Horeb. Strike the rock, and water will come out of it, so that the people may drink." Moses did so, in the sight of the elders of Israel. He called the place Massah and Meribah, because the Israelites quarreled and tested the Lord, saying, "Is the Lord among us or not?"

The Israelites journeyed until, finally, they arrived at Mount Sinai. The people of Israel camped at the base of the mountain, and Moses went up the mountain, and there, God spoke to Moses.

Then God spoke all these words:

I am the Lord your God, who brought you out of the land of Egypt, out of the house of slavery; you shall have no other gods before me.

POINT OF INTEREST

The Ten Commandments are so important that they are described twice. The list here is from Exodus 20; they appear again in Deuteronomy 5:6-21. The wording and order of the commandments is slightly different in the two accounts. Read them both and see what you notice.

You shall not make for yourself an idol, whether in the form of anything that is in heaven above, or that is on the earth beneath, or that is in the water under the earth. You shall not bow down to them or worship them; for I the Lord your God am a jealous God, punishing children for the iniquity of parents, to the third and the fourth generation of those who reject me, but showing steadfast love to the thousandth generation of those who love me and keep my commandments.

You shall not make wrongful use of the name of the Lord your God, for the Lord will not acquit anyone who misuses his name.

Remember the sabbath day, and keep it holy. Six days you shall labor and do all your work. But the seventh day is a sabbath to the Lord your God; you shall not do any work—you, your son or your daughter, your male or female slave, your livestock, or the alien resident in your towns. For in six days the Lord made heaven and earth, the sea, and all that is in them, but rested the seventh day; therefore the Lord blessed the sabbath day and consecrated it.

Honor your father and your mother, so that your days may be long in the land that the Lord your God is giving you.

You shall not murder.

You shall not commit adultery.

You shall not steal.

You shall not bear false witness against your neighbor.

You shall not covet your neighbor's house; you shall not covet your neighbor's wife, or male or female slave, or ox, or donkey, or anything that belongs to your neighbor.

When all the people witnessed the thunder and lightning, the sound of the trumpet, and the mountain smoking, they were afraid and trembled and stood at a distance, and said to Moses, "You speak to us, and we will listen; but do not let God speak to us, or we will die." Moses said to the people, "Do not be afraid; for God has come only to test you and to put the fear of him upon you so that you do not sin." Then the people stood at a distance, while Moses drew near to the thick darkness where God was.

God gave Moses far more than the Ten Commandments; God continued to speak to Moses, and gave him many other laws and statutes for the people: laws about what to eat and what to wear, laws about how to treat people and how to worship; laws about offerings and tithes, laws about justice and social responsibility. Some of the laws seemed obvious, like: "You shall not abuse any widow or orphan." Others seemed more arcane, like: "You shall be people consecrated to me; therefore you shall not eat any meat that is mangled by beasts in the field; you shall throw it to the dogs." But at the heart, all the laws were about how to live holy lives, lives dedicated to God; the people should be holy because God, their God, is holy. The people were being called to live as a witness of God's holiness to the world.

In particular, God talked to Moses about how and when the people of God should worship. God established a priesthood, setting aside the Levites, the descendants of Aaron, to serve as priests. God appointed the sacrifices and festivals that the people should observe. And God gave Moses specific instructions for building the ark of the covenant, a chest to carry the tablets of the law, and the tabernacle, a movable tent of dwelling for God. Since Moses and the people were nomads, God would travel with them, present and real in the midst of them in this movable dwelling. God described the ark and the tabernacle down to the most intimate detail: from the fifty loops that should be on the edge of the curtain of the tabernacle to the exact spices that should be used to make the incense. Every detail was accounted for.

TRAIL CROSSING

The promises exchanged between God and Moses on Mount Sinai are the third covenant in the Bible, the Mosaic covenant. The earlier covenants are the Noahic covenant (Genesis 9:8-17) and the Abrahamic covenant (Genesis 12-17). In the Mosaic covenant God gives people the Ten Commandments and other laws to follow and calls them to be holy as God is holy (Leviticus 19:2). In return, God promises that Israel will be God's treasured possession and a kingdom of priests (Exodus 19:5-6).

After receiving these laws, Moses went down from the mountain and shared them with the leaders. Then God summoned Moses to the highest part of the mountain, to receive the tablets of stone, with the law and the commandments God had given to the people.

Then Moses went up on the mountain, and the cloud covered the mountain. The glory of the Lord settled on Mount Sinai, and the cloud covered it for six days; on the seventh day he called to Moses out of the cloud. Now the appearance of the glory of the Lord was like a devouring fire on the top of the mountain in the sight of the people of Israel. Moses entered the cloud, and went up on the mountain. Moses was on the mountain for forty days and forty nights. When God finished speaking with Moses on Mount Sinai, he gave him the two tablets of the covenant, tablets of stone, written with the finger of God.

While God was speaking with Moses on Mount Sinai, the people below grew restless. They approached Aaron and asked him to make a god for them. Aaron took the people's gold rings and earrings and formed them in a mold and made an image of a calf. The people built an altar before the calf and began to bring it offerings, to worship it, and to drink and revel. Moses was so angered when he came down the mountain that he threw down the tablets that God had made, breaking them in the process. Moses destroyed the calf, and called the people to repent and return to God. The people received God's forgiveness, but their disobedience was not without cost. The stiff-necked people of God still had a lot to learn, but God was not ready to abandon them.

So Moses cut two tablets of stone like the former ones; and he rose early in the morning and went up on Mount Sinai, as the Lord had commanded him, and took in his hand the two tablets of stone. The Lord descended in the cloud and stood with him there, and proclaimed the name, "The Lord." The Lord passed before him, and proclaimed,

> **TRAIL CROSSING**
> Moses is changed after his encounter with God; from this point onward, the skin of his face shines. Compare this to Jacob's encounter with God in Genesis 32:22-32.

> "The Lord, the Lord,
>   a God merciful and gracious,
>   slow to anger,
>   and abounding in steadfast love and faithfulness,
>   keeping steadfast love for the thousandth generation,
>   forgiving iniquity and transgression and sin,
>   yet by no means clearing the guilty,
>   but visiting the iniquity of the parents
>   upon the children
>   and the children's children,
>   to the third and the fourth generation."

And Moses quickly bowed his head toward the earth, and worshiped. He said, "If now I have found favor in your sight, O Lord, I pray, let the Lord go with us. Although this is a stiff-necked people, pardon our iniquity and our sin, and take us for your inheritance."

On Mount Sinai, God renewed his covenant with the people in spite of their unfaithfulness. God called the people once again to holiness of life and gave the law again to Moses, on two tablets of stone. When he came down from encountering God on the holy mountain, the skin of Moses' face shone, and the people were afraid to come near him. So Moses would cover his face with a veil, when he stood before the people. Moses came before them to remind them of the essence of God's laws, and call them to obedience.

SCENIC VIEW

This passage is called the *Shema,* the Hebrew word for hear. Many Jews recite this prayer day and night, and have prayer practices for binding it to their foreheads with *tefillin* and putting it on their doorposts with *mezuzah.* Jesus calls this the greatest commandment in Matthew 22:34-40.

Hear, O Israel: The Lord is our God, the Lord alone. You shall love the Lord your God with all your heart, and with all your soul, and with all your might. Keep these words that I am commanding you today in your heart. Recite them to your children and talk about them when you are at home and when you are away, when you lie down and when you rise. Bind them as a sign on your hand, fix them as an emblem on your forehead, and write them on the doorposts of your house and on your gates.

So now, O Israel, what does the Lord your God require of you? Only to fear the Lord your God, to walk in all his ways, to love him, to serve the Lord your God with all your heart and with all your soul, and to keep the commandments of the Lord your God and his decrees that I am commanding you today, for your own well-being. Although heaven and the heaven of heavens belong to the Lord your God, the earth with all that is in it, yet the Lord set his heart in love on your ancestors alone and chose you, their descendants after them, out of all the peoples, as it is today. Circumcise, then, the foreskin of your heart, and do not be stubborn any longer. For the Lord your God is God of gods and Lord of lords, the great God, mighty and awesome, who is not partial and takes no bribe, who executes justice for the orphan and the widow, and who loves the strangers, providing them food and clothing. You shall also love the stranger, for you were strangers in the land of Egypt. You shall fear the Lord your God; him alone you shall worship; to him you shall hold fast, and by his name you shall swear. He is your praise; he is your God, who has done for you these great and awesome things that your own eyes have seen.

For forty years, Moses led the people of Israel as they wandered in the desert. In spite of God's promise and presence with them, the Israelites struggled to trust and obey God. Though God provided them with manna from heaven, they grew tired of eating it, weeping and complaining that they wanted meat. So God provided quail for them to eat as well. The people's complaints and rebellion grew so extreme that God became angry and Moses had to intercede for the people yet again. God relented and promised forgiveness, but as a consequence for their faithlessness, God said that none of the people who had seen God's glory in the escape from Egypt or the wilderness would enter the promised land; only their descendants would receive that promise. As the people neared the end of their journey and Moses neared the end of his life, he cautioned the people not to forget God in prosperity and to remember God, even when life became easier and they reached the land of promise.

Then Moses went up from the plains of Moab to Mount Nebo, to the top of Pisgah, which is opposite Jericho, and the Lord showed him the whole land: Gilead as far as Dan, all Naphtali, the land of Ephraim and Manasseh, all the land of Judah as far as the Western Sea, the Negeb, and the Plain—that is, the valley of Jericho, the city of palm trees—as far as Zoar. The Lord said to him, "This is the land of which I swore to Abraham, to Isaac, and to Jacob, saying, 'I will give it to your descendants';

I have let you see it with your eyes, but you shall not cross over there." Then Moses, the servant of the Lord, died there in the land of Moab, at the Lord's command. Moses was one hundred twenty years old when he died; his sight was unimpaired and his vigor had not abated. The Israelites wept for Moses in the plains of Moab thirty days; then the period of mourning for Moses was ended.

Joshua son of Nun was full of the spirit of wisdom, because Moses had laid his hands on him; and the Israelites obeyed him, doing as the Lord had commanded Moses. Never since has there arisen a prophet in Israel like Moses, whom the Lord knew face to face. He was unequaled for all the signs and wonders that the Lord sent him to perform in the land of Egypt, against Pharaoh and all his servants and his entire land, and for all the mighty deeds and all the terrifying displays of power that Moses performed in the sight of all Israel.

Scripture Citations
Exodus 14:5-31 | 15:20-21 | 16:2-4a, 12-26, 30-31, 35 | 17:1-7 | 20:1-21 | 22:22, 31 | 24:15-18 | 31:18 | 34: 4-9
Deuteronomy 6:4-9 | 10:12-21 | 34:1-5, 7-12

QUESTIONS FOR THE JOURNEY

1. The journey of the people of God features amazing deliverance, but it also involves wandering in the wilderness for forty years. When has your journey with God felt more like wandering? How has the experience of wandering impacted your faith?

2. In spite of God's presence and promise to them, the people struggle to trust God, and it doesn't take long after their miraculous deliverance for the people to begin complaining,

quarreling, and fighting against God and one another. Why do you think that is? When have you struggled to trust God? How might you focus on the glorious things that God has done rather than complain about the things you don't have?

3. When God rains down manna from heaven, the people are instructed to only take enough for food each day, and nothing more, but they find it difficult to do. Why do you think God asks them to do that? Why do you think it's so difficult? Compare this to Matthew 6:9-13. What might these passages say to us today?

4. In Exodus, Leviticus, and Deuteronomy, God is very specific, describing in great detail the tabernacle and vestments and what to eat and what to wear. What might God be saying to us about our lives by listing the laws so specifically? Even though we live in a different time, how might those laws speak to us today?

5. Moses leads the people for forty years, sticking with them even when they grumble, complain, and sin. Yet he doesn't get to see the people make it all the way into the promised land. What do you think about that? What might that say to us about our own service to God?

6. The Bible retells the story of Moses and the people in the wilderness again and again; it becomes a touchstone for the story of the people of God. Look at the way the story is told in Psalm 78. How does it compare with the story in this chapter? What do you notice about that version of the story?

NEXT STEPS

- Again and again in this chapter, Moses pleads with God on behalf of the people who have sinned. What might this say to us about how we are called to pray and relate to one another? Make a list of some people you are called to pray for or ask someone else to pray for you.

- Many of the Ten Commandments seem straightforward and obvious, if not easy. But one of the most overlooked is the command to remember the sabbath. Read that commandment closely; what do you notice? Why do you think God commanded, rather than requested, sabbath observance? How do you— or could you—observe sabbath in your life? Set a goal for observing the sabbath in your coming week.

7

The Wall Fell Down Flat

Moses had died, and the people he had been leading were poised on the edge of the land of promise. But God's promise to his people was not contingent upon any one person, even a great leader like Moses. The story of God and God's people continued with new leadership, as they entered a new chapter of life together.

After the death of Moses the servant of the Lord, the Lord spoke to Joshua son of Nun, Moses' assistant, saying, "My servant Moses is dead. Now proceed to cross the Jordan, you and all this people, into the land that I am giving to them, to the Israelites. Every place that the sole of your foot will tread upon I have given to you, as I promised to Moses. From the wilderness and the Lebanon as far as the great river, the river Euphrates, all the land of the Hittites, to the Great Sea in the west shall be your territory. No one shall be able to stand against you all the days of your life. As I was with Moses, so I will be with you; I will not fail you or forsake you. Be strong and courageous; for you shall put this people in possession of the land that I swore to their ancestors to give them. Only be strong and very courageous, being careful to act in accordance with all the law that my servant Moses commanded you; do not turn from it to the right hand or to the left, so that you may be successful wherever you go. This book of the law shall not depart out of your mouth; you shall meditate on it day and night, so that you may be careful to act in accordance with all that is written in it. For then you shall make your way prosperous, and then you shall be successful. I hereby command you: Be strong and courageous; do not be frightened or dismayed, for the Lord your God is with you wherever you go."

Then Joshua son of Nun sent two men secretly from Shittim as spies, saying, "Go, view the land, especially Jericho." So they went, and entered the house of a prostitute whose name was Rahab, and spent the night there. The king of Jericho was told, "Some Israelites have come here tonight to search out the land." Then the king of Jericho sent orders to Rahab, "Bring out the men who have come to you, who entered your house, for they have come only to search out the whole land." But the woman took the two men and hid them. Then she said, "True, the men came to me, but I did not know where they came from. And when it was time to close the gate at dark, the men went out. Where the men went I do not know. Pursue them quickly, for you can overtake them." She had, however, brought them up to the roof and hidden them with the stalks of flax that she had laid out on the roof. So the men pursued them on the way to the Jordan as far as the fords. As soon as the pursuers had gone out, the gate was shut.

SCENIC VIEW

God uses many unlikely people in the arc of salvation history. Rahab, a foreigner and a prostitute, might not seem like a good candidate for God to use. Yet her part in the story is so important that she is named in the genealogy of Jesus (Matthew 1:5).

Before they went to sleep, she came up to them on the roof and said to the men: "I know that the Lord has given you the land, and that dread of you has fallen on us, and that all the inhabitants of the land melt in fear before you. For we have heard how the Lord dried up the water of the Red Sea before you when you came out of Egypt, and what you did to the two kings of the Amorites that were beyond the Jordan, to Sihon and Og, whom you utterly destroyed. As soon as we heard it, our hearts melted, and there was no courage left in any of us because of you. The Lord your God is indeed God in heaven above and on earth below. Now then, since I have dealt kindly with you, swear to me by the Lord that you in turn will deal kindly with my family. Give me a sign of good faith that you will spare my father and mother, my brothers and sisters, and all who belong to them, and deliver our lives from death." The men said to her, "Our life for yours! If you do not tell this business of ours, then we will deal kindly and faithfully with you when the Lord gives us the land."

Then she let them down by a rope through the window, for her house was on the outer side of the city wall and she resided within the wall itself. She said to them, "Go toward the hill country, so that the pursuers may not come upon you. Hide yourselves there three days, until the pursuers have returned; then afterward you may go your way." The men said to her, "We will be released from this oath that you have made us swear to you if we invade the land and you do not tie this crimson cord in the window through which you let us down, and you do not gather into your house your father and mother, your brothers, and all your family. If any of you go out of the doors of your house into the street, they shall be responsible for their own death, and we shall be innocent; but if a hand is laid upon any who are with you in the house, we shall bear the responsibility for their death. But if you tell this business of

> **TRAIL CROSSING**
> The Bible tells the story of another crimson cord in Genesis 38:27-30, when Tamar's midwife uses a crimson thread to mark the birth order of Tamar's twin boys. Exodus 12:7-13 tells of another important red mark— the blood that marks the doors of the Israelites to spare them from the plague of the first-born. What connections do you hear between these stories? What might be the meaning of a crimson (sometimes called scarlet) cord?

ours, then we shall be released from this oath that you made us swear to you." She said, "According to your words, so be it." She sent them away and they departed. Then she tied the crimson cord in the window.

They departed and went into the hill country and stayed there three days, until the pursuers returned. The pursuers had searched all along the way and found nothing. Then the two men came down again from the hill country. They crossed over, came to Joshua son of Nun, and told him all that had happened to them. They said to Joshua, "Truly the Lord has given all the land into our hands; moreover all the inhabitants of the land melt in fear before us."

Early in the morning Joshua rose and set out from Shittim with all the Israelites, and they came to the Jordan. They camped there before crossing over. Then Joshua said to the people, "Sanctify yourselves; for tomorrow the Lord will do wonders among you." To the priests Joshua said, "Take up the ark of the covenant, and pass on in front of the people." So they took up the ark of the covenant and went in front of the people.

The Lord said to Joshua, "This day I will begin to exalt you in the sight of all Israel, so that they may know that I will be with you as I was with Moses. You are the one who shall command the priests who bear the ark of the covenant, 'When you come to the edge of the waters of the Jordan, you shall stand still in the Jordan.'" Joshua then said to the Israelites, "Draw near and hear the words of the Lord your God." Joshua said, "By this you shall know that among you is the living God who without fail will drive out from before you the Canaanites, Hittites, Hivites, Perizzites, Girgashites, Amorites, and Jebusites: the ark of the covenant of the Lord of all the earth is going to pass before you into the Jordan. So now select twelve men from the tribes of Israel, one from each tribe. When the soles of the feet of the priests who bear the ark of the Lord, the Lord of all the earth, rest in the waters of the Jordan, the waters of the Jordan flowing from above shall be cut off; they shall stand in a single heap."

When the people set out from their tents to cross over the Jordan, the priests bearing the ark of the covenant were in front of the people. Now the Jordan overflows all its banks throughout the time of harvest. So when those who bore the ark had come to the Jordan, and the feet of the priests bearing the ark were dipped in the edge of the water, the waters flowing from above stood still, rising up in a single heap far off at Adam, the city that is beside Zarethan, while those flowing toward the sea of the Arabah, the Dead Sea, were wholly cut off. Then the people crossed over opposite Jericho. While all Israel were crossing over on dry ground, the priests who bore the ark of the covenant of the Lord stood on dry ground in the middle of the Jordan, until the entire nation finished crossing over the Jordan.

> **TRAIL CROSSING**
> The miracle that God performs here as the people enter the promised land is a parallel to the miraculous crossing of the Red Sea when the people exited Egypt (Exodus 14:15-31). Go back and read that story. What are some of the similarities? What are the differences?

The new generation was circumcised and began to plant and harvest in the land. On the first Passover in Canaan, the people ate of their own harvest, and the manna that God had provided for forty years ceased. The people traveled on until they reached the city of Jericho, a walled city.

Now Jericho was shut up inside and out because of the Israelites; no one came out and no one went in. The Lord said to Joshua, "See, I have handed Jericho over to you, along with its king and soldiers. You shall march around the city, all the warriors circling the city once. Thus you shall do for six days, with seven priests bearing seven trumpets of rams' horns before the ark. On the seventh day you shall march around the city seven times, the priests blowing the trumpets. When they make a long blast with the ram's horn, as soon as you hear the sound of the trumpet, then all the people shall shout with a great shout; and the wall of the city will fall down flat, and all the people shall charge straight ahead." So Joshua son of Nun summoned the priests and said to them, "Take up the ark of the covenant, and have seven priests carry seven trumpets of rams' horns in front of the ark of the Lord." To the people he said, "Go forward and march around the city; have the armed men pass on before the ark of the Lord."

As Joshua had commanded the people, the seven priests carrying the seven trumpets of rams' horns before the Lord went forward, blowing the trumpets, with the ark of the covenant of the Lord following them. And the armed men went before the priests who blew the trumpets; the rear guard came after the ark, while the trumpets blew continually. To the people Joshua gave this command: "You shall not shout or let your voice be heard, nor shall you utter a word, until the day I tell you to shout. Then you shall shout." So the ark of the Lord went around the city, circling it once; and they came into the camp, and spent the night in the camp.

Then Joshua rose early in the morning, and the priests took up the ark of the Lord. The seven priests carrying the seven trumpets of rams' horns before the ark of the Lord passed on, blowing the trumpets continually. The armed men went before them, and the rear guard came after the ark of the Lord, while the trumpets blew continually. On the second day they marched around the city once and then returned to the camp. They did this for six days.

On the seventh day they rose early, at dawn, and marched around the city in the same manner seven times. It was only on that day that they marched around the city seven times. And at the seventh time, when the priests had blown the trumpets, Joshua said to the people, "Shout! For the Lord has given you the city. The city and all that is in it shall be devoted to the Lord for destruction. Only Rahab the prostitute and all who are with her in her house shall live because she hid the messengers we sent. As for you, keep away from the things devoted to destruction, so as not to covet and take any of the devoted things and make the camp of Israel an object for destruction, bringing trouble upon it. But all silver and gold, and vessels of bronze and iron, are sacred to the Lord; they shall go into the treasury of the Lord." So the people shouted, and the trumpets were blown. As soon as the people heard the sound of the trumpets, they raised a great shout, and the wall fell down flat; so the people charged straight ahead into the city and

POINT OF INTEREST
The walls of Jericho fall without any violence, merely by the sound of trumpets and the shouts of the people. Yet the Israelites kill those inside the city, saving only Rahab and her family. This legacy of violence, very present in the book of Joshua, is a difficult part of our tradition.

captured it. Then they devoted to destruction by the edge of the sword all in the city, both men and women, young and old, oxen, sheep, and donkeys.

Joshua said to the two men who had spied out the land, "Go into the prostitute's house, and bring the woman out of it and all who belong to her, as you swore to her." So the young men who had been spies went in and brought Rahab out, along with her father, her mother, her brothers, and all who belonged to her—they brought all her kindred out—and set them outside the camp of Israel. They burned down the city, and everything in it; only the silver and gold, and the vessels of bronze and iron, they put into the treasury of the house of the Lord. But Rahab the prostitute, with her family and all who belonged to her, Joshua spared. Her family has lived in Israel ever since. For she hid the messengers whom Joshua sent to spy out Jericho.

Not all of Israel's conquests went so smoothly. When Achan, a member of the tribe of Judah, disobeyed God's command and took some of the spoils that God had told the people to leave behind, the Israelites were defeated in battle at Ai.

Again and again, Joshua led the people in battles and conquests. Some were successful, and others were less so. With each battle, the people were confronted with the difficulty that the land that God had promised the Israelites was already occupied by the Canaanites, the Amorites, the Amalakites, the Gibeonites, the Hittites, and others. So there were battles and sieges; cities were laid to waste, and people were slaughtered. In each place, the Israelites destroyed not only the cities and the people, but also the altars and offerings to foreign gods.

So Joshua took all that land, the hill country and all the Negeb and all the land of Goshen and the lowland and the Arabah and the hill country of Israel and its lowland, from Mount Halak, which rises toward Seir, as far as Baal-gad in the valley of Lebanon below Mount Hermon. He took all their kings, struck them down, and put them to death. Joshua made war a long time with all those kings. There was not a town that made peace with the Israelites, except the Hivites, the inhabitants of Gibeon; all were taken in battle. For it was the Lord's doing to harden their hearts so that they would come against Israel in battle, in order that they might be utterly destroyed, and might receive no mercy, but be exterminated, just as the Lord had commanded Moses.

At that time Joshua came and wiped out the Anakim from the hill country, from Hebron, from Debir, from Anab, and from all the hill country of Judah, and from all the hill country of Israel; Joshua utterly destroyed them with their towns. None of the Anakim was left in the land of the Israelites; some remained only in Gaza, in Gath, and in Ashdod. So Joshua took the whole land, according to all that the Lord had spoken to Moses; and Joshua gave it for an inheritance to Israel according to their tribal allotments. And the land had rest from war.

Joshua divided the territory of the Land of Canaan among the tribes of Israel, apportioning certain parts of the land to each tribe, as God commanded him. Yet many parts of the promised land remained occupied by others; Israel had not driven out all of the people who already lived in the land. So it was that, though they had entered the land that God had promised them, the Israelites did not possess all of it. Instead they lived as a people in the midst of many other peoples.

A long time afterward, when the Lord had given rest to Israel from all their enemies all around, and Joshua was old and well advanced in years, Joshua summoned all Israel, their elders and heads, their judges and officers, and said to them, "I am now old and well advanced in years; and you have seen all that the Lord your God has done to all these nations for your sake, for it is the Lord your God who has fought for you. I have allotted to you as an inheritance for your tribes those nations that remain, along with all the nations that I have already cut off, from the Jordan to the Great Sea in the west. The Lord your God will push them back before you, and drive them out of your sight; and you shall possess their land, as the Lord your God promised you. Therefore be very steadfast to observe and do all that is written in the book of the law of Moses, turning aside from it neither to the right nor to the left, so that you may not be mixed with these nations left here among you, or make mention of the names of their gods, or swear by them, or serve them, or bow yourselves down to them, but hold fast to the Lord your God, as you have done to this day. For the Lord has driven out before you great and strong nations; and as for you, no one has been able to withstand you to this day. One of you puts to flight a thousand, since it is the Lord your God who fights for you, as he promised you. Be very careful, therefore, to love the Lord your God. For if you turn back, and join the survivors of these nations left here among you, and intermarry with them, so that you marry their women and they yours, know assuredly that the Lord your God will not continue to drive out these nations before you; but they shall be a snare and a trap for you, a scourge on your sides, and thorns in your eyes, until you perish from this good land that the Lord your God has given you.

"And now I am about to go the way of all the earth, and you know in your hearts and souls, all of you, that not one thing has failed of all the good things that the Lord your God promised concerning you; all have come to pass for you, not one of them has failed. But just as all the good things that the Lord your God promised concerning you have been fulfilled for you, so the Lord will bring upon you all the bad things, until he has destroyed you from this good land that the Lord your God has given you. If you transgress the covenant of the Lord your God, which he enjoined on you, and go and serve other gods and bow down to them, then the anger of the Lord will be kindled against you, and you shall perish quickly from the good land that he has given to you."

Then Joshua gathered all the tribes of Israel to Shechem, and summoned the elders, the heads, the judges, and the officers of Israel; and they presented themselves before God.

"Now therefore revere the Lord, and serve him in sincerity and in faithfulness; put away the gods that your ancestors served beyond the River and in Egypt, and serve the Lord. Now if you are unwilling to serve the Lord, choose this day whom you will serve, whether the gods your ancestors served in the region beyond the River or the gods of the Amorites in whose land you are living; but as for me and my household, we will serve the Lord."

Then the people answered, "Far be it from us that we should forsake the Lord to serve other gods; for it is the Lord our God who brought us and our ancestors up from the land of Egypt, out of the house of slavery, and who did those great signs in our sight. He protected us along all the way that we went, and among all the peoples through whom we passed; and the Lord drove out before us all the peoples, the Amorites who lived in the land. Therefore we also will serve the Lord, for he is our God."

But Joshua said to the people, "You cannot serve the Lord, for he is a holy God. He is a jealous God; he will not forgive your transgressions or your sins. If you forsake the Lord and serve foreign gods, then he will turn and do you harm, and consume you, after having done you good." And the people said to Joshua, "No, we will serve the Lord!" Then Joshua said to the people, "You are witnesses against yourselves that you have chosen the Lord, to serve him." And they said, "We are witnesses." He said, "Then put away the foreign gods that are among you, and incline your hearts to the Lord, the God of Israel." The people said to Joshua, "The Lord our God we will serve, and him we will obey." So Joshua made a covenant with the people that day, and made statutes and ordinances for them at Shechem. Joshua wrote these words in the book of the law of God; and he took a large stone, and set it up there under the oak in the sanctuary of the Lord. Joshua said to all the people, "See, this stone shall be a witness against us; for it has heard all the words of the Lord that he spoke to us; therefore it shall be a witness against you, if you deal falsely with your God." So Joshua sent the people away to their inheritances.

DEATH OF JOSHUA

After these things Joshua son of Nun, the servant of the Lord, died, being one hundred ten years old. They buried him in his own inheritance at Timnath-serah, which is in the hill country of Ephraim, north of Mount Gaash. Israel served the Lord all the days of Joshua, and all the days of the elders who outlived Joshua and had known all the work that the Lord did for Israel.

Scripture Citations
Joshua 1:1-9 | 2:1-24 | 3:1, 5-17 | 6:1-25 | 11:16-23 |
23:1-16 | 24:1, 14-31

QUESTIONS FOR THE JOURNEY

1. Joshua contains a lot of violence and descriptions of "holy wars," reminding us that it is not only "other people" who engage in holy war; in our Bible we are implicated in holy war. How can we wrestle with this difficult part of our holy scriptures? What might the presence of these stories say to us about our history? What might we learn from them?

2. At the end of each of the conflicts in Joshua, the biblical text says, "And the land had rest from war." How do wars impact the people as well as the natural world and the land? What might the presence of these verses tell us about humanity's impact on and responsibility for the land?

3. In his final speech to the people, Joshua tells them that they can serve either God or foreign gods, and they must "choose this day whom you will serve." What do you think about his description of following God as a choice about whom you will serve? What are some of the other "gods" that you might be tempted to serve in today's world?

4. The Collect for Peace in *The Book of Common Prayer* says, "O God, the author of peace and lover of concord, to know you is eternal life and to serve you is perfect freedom…" How might serving God, instead of the gods of this world, bring you deeper freedom?

NEXT STEPS

- Two of the most important theological documents in our lives are our calendars and our checkbooks; they tell us where we spend our time and where we spend our money. Set aside time this week to look at your checkbook and your calendar. What do they say about who you are serving? Are you spending your time and money on the things you value most? In what ways could you change your allocation of time and money to more accurately reflect your priorities?

- Joshua is not the only one to speak about serving God; Jesus will underscore the importance of serving God with both his words and his life. Read Matthew 20:20-28 and Luke 16:13. How do Jesus' words compare to Joshua's?

8

The Lord Raised Up Judges

When Joshua dismissed the people, the Israelites all went to their own inheritances to take possession of the land. The people worshiped the Lord all the days of Joshua, and all the days of the elders who outlived Joshua, who had seen all the great work that the Lord had done for Israel. Joshua son of Nun, the servant of the Lord, died at the age of one hundred ten years. So they buried him within the bounds of his inheritance in Timnath-heres, in the hill country of Ephraim, north of Mount Gaash. Moreover, that whole generation was gathered to their ancestors, and another generation grew up after them, who did not know the Lord or the work that he had done for Israel.

AFTER THE DEATH OF JOSHUA

Then the Israelites did what was evil in the sight of the Lord and worshiped the Baals; and they abandoned the Lord, the God of their ancestors, who had brought them out of the land of Egypt; they followed other gods, from among the gods of the peoples who were all around them, and bowed down to them; and they provoked the Lord to anger. They abandoned the Lord, and worshiped Baal and the Astartes. So the anger of the Lord was kindled against Israel, and he gave them over to plunderers who plundered them, and he sold them into the power of their enemies all around, so that they could no longer withstand their enemies. Whenever they marched out, the hand of the Lord was against them to bring misfortune, as the Lord had warned them and sworn to them; and they were in great distress.

Then the Lord raised up judges, who delivered them out of the power of those who plundered them. Yet they did not listen even to their judges; for they lusted after other gods and bowed down to them. They soon turned aside from the way in which their ancestors had walked, who had obeyed the commandments of the Lord; they did not follow their example. Whenever the Lord raised up judges for them, the Lord was with the judge, and he delivered them from the hand of their enemies all the days of the judge; for the Lord would be moved to pity by their groaning because of those who persecuted and oppressed them. But whenever the judge died, they would relapse and behave worse than their ancestors, following other gods, worshiping them and bowing down to them. They would not drop any of their practices or their stubborn ways. So the anger of the Lord was kindled against Israel; and he said, "Because this people have transgressed my covenant that I commanded their ancestors, and have not obeyed my voice, I will no longer drive out before them any of the nations that Joshua left when he died." In order to test Israel, whether or not they would take care to walk in the way of the Lord as their ancestors did, the Lord had left those nations, not driving them out at once, and had not handed them over to Joshua.

The Israelites did what was evil in the sight of the Lord, forgetting the Lord their God, and worshiping the Baals and the Asherahs. Therefore the anger of the Lord was kindled against Israel, and he sold them into the hand of King Cushan-rishathaim of Aram-naharaim; and the Israelites served Cushan-rishathaim eight years. But when the Israelites cried out to the Lord, the Lord raised up a deliverer for the Israelites, who delivered them, Othniel son of Kenaz, Caleb's younger brother. The spirit of the Lord came upon him, and he judged Israel; he went out to war, and the Lord gave King Cushan-rishathaim of Aram into his hand; and his hand prevailed over Cushan-rishathaim. So the land had rest forty years. Then Othniel son of Kenaz died.

EGLON AND EHUD

The Israelites again did what was evil in the sight of the Lord; and the Lord strengthened King Eglon of Moab against Israel, because they had done what was evil in the sight of the Lord. In alliance with the Ammonites and the Amalekites, he went and defeated Israel; and they took possession of the city of palms. So the Israelites served King Eglon of Moab eighteen years.

But when the Israelites cried out to the Lord, the Lord raised up for them a deliverer, Ehud son of Gera, the Benjaminite, a left-handed man. The Israelites sent tribute by him to King Eglon of Moab. Ehud made for himself a sword with two edges, a cubit in length; and he fastened it on his right thigh under his clothes. Then he presented the tribute to King Eglon of Moab. Now Eglon was a very fat man. When Ehud had finished presenting the tribute, he sent the people

> **POINT OF INTEREST**
> The first time the Israelites sinned, they served a foreign king for eight years. This time, their captivity lasts for eighteen years. Each time they wander farther from God in the book of Judges, the time of servitude increases.

who carried the tribute on their way. But he himself turned back at the sculptured stones near Gilgal, and said, "I have a secret message for you, O king." So the king said, "Silence!" and all his attendants went out from his presence. Ehud came to him, while he was sitting alone in his cool roof chamber, and said, "I have a message from God for you." So he rose from his seat. Then Ehud reached with his left hand, took the sword from his right thigh, and thrust it into Eglon's belly; the hilt also went in after the blade, and the fat closed over the blade, for he did not draw the sword out of his belly; and the dirt came out. Then Ehud went out into the vestibule, and closed the doors of the roof chamber on him, and locked them.

After he had gone, the servants came. When they saw that the doors of the roof chamber were locked, they thought, "He must be relieving himself in the cool chamber." So they waited until they were embarrassed. When he still did not open the doors of the roof chamber, they took the key and opened them. There was their lord lying dead on the floor.

> **SCENIC VIEW**
>
> This story is supposed to be humorous and even a little bit crass. After all, Eglon is killed in the bathroom! People are often surprised to find humor in the Bible, but the Bible contains the full gamut of human emotion, including a great deal of humor. Sarah laughed at God (Genesis 18:9-15, 21:1-7). Check out 1 Samuel 21:14-15 for a little bit of sarcasm or Numbers 22:21-35 for the silly story of a man and his talking donkey.

Ehud escaped while they delayed, and passed beyond the sculptured stones, and escaped to Seirah. When he arrived, he sounded the trumpet in the hill country of Ephraim; and the Israelites went down with him from the hill country, having him at their head. He said to them, "Follow after me; for the Lord has given your enemies the Moabites into your hand." So they went down after him, and seized the fords of the Jordan against the Moabites, and allowed no one to cross over. At that time they killed about ten thousand of the Moabites, all strong, able-bodied men; no one escaped. So Moab was subdued that day under the hand of Israel. And the land had rest eighty years.

The Israelites again did what was evil in the sight of the Lord, after Ehud died. So the Lord sold them into the hand of King Jabin of Canaan, who reigned in Hazor; the commander of his army was Sisera, who lived in Harosheth-ha-goiim. Then the Israelites cried out to the Lord for help; for he had nine hundred chariots of iron, and had oppressed the Israelites cruelly twenty years.

DEBORAH, SISERA, AND JAEL

At that time Deborah, a prophetess, wife of Lappidoth, was judging Israel. She used to sit under the palm of Deborah between Ramah and Bethel in the hill country of Ephraim; and the Israelites came up to her for judgment. She sent and summoned Barak son of Abinoam from Kedesh in Naphtali, and said to him, "The Lord, the God of Israel, commands you, 'Go, take position at Mount Tabor, bringing ten thousand from the tribe of Naphtali and the tribe of Zebulun. I will draw out Sisera, the general of Jabin's army, to meet you by the Wadi Kishon with his chariots and his troops; and I will give him into your hand.'" Barak said to her, "If you will go with me, I will go; but if you will not go with me, I will not go." And she said, "I will surely go with you; nevertheless, the road on which you are going will not lead to your glory, for the Lord will sell Sisera into the hand of a woman." Then Deborah got up and went with Barak to Kedesh. Barak summoned Zebulun and Naphtali to Kedesh; and ten thousand warriors went up behind him; and Deborah went up with him.

> **POINT OF INTEREST**
>
> In this story in Judges, women take a leading role in bringing about God's salvation. Deborah is a judge and prophet, leading the people, and Jael defeats General Sisera when the army fails.

When Sisera was told that Barak son of Abinoam had gone up to Mount Tabor, Sisera called out all his chariots, nine hundred chariots of iron, and all the troops who were with him, from Harosheth-ha-goiim to the Wadi Kishon. Then Deborah said to Barak, "Up! For this is the day on which the Lord has given

Sisera into your hand. The Lord is indeed going out before you." So Barak went down from Mount Tabor with ten thousand warriors following him. And the Lord threw Sisera and all his chariots and all his army into a panic before Barak; Sisera got down from his chariot and fled away on foot, while Barak pursued the chariots and the army to Harosheth-ha-goiim. All the army of Sisera fell by the sword; no one was left.

Now Sisera had fled away on foot to the tent of Jael wife of Heber the Kenite; for there was peace between King Jabin of Hazor and the clan of Heber the Kenite. Jael came out to meet Sisera, and said to him, "Turn aside, my lord, turn aside to me; have no fear." So he turned aside to her into the tent, and she covered him with a rug. Then he said to her, "Please give me a little water to drink; for I am thirsty." So she opened a skin of milk and gave him a drink and covered him. He said to her, "Stand at the entrance of the tent, and if anybody comes and asks you, 'Is anyone here?' say, 'No.'" But Jael wife of Heber took a tent peg, and took a hammer in her hand, and went softly to him and drove the peg into his temple, until it went down into the ground—he was lying fast asleep from weariness—and he died. Then, as Barak came in pursuit of Sisera, Jael went out to meet him, and said to him, "Come, and I will show you the man whom you are seeking." So he went into her tent; and there was Sisera lying dead, with the tent peg in his temple.

So on that day God subdued King Jabin of Canaan before the Israelites.

In the wake of the victory, Deborah sang a song of triumph, proclaiming the good news that God had indeed delivered the Israelites by the hand of a woman, and the land had rest for forty years. Yet the Israelites had not learned their lesson. Again and again, they repeated the same cycle. The Israelites would sin, failing to be faithful to God. In return, God would hand them over to their enemies as punishment. Then the Israelites would cry out to God, at which point God would send a judge to deliver them.

The judge would lead them to victory, and the land would have rest for a time. Then Israel would forget and fall into sin, and the cycle would begin again. It happened first with Othniel, then Ehud, then Shamgar, then Deborah, then Gideon, then Tola, then Jair, then Jephthah, then Ibzan, then Elon, and then Abdon. With each successive cycle, the Israelites would move farther and further away from God, as they failed to live into their identity as God's covenant people.

Yet God continued to hear and respond to the cry of his people, in spite of their faithlessness. After the death of Abdon, the Israelites had once again fallen into sin, and for forty years were sorely oppressed by the Philistines. When they cried out, God sent Samson to be judge over Israel.

SAMSON AND DELILAH

Born to a barren mother, Samson was set aside as special even before his birth. His mother promised to raise him as a Nazirite; he must not come into contact with a corpse, drink alcohol, or shave the hair of his head. These three things were signs of his special relationship with God. Samson was a true warrior for the people, a man of superhuman strength who defeated a lion with his bare hands and killed a thousand Philistines with only the jawbone of a donkey as a weapon. It seemed that Samson could not be stopped and would lead the Israelites to victory over the Philistines. And yet, Samson failed to live up to the Nazirite vow. First he touched the body of the lion that he killed, then he had a wild drinking party.

> **TRAIL CROSSING**
> Nazirite vows are described in Numbers 6:1-21 and are a special way of setting people apart for service to God. Samuel (1 Samuel 1) and John (Luke 1:5-25) are two other special children dedicated as Nazirites before their birth.

After this he fell in love with a woman in the valley of Sorek, whose name was Delilah. The lords of the Philistines came to her and said to her, "Coax him, and find out what makes his strength so great, and how we may overpower him, so that we may bind him in order to subdue him; and we will each give you eleven hundred pieces of silver." So Delilah said to Samson, "Please tell me what makes your strength so great, and how you could be bound, so that one could subdue you." Samson said to her, "If they bind me with seven fresh bowstrings that are not dried out, then I shall become weak, and be like anyone else." Then the lords of the Philistines brought her seven fresh bowstrings that had not dried out, and she bound him with them. While men were lying in wait in an inner chamber, she said to him, "The Philistines are upon you, Samson!" But he snapped the bowstrings, as a strand of fiber snaps when it touches the fire. So the secret of his strength was not known.

Then Delilah said to Samson, "You have mocked me and told me lies; please tell me how you could be bound." He said to her, "If they bind me with new ropes that have not been used, then I shall become weak, and be like anyone else." So Delilah took new ropes and bound him with them, and said to him, "The Philistines are upon you, Samson!" (The men lying in wait were in an inner chamber.) But he snapped the ropes off his arms like a thread.

Then Delilah said to Samson, "Until now you have mocked me and told me lies; tell me how you could be bound." He said to her, "If you weave the seven locks of my head with the web and make it tight with the pin, then I shall become weak, and be like anyone else." So while he slept, Delilah took the seven locks of his head and wove them into the web, and made them tight with the pin. Then she said to him, "The Philistines are upon you, Samson!" But he awoke from his sleep, and pulled away the pin, the loom, and the web.

Then she said to him, "How can you say, 'I love you,' when your heart is not with me? You have mocked me three times now and have not told me what makes your strength so great." Finally, after she had nagged him with her words day after day, and pestered him, he was tired to death. So he told her his whole secret, and said to her, "A razor has never come upon my head; for I have been a nazirite to God from my mother's womb. If my head were shaved, then my strength would leave me; I would become weak, and be like anyone else."

When Delilah realized that he had told her his whole secret, she sent and called the lords of the Philistines, saying, "This time come up, for he has told his whole secret to me." Then the lords of the Philistines came up to her, and brought the money in their hands. She let him fall asleep on her lap; and she called a man, and had him shave off the seven locks of his head. He began to weaken, and his strength left him. Then she said, "The Philistines are upon you, Samson!" When he awoke from his sleep, he thought, "I will go out as at other times, and shake myself free." But he did not know that the Lord had left him. So the Philistines seized him and gouged out his eyes. They brought him down to Gaza and bound him with bronze shackles; and he ground at the mill in the prison. But the hair of his head began to grow again after it had been shaved.

SAMSON'S DEATH

Now the lords of the Philistines gathered to offer a great sacrifice to their god Dagon, and to rejoice; for they said, "Our god has given Samson our enemy into our hand." When the people saw him, they praised their god; for they said, "Our god has given our enemy into our hand, the ravager of our country, who has killed many of us." And when their hearts were merry, they said, "Call Samson, and let him entertain us." So they called Samson out of the prison, and he performed for them. They made him stand between the pillars; and Samson said to the attendant who held him by the hand, "Let me feel the pillars on which the house rests, so that I may lean against them." Now the house was full of men and women; all the lords of the Philistines were there, and on the roof there were about three thousand men and women, who looked on while Samson performed.

Then Samson called to the Lord and said, "Lord God, remember me and strengthen me only this once, O God, so that with this one act of revenge I may pay back the Philistines for my two eyes." And Samson grasped the two middle pillars on which the house rested, and he leaned his weight against them, his right hand on the one and his left hand on the other. Then Samson said, "Let me die with the Philistines." He strained with all his might; and the house fell on the lords and all the people who were in it. So those he killed at his death were more than those he had killed during his life. Then his brothers and all his family came down and took him and brought him up and buried him between Zorah and Eshtaol in the tomb of his father Manoah. He had judged Israel twenty years.

In those days there was no king in Israel; all the people did what was right in their own eyes.

Scripture Citations
JUDGES 2:6-23 | 3:7-30 | 4:1-10, 12-23 | 16:4-31 | 21:25

QUESTIONS FOR THE JOURNEY

1. The book of Judges tells the story of a continuous cycle of sin-judgment-repentance-forgiveness-sin, which gets played out over and over. What does this cycle tell us about the people of Israel? What does it tell us about God? Where have you seen this cycle in your life or the world today?

2. When the people have a leader in their lives, like Moses or Joshua or some of the judges, they find it easier to follow God. Who are some of the spiritual leaders in your life who have helped you to follow God more closely?

3. God yearns for the people to turn to him as their leader, their judge, and their king, rather than needing earthly judges and kings to tell them how to live. Why do you think that is so difficult for the people? How do we struggle with this same challenge in our day and time?

4. The book of Judges has many stories that might seem more at home in a soap opera or blockbuster film. Ehud kills Eglon in the bathroom, then sneaks out the window; Jael kills the king after lulling him to sleep in her lap, and Samson falls for Delilah's ridiculous tricks again and again. How do you wrestle with these stories as part of our holy scriptures? What might the presence of these kinds of stories (and these kinds of people) tell us about salvation history?

NEXT STEPS

- One of the judges in the Bible, Gideon, takes a bit of persuading before he trusts God. Read Gideon's story in Judges 6:11-8:28. What do you notice? How does Gideon compare to other judges we read about? How does God respond to Gideon's tests?

- We often have a deep discomfort with the idea of being judged. Yet the Bible is clear that God will judge us. Read Psalm 51 and Romans 14:1-13. How might we hear God's judgment as good news? How might turning to God instead of earthly judges bring us deeper peace?

9

Speak, For Your Servant Is Listening

In the time when the judges ruled and the Israelites turned further and further away from God, a man named Elimelech, from Bethlehem in Judah, went to live in the country of Moab with his wife, Naomi, and two sons, Mahlon and Chilion. Mahlon and Chilion met and married two Moabite women, Orpah and Ruth. But Elimelech, Mahlon, and Chilion all died in Moab, leaving Naomi without her husband or her two sons. So Naomi decided to leave Moab and return to her home in Judah, where she had learned that the Lord had heard the cry of the people and lifted the famine that afflicted the land.

NAOMI AND HER DAUGHTERS-IN-LAW

So Naomi set out from the place where she had been living, she and her two daughters-in-law, and they went on their way to go back to the land of Judah. But Naomi said to her two daughters-in-law, "Go back each of you to your mother's house. May the Lord deal kindly with you, as you have dealt with the dead and with me. The Lord grant that you may find security, each of you in the house of your husband." Then she kissed them, and they wept aloud. They said to her, "No, we will return with you to your people." But Naomi said, "Turn back, my daughters, why will you go with me? Do I still have sons in my womb that they may become your husbands? Turn back, my daughters, go your way, for I am too old to have a husband. Even if I thought there was hope for me, even if I should have a husband tonight and bear sons, would you then wait until they were grown? Would you then refrain from marrying? No, my daughters, it has been far more bitter for me than for you, because the hand of the Lord has turned against me." Then they wept aloud again. Orpah kissed her mother-in-law, but Ruth clung to her.

So she said, "See, your sister-in-law has gone back to her people and to her gods; return after your sister-in-law." But Ruth said,

> "Do not press me to leave you
> > or to turn back from following you!
> Where you go, I will go;
> > where you lodge, I will lodge;
> your people shall be my people,
> > and your God my God.
> Where you die, I will die—
> > there will I be buried.
> May the Lord do thus and so to me,
> > and more as well,
> if even death parts me from you!"

When Naomi saw that she was determined to go with her, she said no more to her.

So Naomi returned together with Ruth the Moabite, her daughter-in-law, who came back with her from the country of Moab. They came to Bethlehem at the beginning of the barley harvest.

Now Naomi had a kinsman on her husband's side, a prominent rich man, of the family of Elimelech, whose name was Boaz. And Ruth the Moabite said to Naomi, "Let me go to the field and glean among the ears of grain, behind someone in whose sight I may find favor." She said to her, "Go, my daughter." So she went. She came and gleaned in the field behind the reapers. As it happened, she came to the part of the field belonging to Boaz, who was of the family of Elimelech. Just then Boaz came from Bethlehem. He said to the reapers, "The Lord be with you." They answered, "The Lord bless you." Then Boaz said to his servant who was in charge of the reapers, "To whom does this young woman belong?" The servant who was in charge of the reapers answered, "She is the Moabite who came back with Naomi from the country of Moab. She said, 'Please, let me glean and gather among the sheaves behind the reapers.' So she came, and she has been on her feet from early this morning until now, without resting even for a moment."

> **POINT OF INTEREST**
> Gleaning is the practice of collecting leftover crops from the fields after the workers have done their picking. In fact, Leviticus 23:22 and Deuteronomy 24:19-22 command workers to be sure not to pick everything when they harvest, so that there will be plenty left behind for the poor.

Then Boaz said to Ruth, "Now listen, my daughter, do not go to glean in another field or leave this one, but keep close to my young women. Keep your eyes on the field that is being reaped, and follow behind them. I have ordered the young men not to bother you. If you get thirsty, go to the vessels and drink from what the young men have drawn." Then she fell prostrate, with her face to the ground, and said to him, "Why have I found favor in your sight, that you should take notice of me, when I am a foreigner?" But Boaz answered her, "All that you have done for your mother-in-law since the death of your husband has been fully told me, and how you left your father and mother and your native land and came to a people that you did not know before. May the Lord reward you for your deeds, and may you have a full reward from the Lord, the God of Israel, under whose wings you have come for refuge!" Then she said, "May I continue to find favor in your sight, my lord, for you have comforted me and spoken kindly to your servant, even though I am not one of your servants."

At mealtime Boaz said to her, "Come here, and eat some of this bread, and dip your morsel in the sour wine." So she sat beside the reapers, and he heaped up for her some parched grain. She ate until she was satisfied, and she had some left over. When she got up to glean, Boaz instructed his young men, "Let her glean even among the standing sheaves, and do not reproach her. You must also pull out some handfuls for her from the bundles, and leave them for her to glean, and do not rebuke her."

So Ruth gleaned in the field until evening. Then she beat out what she had gleaned, and it was about an ephah of barley. She picked it up and came into the town, and her mother-in-law saw how much she had gleaned. Then she took out and gave her what was left over after she herself had been satisfied. Her mother-in-law said to her, "Where did you glean today? And where have you worked? Blessed be the man who took notice of you." So she told her mother-in-law with whom she had worked, and said, "The name of the man with whom I worked today is Boaz." Then Naomi said to her daughter-in-law, "Blessed be he by the Lord, whose kindness has not forsaken the living or the dead!" Naomi also said to her, "The man is a relative of ours, one of our nearest kin." Then Ruth the Moabite said, "He even said to me, 'Stay close by my servants, until they have finished all my harvest.'" Naomi said to Ruth, her daughter-in-law, "It is better, my daughter, that you go out with his young women, otherwise you might be bothered in another field." So she stayed close to the young women of Boaz, gleaning until the end of the barley and wheat harvests; and she lived with her mother-in-law.

Boaz continued to be kind and generous with Ruth, just as she had been faithful and generous with her mother-in-law. Naomi wanted to help secure Ruth's future and came up with a plan for Ruth to go to Boaz at night, on the threshing floor, and ask Boaz for his protection. Ruth did as Naomi instructed, and Boaz, deeply impressed by Ruth's loyalty, agreed to be her redeemer. In Israelite custom, a redeemer was the nearest relative of a deceased male, who married the man's widow in order to carry on his dead relative's lineage. Boaz realized that there was another male relative more closely related to Naomi who had first claim on Ruth, so Boaz went to meet with the next of kin in order to come to an agreement.

> **SCENIC VIEW**
> The custom of Levirate marriage is described in Deuteronomy 25:5-10. Though this may seem strange to us, this law helped to protect widows, who had no source of income after their husbands died.

No sooner had Boaz gone up to the gate and sat down there than the next-of-kin, of whom Boaz had spoken, came passing by. So Boaz said, "Come over, friend; sit down here." And he went over and sat down. Then Boaz took ten men of the elders of the city, and said, "Sit down here"; so they sat down. He then said to the next-of-kin, "Naomi, who has come back from the country of Moab, is selling the parcel of land that belonged to our kinsman Elimelech. So I thought I would tell you of it, and say: Buy it in the presence of those sitting here, and in the presence of the elders of my people. If you will redeem it, redeem it; but if you will not, tell me, so that I may know; for there is no one prior to you to redeem it, and I come after you." So he said, "I will redeem it." Then Boaz said, "The day you acquire the field from the hand of Naomi, you are also acquiring Ruth the Moabite, the widow of the dead man, to maintain the dead man's name on his inheritance." At this, the next-of-kin said, "I cannot redeem it for myself without damaging my own inheritance. Take my right of redemption yourself, for I cannot redeem it."

Now this was the custom in former times in Israel concerning redeeming and exchanging: to confirm a transaction, the one took off a sandal and gave it to the other; this was the manner of attesting in Israel. So when the next-of-kin said to Boaz, "Acquire it for yourself," he took off his sandal. Then Boaz said to the elders and all the people, "Today you are witnesses that I have acquired from the hand of Naomi all that belonged to Elimelech and all that belonged to Chilion and Mahlon. I have also acquired Ruth the Moabite, the wife of Mahlon, to be my wife, to maintain the dead man's name on his inheritance, in order that the name of the dead may not be cut off from his kindred and from the gate of his native place; today you are witnesses." Then all the people who were at the gate, along with the elders, said, "We are witnesses. May the Lord make the woman who is coming into your house like Rachel and Leah, who together built up the house of Israel. May you produce children in Ephrathah and bestow a name in Bethlehem; and, through the children that the Lord will give you by this young woman, may your house be like the house of Perez, whom Tamar bore to Judah."

> **POINT OF INTEREST**
> The people and elders pray that Ruth will be like Rachel and Leah, two women who built up the house of Israel. Go back and read their story in Genesis 29-30.

THE GENEALOGY OF DAVID

So Boaz took Ruth and she became his wife. When they came together, the Lord made her conceive, and she bore a son. Then the women said to Naomi, "Blessed be the Lord, who has not left you this day without next-of-kin; and may his name be renowned in Israel! He shall be to you a restorer of life and a nourisher of your old age; for your daughter-in-law who loves you, who is more to you than seven sons, has borne him." Then Naomi took the child and laid him in her bosom, and became his nurse. The women of the neighborhood gave him a name, saying, "A son has been born to Naomi." They named him Obed; he became the father of Jesse, the father of David.

Not long after this, in the nearby hill country of Ephraim, another remarkable and faithful woman was enduring great hardship. Hannah was wife to Elkanah, a faithful man who would go every year to worship the Lord of hosts at Shiloh. Though she desired a child very much, Hannah was barren, which grieved her deeply. Yet even in her grief, Hannah went to worship the Lord at Shiloh year after year, hoping against hope that things would change. And then, one year, they did.

After they had eaten and drunk at Shiloh, Hannah rose and presented herself before the Lord. Now Eli the priest was sitting on the seat beside the doorpost of the temple of the Lord. [Hannah] was deeply distressed and prayed to the Lord, and wept bitterly. She made this vow: "O Lord of hosts, if only you will look on the misery of your servant, and remember me, and not forget your servant, but will give to your servant a male child, then I will set him before you as a nazirite until the day of his death. He shall drink neither wine nor intoxicants, and no razor shall touch his head."

As she continued praying before the Lord, Eli observed her mouth. Hannah was praying silently; only her lips moved, but her voice was not heard; therefore Eli thought she was drunk. So Eli said to her, "How long will you make a drunken spectacle of yourself? Put away your wine." But Hannah answered, "No, my lord, I am a woman deeply troubled; I have drunk neither wine nor strong drink, but I have been pouring out my soul before the Lord. Do not regard your servant as a worthless woman, for I have been speaking out of my great anxiety and vexation all this time." Then Eli answered, "Go in peace; the God of Israel grant the petition you have made to him." And she said, "Let your servant find favor in your sight." Then the woman went to her quarters, ate and drank with her husband, and her countenance was sad no longer.

> **TRAIL CROSSING**
> Hannah was praying so passionately that Eli thought she was drunk! Read Acts 2 to hear another story of people praying so passionately that bystanders believed they were drunk.

They rose early in the morning and worshiped before the Lord; then they went back to their house at Ramah. Elkanah knew his wife Hannah, and the Lord remembered her. In due time Hannah conceived and bore a son. She named him Samuel, for she said, "I have asked him of the Lord."

The man Elkanah and all his household went up to offer to the Lord the yearly sacrifice, and to pay his vow. But Hannah did not go up, for she said to her husband, "As soon as the child is weaned, I will bring him, that he may appear in the presence of the Lord, and remain there forever; I will offer him as a nazirite for all time." Her husband Elkanah said to her, "Do what seems best to you, wait until you have weaned him; only—may the Lord establish his word." So the woman remained and nursed her son, until she weaned him. When she had weaned him, she took him up with her, along with a three-year-old bull, an ephah of flour, and a skin of wine. She brought him to the house of the Lord at Shiloh; and the child was young. Then they slaughtered the bull, and they brought the child to Eli. And she said, "Oh, my lord! As you live, my lord, I am the woman who was standing here in your presence, praying to the Lord. For this child I prayed; and the Lord has granted me the petition that I made to him. Therefore I have lent him to the Lord; as long as he lives, he is given to the Lord." She left him there for the Lord.

Hannah returned home and sang to the Lord a song of great joy. Samuel remained with Eli, ministering before the Lord, and every year, Hannah visited with her husband to offer their sacrifice and bring Samuel a new robe. Eli was impressed by Hannah's faithfulness and blessed her. And God blessed Hannah as well; she had more children: three sons and two daughters.

Unfortunately, Eli's sons were nothing like him. They were scoundrels who had no regard for God or for the duties of the priests to the people. So God told Eli that his sons would not be the priests to lead the people, and instead God would call another to be the chief priest.

GOD CALLS SAMUEL

Now the boy Samuel was ministering to the Lord under Eli. The word of the Lord was rare in those days; visions were not widespread. At that time Eli, whose eyesight had begun to grow dim so that he could not see, was lying down in his room; the lamp of God had not yet gone out, and Samuel was lying down in the temple of the Lord, where the ark of God was. Then the Lord called, "Samuel! Samuel!" and he said, "Here I am!" and ran to Eli, and said, "Here I am, for you called me." But he said, "I did not call; lie down again." So he went and lay down. The Lord called again, "Samuel!" Samuel got up and went to Eli, and said, "Here I am, for you called me." But he said, "I did not call, my son; lie down again." Now Samuel did not yet know the Lord, and the word of the Lord had not yet been revealed to him. The Lord called Samuel again, a third time. And he got up and went to Eli, and said, "Here I am, for you called me." Then Eli perceived that the Lord was calling the boy. Therefore Eli said to Samuel, "Go, lie down; and if he calls you, you shall say, 'Speak, Lord, for your servant is listening.'" So Samuel went and lay down in his place.

> **TRAIL CROSSING**
> In the Bible, when people hear the voice of God, the faithful response is, "Here I am!" This stands in contrast to the response of Adam and Eve in the Garden, who hide when they hear the voice of God (Genesis 3:8-9) Check out Genesis 22:1, Genesis 31:11, Exodus 3:4, and Isaiah 6:8 to hear other faithful people who respond "Here I am!" to God.

Now the Lord came and stood there, calling as before, "Samuel! Samuel!" And Samuel said, "Speak, for your servant is listening." Then the Lord said to Samuel, "See, I am about to do something in Israel that will make both ears of anyone who hears of it tingle. On that day I will fulfill against Eli all that I have spoken concerning his house, from beginning to end. For I have told him that I am about to punish his house forever, for the iniquity that he knew, because his sons were blaspheming God, and he did not restrain them. Therefore I swear to the house of Eli that the iniquity of Eli's house shall not be expiated by sacrifice or offering forever."

Samuel lay there until morning; then he opened the doors of the house of the Lord. Samuel was afraid to tell the vision to Eli. But Eli called Samuel and said, "Samuel, my son." He said, "Here I am." Eli said, "What was it that he told you? Do not hide it from me. May God do so to you and more also, if you hide anything from me of all that he told you." So Samuel told him everything and hid nothing from him. Then he said, "It is the Lord; let him do what seems good to him."

As Samuel grew up, the Lord was with him and let none of his words fall to the ground. And all Israel from Dan to Beer-sheba knew that Samuel was a trustworthy prophet of the Lord. The Lord continued to appear at Shiloh, for the Lord revealed himself to Samuel at Shiloh by the word of the Lord.

Scripture Citations
RUTH 1:7-18, 22 | 2:1-23 | 4:1-17
1 SAMUEL 1:9-28 | 2:12-13a | 3:1-21

QUESTIONS FOR THE JOURNEY

1. Ruth famously says, "For wherever you go, I will go; wherever you lodge, I will lodge; your people shall be my people, and your God my God." This passage is often understood in the context of marriage, but that misses the larger meaning. What do you imagine it was like for Ruth to make this declaration and to do what it says? What was she giving up? What was she gaining?

2. Ruth chooses to be a part of Naomi's family, even though they are not related by blood, and their social ties have been broken. Who are some of the people in your "family" who are related, not by blood, but by choice? What might these relationships teach us about the family of God?

3. Hannah prays and longs for a son for many years. When he is finally born, she gives him up to serve God, and it brings her deep joy. What might we learn from her faithful example?

4. When Samuel hears the voice of God calling him, at first he thinks it is the voice of Eli, his trusted mentor. What does the voice of God sound like to you? Has the voice of God ever spoken to you through other people? What was that experience like?

5. It takes four tries for the Lord to reach Samuel. Have you ever experienced God speaking to you persistently? Has it ever taken a few attempts for God to get through?

NEXT STEPS

• After Hannah dedicates her son to God and leaves him with Eli to serve the Lord, she sings a song of praise. Read her song in 1 Samuel 2:1-10. What do you notice about her prayer? How might her example inspire and challenge you? Then read Luke 1:26-56 to hear another story about an inspiring mother and the song she sings in praise of God.

• Both Hannah and Ruth have to give things up in order to love and serve God: Ruth gives up her homeland and her family, and Hannah offers up her beloved son. Yet they both find, not resentment, but joy in offering those things to God. Reflect on some things that you might have given up (or might be called to let go of) in order to follow God more fully. Pray for God's grace, not only to let go of those things, but also to do so with a joyful heart.

10
Determined to Have a King

While Samuel was growing up in Eli's household, disaster struck the people of Israel. In the midst of a battle with the Philistines, the ark of the Lord was captured. When Eli heard the news, he fell over backward and broke his neck, dying on the spot. The ark of the Lord stayed with the Philistines seven months, but during that time they suffered: their gods fell on their faces, and the people broke out in tumors. Finally, in desperation, the Philistines returned the ark to Israel, in an attempt to avoid God's wrath. There was much rejoicing in Israel, as they welcomed the ark home. The ark would remain safely in Shiloh until David would later bring it into Jerusalem. Samuel took Eli's place as chief priest and judge and lived his life just as he began it: faithful to the Lord, following his ways, and teaching the people to do the same. He called the people to put away foreign gods and direct their hearts fully to the Lord, and they did. He called them to repent and return to the Lord, and they did.

When Samuel became old, he made his sons judges over Israel. Yet his sons did not follow in his ways, but turned aside after gain; they took bribes and perverted justice. Then all the elders of Israel gathered together and came to Samuel at Ramah, and said to him, "You are old and your sons do not follow in your ways; appoint for us, then, a king to govern us, like other nations." But the thing displeased Samuel when they said, "Give us a king to govern us." Samuel prayed to the Lord, and the Lord said to Samuel, "Listen to the voice of the people in all that they say to you; for they have not rejected you, but they have rejected me from being king over them. Just as they have done to me, from the day I brought them up out of Egypt to this day, forsaking me and serving other gods, so also they are doing to you. Now then, listen to their voice; only— you shall solemnly warn them, and show them the ways of the king who shall reign over them."

So Samuel reported all the words of the Lord to the people who were asking him for a king. He said, "These will be the ways of the king who will reign over you: he will take your sons and appoint them to his chariots and to be his horsemen, and to run before his chariots; and he will appoint for himself commanders of thousands and commanders of fifties, and some to plow his ground and to reap his harvest, and to make his implements of war and the equipment of his chariots. He will take your daughters to be perfumers and cooks and bakers. He will take the best of your fields and vineyards and olive orchards and give them to his courtiers. He will take one-tenth of your grain and of your vineyards and give it to his officers and his courtiers. He will take your male and female slaves, and the best of your cattle and donkeys, and put them to his work. He will take one-tenth of your flocks, and you shall be his slaves. And in that day you will cry out because of your king, whom you have chosen for yourselves; but the Lord will not answer you in that day."

ISRAEL'S REQUEST FOR A KING GRANTED

But the people refused to listen to the voice of Samuel; they said, "No! but we are determined to have a king over us, so that we also may be like other nations, and that our king may govern us and go out before us and fight our battles." When Samuel had heard all the words of the people, he repeated them in the ears of the Lord. The Lord said to Samuel, "Listen to their voice and set a king over them."

There was a man of Benjamin whose name was Kish son of Abiel son of Zeror son of Becorath son of Aphiah, a Benjaminite, a man of wealth. He had a son whose name was Saul, a handsome young man. There was not a man among the people of Israel more handsome than he; he stood head and shoulders above everyone else.

One day, Saul went looking for one of his father's donkeys, which was lost, and traveled to the town where Samuel was staying.

Now the day before Saul came, the Lord had revealed to Samuel: "Tomorrow about this time I will send to you a man from the land of Benjamin, and you shall anoint him to be ruler over my people Israel. He shall save my people from the hand of the Philistines; for I have seen the suffering of my people, because their

> **TRAIL CROSSING**
> Donkeys play an important role in a number of biblical stories. Check out Numbers 22:22-35 and Matthew 21:1-11 to learn more.

outcry has come to me." When Samuel saw Saul, the Lord told him, "Here is the man of whom I spoke to you. He it is who shall rule over my people." Then Saul approached Samuel inside the gate, and said, "Tell me, please, where is the house of the seer?" Samuel answered Saul, "I am the seer; go up before me to the shrine, for today you shall eat with me, and in the morning I will let you go and will tell you all that is on your mind. As for your donkeys that were lost three days ago, give no further thought to them, for they have been found. And on whom is all Israel's desire fixed, if not on you and on all your ancestral house?" Saul answered, "I am only a Benjaminite, from the least of the tribes of Israel, and my family is the humblest of all the families of the tribe of Benjamin. Why then have you spoken to me in this way?"

Samuel took a vial of oil and poured it on his head, and kissed him; he said, "The Lord has anointed you ruler over his people Israel. You shall reign over the people of the Lord and you will save them from the hand of their enemies all around. Now this shall be the sign to you that the Lord has anointed you ruler over his heritage: When you depart from me today you will meet two men by Rachel's tomb in the territory of Benjamin at Zelzah; they will say to you, 'The donkeys that you went to seek are found, and now your father has stopped worrying about them and is worrying about you, saying: What shall I do about my son?' Then you shall go on from there further and come to the oak of Tabor; three men going up to God at Bethel will meet you there, one carrying three kids, another carrying three loaves of bread, and another carrying a skin of wine. They will greet you and give you two loaves of bread, which you shall accept from them. After that you shall come to Gibeath-elohim, at the place where the Philistine garrison is; there, as you come to the town, you will meet a band of prophets coming down from the shrine with harp, tambourine, flute, and lyre playing in front of them; they will be in a prophetic frenzy. Then the spirit of the Lord will possess you, and you will be in a prophetic frenzy along with them and be turned into a different person. Now when these signs meet you, do whatever you see fit to do, for God is with you. And you shall go down to Gilgal ahead of me; then I will come down to you to present burnt offerings and offer sacrifices of well-being. Seven days you shall wait, until I come to you and show you what you shall do."

SAUL PROPHESIES

As he turned away to leave Samuel, God gave him another heart; and all these signs were fulfilled that day. When they were going from there to Gibeah, a band of prophets met him; and the spirit of God possessed him, and he fell into a prophetic frenzy along with them. When all who knew him before saw how he prophesied with the prophets, the people said to one another, "What has come over the son of Kish? Is Saul also among the prophets?"

SAUL PROCLAIMED KING

Samuel summoned the people to the Lord at Mizpah and said to them, "Thus says the Lord, the God of Israel, 'I brought up Israel out of Egypt, and I rescued you from the hand of the Egyptians and from the hand of all the kingdoms that were oppressing you.' But today you have rejected your God, who saves you from all your calamities and your distresses; and you have said, 'No! but set a king over us.' Now therefore present yourselves before the Lord by your tribes and by your clans."

> **SCENIC VIEW**
> One of the things that the people like about Saul is how "kingly" he looks. When God sends Samuel to select Saul's successor, God will caution Samuel to choose based not on looks but on the heart (1 Samuel 16:7).

Then Samuel brought all the tribes of Israel near, and the tribe of Benjamin was taken by lot. He brought the tribe of Benjamin near by its families, and the family of the Matrites was taken by lot. Finally he brought the family of the Matrites near man by man, and Saul the son of Kish was taken by lot. But when they sought him, he could not be found. So they inquired again of the Lord, "Did the man come here?" and the Lord said, "See, he has hidden himself among the baggage." Then they ran and brought him from there. When he took his stand among the people, he was head and shoulders taller than any of them. Samuel said to all the people, "Do you see the one whom the Lord has chosen?

There is no one like him among all the people." And all the people shouted, "Long live the king!"

Saul gathered together warriors whose hearts God had touched. He marshaled them to fight against the Ammonites, whose king had been gouging out the eyes of the Israelites. Under Saul the Israelites were victorious against the Ammonites and drove them out. Then Saul, his son Jonathan, and the Israelite army went to face the Philistines. The Philistine army was massive: thirty thousand chariots, six thousand horsemen, and troops like the sand on the seashore in multitude; when the Israelites saw them, they were terrified. Saul stopped at Gilgal to wait, as Samuel had instructed him to do out of faithfulness to God.

Saul waited seven days, the time appointed by Samuel; but Samuel did not come to Gilgal, and the people began to slip away from Saul. So Saul said, "Bring the burnt offering here to me, and the offerings of well-being." And he offered the burnt offering. As soon as he had finished offering the burnt offering, Samuel arrived; and Saul went out to meet him and salute him. Samuel said, "What have you done?" Saul replied, "When I saw that the people were slipping away from me, and that you did not come within the days appointed, and that the Philistines were mustering at Michmash, I said, 'Now the Philistines will come down upon me at Gilgal, and I have not entreated the favor of the Lord'; so I forced myself, and offered the burnt offering." Samuel said to Saul, "You have done foolishly; you have not kept the commandment of the Lord your God, which he commanded you. The Lord would have established your kingdom over Israel forever, but now your kingdom will not continue; the Lord has sought out a man after his own heart; and the Lord has appointed him to be ruler over his people, because you have not kept what the Lord commanded you." And Samuel left and went on his way from Gilgal. The rest of the people followed Saul to join the army; they went up from Gilgal toward Gibeah of Benjamin.

Now Saul committed a very rash act on that day. He had laid an oath on the troops, saying, "Cursed be anyone who eats food before it is evening and I have been avenged on my enemies." So none of the troops tasted food. All the troops came upon a honeycomb; and there was honey on the ground. When the troops came upon the honeycomb, the honey was dripping out; but they did not put their hands to their mouths, for they feared the oath. But Jonathan had not heard his father charge the troops with the oath; so he extended the staff that was in his hand, and dipped the tip of it in the honeycomb, and put his hand to his mouth; and his eyes brightened. Then one of the soldiers said, "Your father strictly charged the troops with an oath, saying, 'Cursed be anyone who eats food this day.' And so the troops are faint." Then Jonathan said, "My father has troubled the land; see how my eyes have brightened because I tasted a little of this honey. How much better if today the troops had eaten freely of the spoil taken from their enemies; for now the slaughter among the Philistines has not been great."

After they had struck down the Philistines that day from Michmash to Aijalon, the troops were very faint; so the troops flew upon the spoil, and took sheep and oxen and calves, and slaughtered them on the ground; and the troops ate them with the blood. Then it was reported to Saul, "Look, the troops are sinning against the Lord by eating with the blood." And he said, "You have dealt treacherously; roll a large stone before me here." Saul said, "Disperse yourselves among the troops, and say to them, 'Let all bring their oxen or their sheep, and slaughter them here, and eat; and do not sin against the Lord by eating with the blood.'" So all of the troops brought their oxen with them that night, and slaughtered them there. And Saul built an altar to the Lord; it was the first altar that he built to the Lord.

> **YOU ARE HERE**
> A number of stories in the Bible feature leaders making promises to God before they think through the consequences. Compare this story to Judges 11. What might these passages teach us about the promises we make to God?

But when Saul prayed and asked God for guidance, he received no response from God. Knowing that something was wrong, Saul recklessly swore to kill whoever had sinned against God, even if it was his own son. After drawing lots, it was revealed that it was indeed his son, Jonathan, who had disobeyed. Saul, bound by his oath to God, said that Jonathan must die. But the Israelites rose in support of Jonathan, who had led them to victory. So the people ransomed Jonathan, and he did not die. Thus Saul, once again, failed to fulfill what he had sworn to God, even as he drove back the Philistines.

SAUL'S CONTINUING WARS

When Saul had taken the kingship over Israel, he fought against all his enemies on every side—against Moab, against the Ammonites, against Edom, against the kings of Zobah, and against the Philistines; wherever he turned he routed them. He did valiantly, and struck down the Amalekites, and rescued Israel out of the hands of those who plundered them.

Samuel said to Saul, "The Lord sent me to anoint you king over his people Israel; now therefore listen to the words of the Lord. Thus says the Lord of hosts, 'I will punish the Amalekites for what they did in opposing the Israelites when they came up out of Egypt. Now go and attack Amalek, and utterly destroy all that they have; do not spare them, but kill both man and woman, child and infant, ox and sheep, camel and donkey.'"

Saul followed the direction of the Lord, leading the Israelite army out and defeating the Amalekites. But once again, Saul failed to do precisely as God had instructed. Rather than destroying everything, as God had commanded, Saul spared King Agag and kept the best of the sheep and cattle, the fatlings and the lambs, and all that was valuable.

SAUL REJECTED AS KING

The word of the Lord came to Samuel: "I regret that I made Saul king, for he has turned back from following me, and has not carried out my commands." Samuel was angry; and he cried out to the Lord all night. Samuel rose early in the morning to meet Saul, and Samuel was told, "Saul went to Carmel, where he set up a monument for himself, and on returning he passed on down to Gilgal." When Samuel came to Saul, Saul said to him, "May you be blessed by the Lord; I have carried out the command of the Lord." But Samuel said, "What then is this bleating of sheep in my ears, and the lowing of cattle that I hear?" Saul said, "They have brought them from the Amalekites; for the people spared the best of the sheep and the cattle, to sacrifice to the Lord your God; but the rest we have utterly destroyed." Then Samuel said to Saul, "Stop! I will tell you what the Lord said to me last night." He replied, "Speak."

> **YOU ARE HERE**
>
> The Bible tells us that Samuel is angry, but it doesn't say at whom. Is he angry at God for changing his mind about Saul? Is he angry at Saul for disobeying God's command? Or is he angry at himself? Regardless, it is what Samuel does with his anger that is important; Samuel turns to God in the midst of his anger and cries out to God. What might this teach us about our anger?

Samuel said, "Though you are little in your own eyes, are you not the head of the tribes of Israel? The Lord anointed you king over Israel. And the Lord sent you on a mission, and said, 'Go, utterly destroy the sinners, the Amalekites, and fight against them until they are consumed.' Why then did you not obey the voice of the Lord? Why did you swoop down on the spoil, and do what was evil in the sight of the Lord?" Saul said to Samuel, "I have obeyed the voice of the Lord, I have gone on the mission on which the Lord sent me, I have brought Agag the king of Amalek, and I have utterly destroyed the Amalekites. But from the spoil the people took sheep and cattle, the best of the things devoted to destruction, to sacrifice to the Lord your God in Gilgal." And Samuel said,

> "Has the Lord as great delight in burnt offerings
> and sacrifices,
> as in obedience to the voice of the Lord?
> Surely, to obey is better than sacrifice,
> and to heed than the fat of rams.
> For rebellion is no less a sin than divination,
> and stubbornness is like iniquity and idolatry.
> Because you have rejected the word of the Lord,
> he has also rejected you from being king."

Saul said to Samuel, "I have sinned; for I have transgressed the commandment of the Lord and your words, because I feared the people and obeyed their voice. Now therefore, I pray, pardon my sin, and return with me, so that I may worship the Lord." Samuel said to Saul, "I will not return with you; for you have rejected the word of the Lord, and the Lord has rejected you from being king over Israel." As Samuel turned to go away, Saul caught hold of the hem of his robe, and it tore. And Samuel said to him, "The Lord has torn the kingdom of Israel from you this very day, and has given it to a neighbor of yours, who is better than you. Moreover the Glory of Israel will not recant or change his mind; for he is not a mortal, that he should change his mind." Then Saul said, "I have sinned; yet honor me now before the elders of my people and before Israel, and return with me, so that I may worship the Lord your God." So Samuel turned back after Saul; and Saul worshiped the Lord.

Then Samuel went to Ramah; and Saul went up to his house in Gibeah of Saul. Samuel did not see Saul again until the day of his death, but Samuel grieved over Saul. And the Lord was sorry that he had made Saul king over Israel.

The Lord said to Samuel, "How long will you grieve over Saul? I have rejected him from being king over Israel. Fill your horn with oil and set out; I will send you to Jesse the Bethlehemite, for I have provided for myself a king among his sons."

When the sons of Jesse came, Samuel looked on Eliab and thought, "Surely the Lord's anointed is now before the Lord." But the Lord said to Samuel, "Do not look on his appearance or on the height of his stature, because I have rejected him; for the Lord does not see as mortals see; they look on the outward appearance, but the Lord looks on the heart." Then Jesse called Abinadab, and made him pass before Samuel. He said, "Neither has the Lord chosen this one." Then Jesse made Shammah pass by. And he said, "Neither has the Lord chosen this one." Jesse made seven of his sons pass before Samuel, and Samuel said to Jesse, "The Lord has not chosen any of these." Samuel said to Jesse, "Are all your sons here?" And he said, "There remains yet the youngest, but he is keeping the sheep." And Samuel said to Jesse, "Send and bring him; for we will not sit down until he comes here." He sent and brought him in. Now he was ruddy, and had beautiful eyes, and was handsome. The Lord said, "Rise and anoint him; for this is the one." Then Samuel took the horn of oil, and anointed him in the presence of his brothers; and the spirit of the Lord came mightily upon David from that day forward. Samuel then set out and went to Ramah.

> **TRAIL CROSSING**
> Anointing with oil is a way of setting people and things apart as holy. Exodus 30 describes using anointing oil to consecrate the Levitical priests, the Tabernacle, and the holy objects. Both David and Saul are anointed with oil as a sign of their kingship. Read Luke 7:36-50 to hear another important story of anointing.

DAVID PLAYS THE LYRE FOR SAUL

Now the spirit of the Lord departed from Saul, and an evil spirit from the Lord tormented him. And Saul's servants said to him, "See now, an evil spirit from God is tormenting you. Let our lord now command the servants who attend you to look for someone who is skillful in playing the lyre; and when the evil spirit from God is upon you, he will play it, and you will feel better." So Saul said to his servants, "Provide for me someone who can play well, and bring him to me." One of the young men answered, "I have seen a son of Jesse the Bethlehemite who is skillful in playing, a man of valor, a warrior, prudent in speech, and a man of good presence; and the Lord is with him." So Saul sent messengers to Jesse, and said, "Send me your son David who is with the sheep." Jesse took a donkey loaded with bread, a skin of wine, and a kid, and sent them by his son David to Saul. And David came to Saul, and entered his service. Saul loved him greatly, and he became his armor-bearer. Saul sent to Jesse, saying, "Let David remain in my service, for he has found favor in my sight." And whenever the evil spirit from God came upon Saul, David took the lyre and played it with his hand, and Saul would be relieved and feel better, and the evil spirit would depart from him.

Scripture Citations

1 SAMUEL 8:1, 3-22a | 9:1-2, 15-21 | 10:1-11, 17-24 | 13:8-15 | 14:24-35, 47-48 | 15:1-3, 10- 31, 34-35 | 16:1, 6-23

QUESTIONS FOR THE JOURNEY

1. Again and again, God gives Saul specific directions to follow, and each time, Saul fails to do precisely as God asks. What might we learn from Saul about the importance of listening closely to God? What might we learn about obedience?

2. Saul is possessed by the spirit of God when he is first chosen by Samuel, and the spirit causes him to praise and prophecy. At the end of Saul's story, the evil spirit that seizes him is also said to come from God. What do you make of this?

3. Do you find Saul to be a sympathetic character? Why or why not?

4. Samuel grieves deeply over Saul's failure as a leader. Samuel had hoped Saul would be more than merely a successful ruler but rather that he would help lead the people closer to God. When have you been disappointed in one of your spiritual or civic leaders in whom you had put a tremendous amount of hope and trust?

5. In spite of his grief, Samuel remains faithful to God and is willing to try again with the leadership of David. When have you moved through grief and disappointment to choose to trust and follow another leader?

6. The stories of Israel's kings raise questions about the relationship between human authority and divine authority. How do you see the relationship of those two things? When have you needed to balance obedience to God with obedience to earthly leaders?

NEXT STEPS

- From the story of Samuel and Saul, we learn about the importance of spiritual leadership, even as we hear about the flawed humanity of our leaders. Take a moment to think about some of the important spiritual leaders in your life. Write or call one of those leaders, and thank him or her for bringing you closer to God.

- Samuel speaks up when Saul's political leadership is not in line with God's commands. How might you be called to speak to your political leaders in a way informed by your faith? Draft a letter to one of your senators or representatives addressing an issue you are passionate about, writing not only as a citizen but also as a Christian.

11

A Man after
God's Own Heart

Saul was deteriorating. The Spirit of the Lord had abandoned him, and it was replaced by evil spirits that tormented him. Samuel, Saul's trusted prophet and advisor, had left him. And the Israelites were still deeply entrenched in a war with the Philistines. The Philistines, with their much more advanced weaponry and aggressive military, continually oppressed and harassed the Israelites, never allowing the people a moment's peace.

DAVID AND GOLIATH

Now the Philistines gathered their armies for battle; they were gathered at Socoh, which belongs to Judah, and encamped between Socoh and Azekah, in Ephes-dammim. Saul and the Israelites gathered and encamped in the valley of Elah, and formed ranks against the Philistines. The Philistines stood on the mountain on the one side, and Israel stood on the mountain on the other side, with a valley between them. And there came out from the camp of the Philistines a champion named Goliath, of Gath, whose height was six cubits and a span.

He had a helmet of bronze on his head, and he was armed with a coat of mail; the weight of the coat was five thousand shekels of bronze. He had greaves of bronze on his legs and a javelin of bronze slung between his shoulders. The shaft of his spear was like a weaver's beam, and his spear's head weighed six hundred shekels of iron; and his shield bearer went before him. He stood and shouted to the ranks of Israel, "Why have you come out to draw up for battle? Am I not a Philistine, and are you not servants of Saul? Choose a man for yourselves, and let him come down to me. If he is able to fight with me and kill me, then we will be your servants; but if I prevail against him and kill him, then you shall be our servants and serve us." And the Philistine said, "Today I defy the ranks of Israel! Give me a man, that we may fight together." When Saul and all Israel heard these words of the Philistine, they were dismayed and greatly afraid.

> **POINT OF INTEREST**
> Six cubits and a span put Goliath anywhere from 6 feet, 9 inches to 10 feet! Clearly, Goliath's size was intimidating and in great contrast to the young David.

Now David, the youngest son of Jesse, the same one whom Samuel had anointed in secret to be the next king, was tending his father's flocks of sheep. But his three oldest brothers were fighting in Saul's army. Jesse sent David into Saul's camp to take food to his brothers. David left his sheep in the care of a keeper and took the provisions to his brothers. As he neared Saul's camp, David saw Goliath and heard him shouting his threats. All the other Israelites were terrified, but David was puzzled and asked the men near him, "Who is this uncircumcised Philistine, that he should defy the armies of the living God?" Others overheard his question and repeated it to Saul, who summoned David to come before him.

David said to Saul, "Let no one's heart fail because of him; your servant will go and fight with this Philistine." Saul said to David, "You are not able to go against this Philistine to fight with him; for you are just a boy, and he has been a warrior from his youth." But David said to Saul, "Your servant used to keep sheep for his father; and whenever a lion or a bear came, and took a lamb from the flock, I went after it and struck it down, rescuing the lamb from its mouth; and if it turned against me, I would catch it by the jaw, strike it down, and kill it. Your servant has killed both lions and bears; and this uncircumcised Philistine shall be like one of them, since he has defied the armies of the living God." David said, "The Lord, who saved me from the paw of the lion and from the paw of the bear, will save me from the hand of this Philistine." So Saul said to David, "Go, and may the Lord be with you!"

Saul clothed David with his armor; he put a bronze helmet on his head and clothed him with a coat of mail. David strapped Saul's sword over the armor, and he tried in vain to walk, for he was not used to them. Then David said to Saul, "I cannot walk with these; for I am not used to them." So David removed them. Then he took his staff in his hand, and chose five smooth stones from the wadi, and put them in his shepherd's bag, in the pouch; his sling was in his hand, and he drew near to the Philistine.

> **TRAIL CROSSING**
> Saul gave David his armor, but it was so heavy and cumbersome that David removed the armor before going to battle Goliath. Instead of using heavy armor, David trusted in God's protection. Read Ephesians 6:10-17 to hear more about the armor of God.

The Philistine came on and drew near to David, with his shield-bearer in front of him. When the Philistine looked and saw David, he disdained him, for he was only a youth, ruddy and handsome in appearance. The Philistine said to David, "Am I a dog, that you come to me with sticks?" And the Philistine cursed David by his gods. The Philistine said to David, "Come to me, and I will give your flesh to the birds of the air and to the wild animals of the field." But David said to the Philistine, "You come to me with sword and spear and javelin; but I come to you in the name of the Lord of hosts, the God of the armies of Israel, whom you have defied. This very day the Lord will deliver you into my hand, and I will strike you down and cut off your head; and I will give the dead bodies of the Philistine army this very day to the birds of the air and to the wild animals of the earth, so that all the earth may know that there is a God in Israel, and that all this assembly may know that the Lord does not save by sword and spear; for the battle is the Lord's and he will give you into our hand."

When the Philistine drew nearer to meet David, David ran quickly toward the battle line to meet the Philistine. David put his hand in his bag, took out a stone, slung it, and struck the Philistine on his forehead; the stone sank into his forehead, and he fell face down on the ground. So David prevailed over the Philistine with a sling and a stone, striking down the Philistine and killing him; there was no sword in David's hand. Then David ran and stood over the Philistine; he grasped his sword, drew it out of its sheath, and killed him; then he cut off his head with it. When the Philistines saw that their champion was dead, they fled. The troops of Israel and Judah rose up with a shout and pursued the Philistines as far as Gath and the gates of Ekron, so that the wounded Philistines fell on the way from Shaaraim as far as Gath and Ekron.

There was great tension between David and Saul. On multiple occasions, Saul tried to have David killed. But David and Jonathan, Saul's son, were beloved friends, and often Jonathan intervened to save David's life. David also had two opportunities to kill Saul, but both times he refused and spared Saul's life. After some time, Samuel died. Saul was so distressed that he consulted a medium, trying to communicate with Samuel after his death. Shortly thereafter, in a terrible battle with the Philistine's, Saul and his sons (including Jonathan) were killed. When David heard the news, he grieved deeply and lamented for Saul and his sons.

SCENIC VIEW

One of the low points of Saul's story is when he consults a medium, someone who claims to speak to the dead, which is strictly prohibited in Leviticus 19:31 and 20:6. Read the story of Saul and the medium at Endor in 1 Samuel 28:3-25.

Even the death of Saul did not immediately clarify the matter of kingship. There was a long war between the house of Saul and the house of David, as they battled to see who would rule Israel. Over time, David grew stronger and stronger, while the house of Saul became weaker and weaker. David's family grew: he married a series of wives (Michal, Ahinoam, Abigail, Maacah, Haggith, Abital, Eglah, and others who are unnamed), and with them, he had many sons (Amnon, Daniel, Absalom, Adonijah, Shephatiah, and Ithream) and a daughter, Tamar.

Finally, Israel was unified under David as king, and Jerusalem was established as the capitol. But safety was not immediately assured. The Philistines gathered to fight David and his army. David asked God for guidance, and God promised to be with him. David and his army defeated the Philistines, destroying their idols and driving them out. As a sign of the triumph of God, David brought the ark of the covenant to Jerusalem in joyful procession.

DAVID BRINGS THE ARK TO JERUSALEM

David and all the house of Israel were dancing before the Lord with all their might, with songs and lyres and harps and tambourines and castanets and cymbals.

When they came to the threshing floor of Nacon, Uzzah reached out his hand to the ark of God and took hold of it, for the oxen shook it. The anger of the Lord was kindled against Uzzah; and God struck him there because he reached out his hand to the ark; and he died there beside the ark of God. David was angry because the Lord had burst forth with an outburst upon Uzzah; so that place is called Perez-uzzah, to this day. David was afraid of the Lord that day; he said, "How can the ark of the Lord come into my care?" So David was unwilling to take the ark of the Lord into his care in the city of David; instead David took it to the house of Obed-edom the Gittite. The ark of the Lord remained in the house of Obed-edom the Gittite three months; and the Lord blessed Obed-edom and all his household.

It was told King David, "The Lord has blessed the household of Obed-edom and all that belongs to him, because of the ark of God." So David went and brought up the ark of God from the house of Obed-edom to the city of David with rejoicing; and when those who bore the ark of the Lord had gone six paces, he sacrificed an ox and a fatling. David danced before the Lord with all his might; David was girded with a linen ephod. So David and all the house of Israel brought up the ark of the Lord with shouting, and with the sound of the trumpet.

As the ark of the Lord came into the city of David, Michal daughter of Saul looked out of the window, and saw King David leaping and dancing before the Lord; and she despised him in her heart. They brought in the ark of the Lord, and set it in its place, inside the tent that David had pitched for it; and David offered burnt offerings and offerings of well-being before the Lord. When David had finished offering the burnt offerings and the offerings of well-being, he blessed the people in the name of the Lord of hosts, and distributed food among all the people, the whole multitude of Israel, both men and women, to each a cake of bread, a portion of meat, and a cake of raisins. Then all the people went back to their homes.

SCENIC VIEW
The psalms that David wrote would become the prayer book of God's people through the centuries, the very same prayers of praise and longing and grief and joy that are sung and said in churches and synagogues around the world today. You can find those psalms of David, as well as some by other, unknown authors, in the Bible's book of Psalms.

When David returned to his home, his wife Michal, the daughter of Saul, mocked him, telling him that he looked silly and shameful, dancing and singing before the ark of God. But David told her that praising God with psalms and songs and dance was more important than what others thought of him. In fact, throughout his life, David would write psalms and songs to God: hymns of glorious praise and prayers of crippling doubt, poems that expressed the whole range of human emotion. David was unfailingly honest with God, laying his heart bare before God just as he laid himself bare that day in the streets of Jerusalem.

GOD'S COVENANT WITH DAVID

Now when the king was settled in his house, and the Lord had given him rest from all his enemies around him, the king said to the prophet Nathan, "See now, I am living in a house of cedar, but the ark of God stays in a tent." Nathan said to the king, "Go, do all that you have in mind; for the Lord is with you."

But that same night the word of the Lord came to Nathan: Go and tell my servant David: Thus says the Lord: Are you the one to build me a house to live in? I have not lived in a house since the day I brought up the people of Israel from Egypt to this day, but I have been moving about in a tent and a tabernacle. Wherever I have moved about among all the people of Israel, did I ever speak a word with any of the tribal leaders of Israel, whom I commanded to shepherd my people Israel, saying, "Why have you not built me a house of cedar?" Now therefore thus you shall say to my servant David: Thus says the Lord of hosts: I took you from the pasture, from following the sheep to be prince over my people Israel; and I have been with you wherever you went, and have cut off all your enemies from before you; and I will make for you a great name, like the name of the great ones of the earth. And I will appoint a place for my people Israel and will plant them, so that they may live in their own place, and be disturbed no more; and evildoers shall afflict them no more, as formerly, from the time that I appointed judges over my people Israel; and I will give you rest from all your enemies. Moreover the Lord declares to you that the Lord will make you a house. When your days are fulfilled and you lie down with your ancestors, I will raise up your offspring after you, who shall come forth from your body, and I will establish his kingdom. He shall build a house for my name, and I will establish the throne of his kingdom forever. I will be a father to him, and he shall be a son to me. When he commits iniquity, I will punish him with a rod such as mortals use, with blows inflicted by human beings. But I will not take my steadfast love from him, as I took it from Saul, whom I put away from before you. Your house and your kingdom shall be made sure forever before me; your throne shall be established forever. In accordance with all these words and with all this vision, Nathan spoke to David.

David was in awe that God had chosen him, that God had promised to build a house for him and that his descendants would build a temple for God. David prayed a prayer of praise and thanksgiving, for all that God had done for Israel from the beginning and all that God was doing in and through David and his family. God was faithful to the promise that he made to David, and David continued to lead the Israelites to victory wherever he went. He defeated the Ammonites and the Arameans, and the territory of Israel spread and expanded. So David reigned over all Israel, and David administered justice and equity to all his people. But even the greatest king that had ever been, a man after God's own heart, wasn't perfect.

In the spring of the year, the time when kings go out to battle, David sent Joab with his officers and all Israel with him; they ravaged the Ammonites, and besieged Rabbah. But David remained at Jerusalem.

It happened, late one afternoon, when David rose from his couch and was walking about on the roof of the king's house, that he saw from the roof a woman bathing; the woman was very beautiful. David sent someone to inquire about the woman. It was reported, "This is Bathsheba daughter of Eliam, the wife of Uriah the Hittite." So David sent messengers to get her, and she came to him, and he lay with her. (Now she was purifying herself after her period.) Then she returned to her house. The woman conceived; and she sent and told David, "I am pregnant."

So David sent word to Joab, "Send me Uriah the Hittite." And Joab sent Uriah to David. When Uriah came to him, David asked how Joab and the people fared, and how the war was going. Then David said to Uriah, "Go down to your house, and wash your feet." Uriah went out of the king's house, and there followed him a present from the king. But Uriah slept at the entrance of the king's house with all the servants of his lord, and did not go down to his house. When they told David, "Uriah did not go down to his house," David said to Uriah, "You have just come from a journey. Why did you not go down to your house?" Uriah said to David, "The ark and Israel and Judah remain in booths; and my lord Joab and the servants of my lord are camping in the open field; shall I then go to my house, to eat and to drink, and to lie with my wife? As you live, and as your soul lives, I will not do such a thing." Then David said to Uriah, "Remain here today also, and tomorrow I will send you back." So Uriah remained in Jerusalem that day. On the next day, David invited him to eat and drink in his presence and made him drunk; and in the evening he went out to lie on his couch with the servants of his lord, but he did not go down to his house.

DAVID HAS URIAH KILLED

In the morning David wrote a letter to Joab, and sent it by the hand of Uriah. In the letter he wrote, "Set Uriah in the forefront of the hardest fighting, and then draw back from him, so that he may be struck down and die." As Joab was besieging the city, he assigned Uriah to the place where he knew there were valiant warriors. The men of the city came out and fought with Joab; and some of the servants of David among the people fell. Uriah the Hittite was killed as well.

When the wife of Uriah heard that her husband was dead, she made lamentation for him. When the mourning was over, David sent and brought her to his house, and she became his wife, and bore him a son.

NATHAN CONDEMNS DAVID

But the thing that David had done displeased the Lord, and the Lord sent Nathan to David. He came to him, and said to him, "There were two men in a certain city, the one rich and the other poor. The rich man had very many flocks and herds; but the poor man had nothing but one little ewe lamb, which he had bought. He brought it up, and it grew up with him and with his children; it used to eat of his meager fare, and drink from his cup, and lie in his bosom, and it was like a daughter to him.

Now there came a traveler to the rich man, and he was loath to take one of his own flock or herd to prepare for the wayfarer who had come to him, but he took the poor man's lamb, and prepared that for the guest who had come to him." Then David's anger was greatly kindled against the man. He said to Nathan, "As the Lord lives, the man who has done this deserves to die; he

> **TRAIL CROSSING**
> The kind of story that Nathan tells David is a parable. It is a little story with a big point that is meant to teach David, the listener, about himself, his actions, and God. Later in the New Testament, we will see that Jesus often teaches through parables.
> Check out a few of Jesus' most famous stories in Luke 15:4-32 and Matthew 13:31-44.

shall restore the lamb fourfold, because he did this thing, and because he had no pity."

Nathan said to David, "You are the man! Thus says the Lord, the God of Israel: I anointed you king over Israel, and I rescued you from the hand of Saul; I gave you your master's house, and your master's wives into your bosom, and gave you the house of Israel and of Judah; and if that had been too little, I would have added as much more. Why have you despised the word of the Lord, to do what is evil in his sight? You have struck down Uriah the Hittite with the sword, and have taken his wife to be your wife, and have killed him with the sword of the Ammonites. Now therefore the sword shall never depart from your house, for you have despised me, and have taken the wife of Uriah the Hittite to be your wife. Thus says the Lord: I will raise up trouble against you from within your own house; and I will take your wives before your eyes, and give them to your neighbor, and he shall lie with your wives in the sight of this very sun. For you did it secretly; but I will do this thing before all Israel, and before the sun."

David said to Nathan, "I have sinned against the Lord." Nathan said to David, "Now the Lord has put away your sin; you shall not die. Nevertheless, because by this deed you have utterly scorned the Lord, the child that is born to you shall die." Then Nathan went to his house.

Just as Nathan had said, Bathsheba and David's child became very ill. David pleaded with God for the life of his child, weeping, fasting, and laying all night on the ground, hoping that God would change his mind. But on the seventh day, the child died. After their child's death, David consoled his wife Bathsheba, and she bore another son, whom they named Solomon. Solomon was beloved, both by his parents and by God.

David had many children with his wives and concubines, at least twenty of whom are named. But David's sons, especially Amnon, Absalom, and Adonijah, could not get along. They fought over who should succeed their father as king, and their disagreements caused division and conflict in the kingdom. God had chosen Solomon to rule after David's death, but his brothers would not relent. Much to the heartbreak of their father, Amnon, Absalom, and Adonijah each died as a result of their treacherous behavior in pursuit of the throne. So it was that, after David died, what God had promised came to pass, and Solomon succeeded him as king

Scripture Citations
1 SAMUEL 17:1-11, 32-52
2 SAMUEL 6:5-19 | 7:1-17 | 11:1-17, 26-27 | 12:1-25

QUESTIONS FOR THE JOURNEY

1. The story of David and Goliath is familiar, and yet most of the time we barely scratch the surface when reading it. What did you notice, reading the story this time, that you might not have noticed before?

2. What does David's relationship with God look like? What impact might the example of his life and relationship with God have on our relationship with God?

3. In what ways are Saul and David similar as leaders? In what ways do they differ? What does each king's reign teach us about God?

4. Nathan tells David a story that helps David see his own life and actions more clearly. Have you ever had a story (from books, movies, or history) that helped you see your life more clearly? What was it and what did it teach you?

5. In our journey with God, there are times when we make a wrong turn, as David does in this story. Repentance means "turning around" and getting back on track. What does turning around look like in David's story? When are some times when you have taken a wrong turn and needed to turn around?

NEXT STEPS

- Many of the most beloved poems and hymns in the book of Psalms are attributed to David. Read a few psalms (Psalm 23, 51, 63, and 139 are good possibilities, among others). What do you notice in reading these psalms? How do they help you understand David? What do they say about David's relationship with God? What might you learn from them about how to talk with God?

- The friendship between David and Jonathan is legendary. Read the story of their friendship in 1 Samuel 18-20. Reflect on some of the central friendships in your life. This week, take time to give thanks for those friendships, remembering them in your prayers. Write your friends a note, telling them what they have meant in your life.

12

The Wisdom of God Was in Him

David's son Solomon followed him as king, as God had promised David.

Solomon made a marriage alliance with Pharaoh king of Egypt; he took Pharaoh's daughter and brought her into the city of David, until he had finished building his own house and the house of the Lord and the wall around Jerusalem. The people were sacrificing at the high places, however, because no house had yet been built for the name of the Lord.

Solomon loved the Lord, walking in the statutes of his father David; only, he sacrificed and offered incense at the high places. The king went to Gibeon to sacrifice there, for that was the principal high place; Solomon used to offer a thousand burnt offerings on that altar. At Gibeon the Lord appeared to Solomon in a dream by night; and God said, "Ask what I should give you."

And Solomon said, "You have shown great and steadfast love to your servant my father David, because he walked before **you** in faithfulness, in righteousness, and in uprightness of heart toward you; and you have kept for him this great and steadfast love, and have given him a son to sit on his throne today. And now, O Lord my God, you have made your servant king in place of my father David, although I am only a little child; I do not know how to go out or come in. And your servant is in the midst of the people whom you have chosen, a great people, so numerous they cannot be numbered or counted. Give your servant therefore an understanding mind to govern your people, able to discern between good and evil; for who can govern this your great people?"

It pleased the Lord that Solomon had asked this. God said to him, "Because you have asked this, and have not asked for yourself long life or riches, or for the life of your enemies, but have asked for yourself understanding to discern what is right, I now do according to your word. Indeed I give you a wise and discerning mind; no one like you has been before you and no one like you shall arise after you. I give you also what you have not asked, both riches and honor all your life; no other king shall compare with you. If you will walk in my ways, keeping my statutes and my commandments, as your father David walked, then I will lengthen your life."

Then Solomon awoke; it had been a dream. He came to Jerusalem where he stood before the ark of the covenant of the Lord. He offered up burnt offerings and offerings of well-being, and provided a feast for all his servants.

YOU ARE HERE

Burnt offerings and offerings of well-being were the sacrifices that faithful Israelites offered according to the commandments that God gave to Moses in Leviticus 1-7. Solomon made these offerings as a tangible demonstration of his gratitude and his faithfulness to God. What are some ways that you make offerings of gratitude and faithfulness to God?

SOLOMON'S WISDOM IN JUDGMENT

Later, two women who were prostitutes came to the king and stood before him. The one woman said, "Please, my lord, this woman and I live in the same house; and I gave birth while she was in the house. Then on the third day after I gave birth, this woman also gave birth. We were together; there was no one else with us in the house, only the two of us were in the house. Then this woman's son died in the night, because she lay on him. She got up in the middle of the night and took my son from beside me while your servant slept. She laid him at her breast, and laid her dead son at my breast. When I rose in the morning to nurse my son, I saw that he was dead; but when I looked at him closely in the morning, clearly it was not the son I had borne." But the other woman said, "No, the living son is mine, and the dead son is yours." The first said, "No, the dead son is yours, and the living son is mine." So they argued before the king.

Then the king said, "The one says, 'This is my son that is alive, and your son is dead'; while the other says, 'Not so! Your son is dead, and my son is the living one.'" So the king said, "Bring me a sword," and they brought a sword before the king. The king said, "Divide the living boy in two; then give half to the one, and half to the other." But the woman whose son was alive said to the king—because compassion for her son burned within her—"Please, my lord, give her the living boy; certainly do not kill him!" The other said, "It shall be neither mine nor yours; divide it."

Then the king responded: "Give the first woman the living boy; do not kill him. She is his mother." All Israel heard of the judgment that the king had rendered; and they stood in awe of the king, because they perceived that the wisdom of God was in him, to execute justice.

God gave Solomon very great wisdom, discernment, and breadth of understanding as vast as the sand on the seashore, so that Solomon's wisdom surpassed the wisdom of all the people of the east, and all the wisdom of Egypt. He composed three thousand proverbs, and his songs numbered a thousand and five. He would speak of trees, from the cedar that is in the Lebanon to the hyssop that grows in the wall; he would speak of animals, and birds, and reptiles, and fish. People came from all the nations to hear the wisdom of Solomon; they came from all the kings of the earth who had heard of his wisdom.

> **SCENIC VIEW**
>
> The biblical books of Proverbs, Song of Songs, and Ecclesiastes are all associated with Solomon. They are collections of the wise proverbs and songs for which he was so renowned. The Wisdom of Solomon is also associated with Solomon. It is part of the Apocrypha, ancient texts often included in Bibles between the Old and New Testaments.

Even the Queen of Sheba came to meet the famously wise King Solomon and test him with questions; he so impressed her with his answers that she praised both Solomon and the Lord his God and showered him with gifts before returning home. King Solomon was king over all Israel, and peace was established in the land and the people of Israel settled in their home, each of the tribes of Israel taking its place in the life and governance of the people of Israel. But though King Solomon had a beautiful palace, and the people of Israel had homes, God's dwelling place was still the tabernacle, the humble tent that the people had carried in the wilderness when they were nomads. During his lifetime, King David had collected everything for the temple: plans, materials, and some of the furnishings. But God had decided that it would be Solomon, not David, who would build the temple, the place where God would rest in the midst of the people Israel, where they might come to worship and encounter God more closely.

> **TRAIL CROSSING**
>
> Mount Moriah is an important place for the people of Israel. In Genesis 22:2, it is where Abraham goes to offer as sacrifice his son, Isaac.

Solomon began to build the house of the Lord in Jerusalem on Mount Moriah, where the Lord had appeared to his father David, at the place that David had designated, on the threshing floor of Ornan the Jebusite. He began to build on the second day of the second month of the fourth year of his reign. These are Solomon's measurements for building the house of God: the length, in cubits of the old standard, was sixty cubits, and the width twenty cubits. The vestibule in front of the nave of the house was twenty cubits long, across the width of the house; and its height was one hundred twenty cubits. He overlaid it on the inside with pure gold. The nave he lined with cypress, covered it with fine gold, and made palms and chains on it. He adorned the house with settings of precious stones. The gold was gold from Parvaim. So he lined the house with gold—its beams, its thresholds, its walls, and its doors; and he carved cherubim on the walls.

He made the most holy place; its length, corresponding to the width of the house, was twenty cubits, and its width was twenty cubits; he overlaid it with six hundred talents of fine gold. The weight of the nails was fifty shekels of gold. He overlaid the upper chambers with gold. In the most holy place he made two carved cherubim and overlaid them with gold. The wings of the cherubim together extended twenty cubits: one wing of the one, five cubits long, touched the wall of the house, and its other wing, five cubits long, touched the wing of the other cherub; and of this cherub, one wing, five cubits long, touched the wall of the house, and the other wing, also five cubits long, was joined to the wing of the first cherub. The wings of these cherubim extended twenty cubits; the cherubim stood on their feet, facing the nave. And Solomon made the curtain of blue and purple and crimson fabrics and fine linen, and worked cherubim into it.

So Solomon made all the things that were in the house of God: the golden altar, the tables for the bread of the Presence, the lampstands and their lamps of pure gold to burn before the inner sanctuary, as

> **YOU ARE HERE**
> The things that are put in the temple are made from gold and finest gemstones.
> It was the people's way of offering their very best to God for his house. What are some ways that we can offer our very best to God?

prescribed; the flowers, the lamps, and the tongs, of purest gold; the snuffers, basins, ladles, and firepans, of pure gold. As for the entrance to the temple: the inner doors to the most holy place and the doors of the nave of the temple were of gold.

Thus all the work that King Solomon did on the house of the Lord was finished. Solomon brought in the things that his father David had dedicated, the silver, the gold, and the vessels, and stored them in the treasuries of the house of the Lord.

THE ARK BROUGHT INTO THE TEMPLE

Then Solomon assembled the elders of Israel and all the heads of the tribes, the leaders of the ancestral houses of the people of Israel, in Jerusalem, to bring up the ark of the covenant of the Lord out of the city of David, which is Zion. King Solomon and all the congregation of Israel, who had assembled before him, were before the ark, sacrificing so many sheep and oxen that they could not be numbered or counted. Then the priests brought the ark of the covenant of the Lord to its place, in the inner sanctuary of the house, in the most holy place, underneath the wings of the cherubim. For the cherubim spread out their wings over the place of the ark, so that the cherubim made a covering above the ark and its poles. There was nothing in the ark except the two tablets that Moses put there at Horeb, where the Lord made a covenant with the people of Israel after they came out of Egypt.

Now when the priests came out of the holy place (for all the priests who were present had sanctified themselves, without regard to their divisions), all the levitical singers, Asaph, Heman, and Jeduthun, their sons and kindred, arrayed in fine linen, with cymbals, harps, and lyres, stood east of the altar with one hundred twenty priests who were trumpeters. It was the duty of the trumpeters and singers to make themselves heard in unison in praise and thanksgiving to the Lord, and when the song was raised, with trumpets and cymbals and other musical instruments, in praise to the Lord,

> "For he is good,
>> for his steadfast love endures forever,"

the house, the house of the Lord, was filled with a cloud, so that the priests could not stand to minister because of the cloud; for the glory of the Lord filled the house of God.

> **TRAIL CROSSING**
> Here we have another early description of people praising and worshiping God through music. This same couplet can be found throughout the psalms (100, 118, 136).

Solomon fell on his knees before all the people of Israel and offered a prayer full of praise and thanksgiving to God. With his prayer, Solomon dedicated the temple, offering both the temple itself and the people of Israel to God.

When Solomon had ended his prayer, fire came down from heaven and consumed the burnt offering and the sacrifices; and the glory of the Lord filled the temple. The priests could not enter the house of the Lord, because the glory of the Lord filled the Lord's house. When all the people of Israel saw the fire come down and the glory of the Lord on the temple, they bowed down on the pavement with their faces to the ground, and worshiped and gave thanks to the Lord, saying,

> "For he is good,
>> for his steadfast love endures forever."

Then the king and all the people offered sacrifice before the Lord. King Solomon offered as a sacrifice twenty-two thousand oxen and one hundred twenty thousand sheep. So the king and all the people dedicated the house of God.

Then the Lord appeared to Solomon in the night and said to him: "I have heard your prayer, and have chosen this place for myself as a house of sacrifice. When I shut up the heavens so that there is no rain, or command the locust to devour the land, or send pestilence among my people, if my people who are called by my name humble themselves, pray, seek my face, and turn from their wicked ways, then I will hear from heaven, and will forgive their sin and heal their land. Now my eyes will be open and my ears attentive to the prayer that is made in this place. For now I have chosen and consecrated this house so that my name may be there forever; my eyes and my heart will be there for all time. As for you, if you walk before me, as your father David walked, doing according to all that I have commanded you and keeping my statutes and my ordinances, then I will establish your royal throne, as I made covenant with your father David saying, 'You shall never lack a successor to rule over Israel.'

"But if you turn aside and forsake my statutes and my commandments that I have set before you, and go and serve other gods and worship them, then I will pluck you up from the land that I have given you; and this house, which I have consecrated for my name, I will cast out of my sight, and will make it a proverb and a byword among all peoples. And regarding this house, now exalted, everyone passing by will be astonished, and say, 'Why has the Lord done such a thing to this land and to this house?' Then they will say, 'Because they abandoned the Lord the God of their ancestors who brought them out of the land of Egypt, and they adopted other gods, and worshiped them and served them; therefore he has brought all this calamity upon them.'"

> **SCENIC VIEW**
>
> Again and again, God promises to be with the people, as long as they remain faithful to him, but that love requires a response from the people. God warns the people clearly of the consequences that will befall them if they turn astray.

In many ways, King Solomon, like his father David before him, was a man after God's own heart. Solomon asked for wisdom instead of riches, and he led the people of Israel into peace and prosperity. He built the glorious temple: a house for the Lord where the people of

Israel would praise and worship God. And yet, Solomon failed to fulfill all that God had asked of him.

King Solomon loved many foreign women along with the daughter of Pharaoh: Moabite, Ammonite, Edomite, Sidonian, and Hittite women, from the nations concerning which the Lord had said to the Israelites, "You shall not enter into marriage with them, neither shall they with you; for they will surely incline your heart to follow their gods"; Solomon clung to these in love. Among his wives were seven hundred princesses and three hundred concubines; and his wives turned away his heart. For when Solomon was old, his wives turned away his heart after other gods; and his heart was not true to the Lord his God, as was the heart of his father David. For Solomon followed Astarte the goddess of the Sidonians, and Milcom the abomination of the Ammonites. So Solomon did what was evil in the sight of the Lord, and did not completely follow the Lord, as his father David had done. Then Solomon built a high place for Chemosh the abomination of Moab, and for Molech the abomination of the Ammonites, on the mountain east of Jerusalem. He did the same for all his foreign wives, who offered incense and sacrificed to their gods.

Then the Lord was angry with Solomon, because his heart had turned away from the Lord, the God of Israel, who had appeared to him twice, and had commanded him concerning this matter, that he should not follow other gods; but he did not observe what the Lord commanded. Therefore the Lord said to Solomon, "Since this has been your mind and you have not kept my covenant and my statutes that I have commanded you, I will surely tear the kingdom from you and give it to your servant. Yet for the sake of your father David I will not do it in your lifetime; I will tear it out of the hand of your son. I will not, however, tear away the entire kingdom; I will give one tribe to your son, for the sake of my servant David and for the sake of Jerusalem, which I have chosen."

Soon, what the Lord had said came to pass. After Solomon died, the northern tribes of Israel, led by Jeroboam, rebelled, and civil war broke out. As a result, the once unified Israel was divided into two kingdoms; Rehoboam, son of Solomon, became king of Judah, the smaller, southern region where Jerusalem and the temple were located. Jeroboam became king of Israel, the larger, northern kingdom. Jeroboam and the people of Israel immediately did what is evil in the sight of God, abandoning the rules for sacrifices, worshiping other gods, and setting up golden calves to worship at Bethel and Dan. And soon, even Rehoboam and the people of Judah went astray, building other high places and worshiping other gods.

Neither of these rulers was a man after God's own heart, and neither of the kingdoms lived into their identity as God's people. There was continual warfare between Rehoboam and Jeroboam, between the northern and southern kingdoms. And when Rehoboam died, and his son Abijah succeeded him, things didn't get any better. The kingdom remained divided and the people continued to sin. The kings of Israel were particularly evil, scorning the ways of God and leading people further and further astray. The kings of Judah were not much better. Occasionally, a good king, like King Asa of Judah, would arise, and do what was right in the sight of the Lord, removing idols and returning to God. But inevitably the people would turn to sin again, either because of, or in spite of, their leader.

The people of Israel, who had clamored for an earthly king, were experiencing that reality. Even the greatest of their kings, David and Solomon, had failed to fulfill their portion of the covenant with God. And now, the kingdom of Israel had fallen into division and disarray, with the people turning against one another, as separated from each other as they were from God. God was not finished with them yet, but it was a dark time, indeed.

Scripture Citations
1 Kings 3:1-28 | 4:29-30, 32-34 | 7:51 | 11:1-13
2 Chronicles 3:1-14, | 4:19-22 | 5:2, 6-8, 10-14 |
7:1-5, 12-22

QUESTIONS FOR THE JOURNEY

1. When God appears to Solomon at Gibeon, he says, "Ask what I should give you." What would you ask God for if he appeared to you in a dream?

2. Solomon is renowned for his wisdom. Who are some of the wise people in your life? What words of wisdom have they spoken to you?

3. Solomon is responsible for building the temple, the sacred place of worship where God chooses to dwell among the people. What do you notice about the temple? How does it compare to the places where you have worshiped God?

4. The story says that "the glory of the Lord filled the temple." Where are some of the places that you have seen "the glory of the Lord"? What was that like?

5. Thus far in the story, we have heard the stories of many different leaders: Abraham, Moses, Deborah, Saul, David, and Solomon. How do these leaders compare to one another? What similarities have you seen, and what differences have you noted?

6. The people of Israel repeatedly beg God for a king, like other nations have, and God gives them what they ask for. How does the reality of kingship compare to what they might have wanted? What might we learn from their experience?

NEXT STEPS

- Solomon is renowned for his wisdom, and many of the books of the Bible known as "wisdom literature," including Proverbs and

Ecclesiastes, are attributed to Solomon. Read Ecclesiastes 5:1-20 or Proverbs 12:1-26. What do these writings say about wisdom? Do you agree or disagree with that assessment?

- In addition to being renowned for wisdom, Solomon is known for his love of women. So it is perhaps no surprise that the Song of Solomon (also called the Song of Songs) is attributed to him. Read Chapters 2, 7, and 8 of the Song of Solomon (or read the whole thing). What do you notice about the poetry of this book? Some say that this is about the love between humans the way that God intended it to be; others say that the poetry is a metaphor for the love between God and God's people. How do you hear this message?

13
Here I Am; Send Me

As the people wandered further and further from God, God's love for them did not wane. Even amid division and turmoil, God sent prophets to call the people to repent and return to the Lord. In the midst of a particularly dark time in Israel, when King Ahab and his wife Jezebel were encouraging worship of other gods like Baal and Asherah and slaughtering prophets and priests who worshiped the Lord, God sent Elijah the Tishbite to speak judgment and truth to the king, and to show by signs and miracles the power of almighty God. God sent ravens to bring food to Elijah in the wilderness where he lived, but one day the river that he drank from dried up, because God had sent a drought upon the land.

Then the word of the Lord came to Elijah, saying, "Go now to Zarephath, which belongs to Sidon, and live there; for I have commanded a widow there to feed you." So he set out and went to Zarephath. When he came to the gate of the town, a widow was there gathering sticks; he called to her and said, "Bring me a little water in a vessel, so that I may drink." As she was going to bring it, he called to her and said, "Bring me a morsel of bread in your hand." But she said, "As the Lord your God lives, I have nothing baked, only a handful of meal in a jar, and a little oil in a jug; I am now gathering a couple of sticks, so that I may go home and prepare it for myself and my son, that we may eat it, and die." Elijah said to her, "Do not be afraid; go and do as you have said; but first make me a little cake of it and bring it to me, and afterwards make something for yourself and your son. For thus says the Lord the God of Israel: The jar of meal will not be emptied and the jug of oil will not fail until the day that the Lord sends rain on the earth." She went and did as Elijah said, so that she as well as he and her household ate for many days. The jar of meal was not emptied, neither did the jug of oil fail, according to the word of the Lord that he spoke by Elijah.

TRAIL CROSSING
There are many feeding miracles in the Bible: from God sending manna from heaven (Exodus 16) to Jesus multiplying loaves and fish to feed 5,000 people (Matthew 14:13-21).

ELIJAH REVIVES THE WIDOW'S SON

After this the son of the woman, the mistress of the house, became ill; his illness was so severe that there was no breath left in him. She then said to Elijah, "What have you against me, O man of God? You have come to me to bring my sin to remembrance, and to cause the death of my son!" But he said to her, "Give me your son." He took him from her bosom, carried him up into the upper chamber where he was lodging, and laid him on his own bed. He cried out to the Lord, "O Lord my God, have you brought calamity even upon the widow with whom I am staying, by killing her son?" Then he stretched himself upon the child three times, and cried out to the Lord, "O Lord my God, let this child's life come into him again." The Lord listened to the voice of Elijah; the life of the child came into him again, and he revived. Elijah took the child, brought him down from the upper chamber into the house, and gave him to his mother; then Elijah said, "See, your son is alive." So the woman said to Elijah, "Now I know that you are a man of God, and that the word of the Lord in your mouth is truth."

After many days the word of the Lord came to Elijah, in the third year of the drought, saying, "Go, present yourself to Ahab; I will send rain on the earth." So Elijah went to present himself to Ahab. The famine was severe in Samaria.

When Ahab saw Elijah, Ahab said to him, "Is it you, you troubler of Israel?" He answered, "I have not troubled Israel; but you have, and your father's house, because you have forsaken the commandments of the Lord and followed the Baals. Now therefore have all Israel assemble for me at Mount Carmel, with the four hundred fifty prophets of Baal and the four hundred prophets of Asherah, who eat at Jezebel's table."

ELIJAH'S TRIUMPH OVER THE PRIESTS OF BAAL

So Ahab sent to all the Israelites, and assembled the prophets at Mount Carmel. Elijah then came near to all the people, and said, "How long will you go limping with two different opinions? If the Lord is God, follow him; but if Baal, then follow him." The people did not answer him a word. Then Elijah said to the people, "I, even I only, am left a prophet of the Lord; but Baal's prophets number four hundred fifty. Let two bulls be given to us; let them choose one bull for themselves, cut it in pieces, and lay it on the wood, but put no fire to it; I will prepare the other bull and lay it on the wood, but put no fire to it. Then you call on the name of your god and I will call on the name of the Lord; the god who answers by fire is indeed God." All the people answered, "Well spoken!" Then Elijah said to the prophets of Baal, "Choose for yourselves one bull and prepare it first, for you are many; then call on the name of your god, but put no fire to it." So they took the bull that was given them, prepared it, and called on the name of Baal from morning until noon, crying, "O Baal, answer us!" But there was no voice, and no answer. They limped about the altar that they had made. At noon Elijah mocked them, saying, "Cry aloud! Surely he is a god; either he is meditating, or he has wandered away, or he is on a journey, or perhaps he is asleep and must be awakened." Then they cried aloud and, as was their custom, they cut themselves with swords and lances until the blood gushed out over them. As midday passed, they raved on until the time of the offering of the oblation, but there was no voice, no answer, and no response.

Then Elijah said to all the people, "Come closer to me"; and all the people came closer to him. First he repaired the altar of the Lord that had been thrown down; Elijah took twelve stones, according to the number of the tribes of the sons of Jacob, to whom the word of the Lord came, saying, "Israel shall be your name"; with the stones he built an altar in the name of the Lord. Then he made a trench around the altar, large enough to contain two measures of seed. Next he put the wood in order, cut the bull in pieces, and laid it on the wood. He said, "Fill four jars with water and pour it on the burnt offering and on the wood." Then he said, "Do it a second time"; and they did it a second time. Again he said, "Do it a third time"; and they did it a third time, so that the water ran all around the altar, and filled the trench also with water.

> ## SCENIC VIEW
> Elijah is going to extremes in order to make a point. By repeatedly dousing the offering with water, he makes it clear that it is God's power, and not some magic trick, that sends fire to burn his offering. Again and again, God's prophets try to convince the people that the power of God is much greater than the power of idols made by human hands.

At the time of the offering of the oblation, the prophet Elijah came near and said, "O Lord, God of Abraham, Isaac, and Israel, let it be known this day that you are God in Israel, that I am your servant, and that I have done all these things at your bidding. Answer me, O Lord, answer me, so that this people may know that you, O Lord, are God, and that you have turned their hearts back." Then the fire of the Lord fell and consumed the burnt offering, the wood, the stones, and the dust, and even licked up the water that was in the trench. When all the people saw it, they fell on their faces and said, "The Lord indeed is God; the Lord indeed is God." Elijah said to them, "Seize the prophets of Baal; do not let one of them escape." Then they seized them; and Elijah brought them down to the Wadi Kishon, and killed them there.

Jezebel was enraged by Elijah's words and actions, and vowed to have him killed. So Elijah fled to the wilderness, alone and endangered. An angel brought him cake and water to sustain him, and he traveled in the wilderness forty days and forty nights until he reached Horeb, the mountain of God.

At that place he came to a cave, and spent the night there.

Then the word of the Lord came to him, saying, "What are you doing here, Elijah?" He answered, "I have been very zealous for the Lord, the God of hosts; for the Israelites have forsaken your covenant, thrown down your altars, and killed your prophets with the sword. I alone am left, and they are seeking my life, to take it away."

ELIJAH MEETS GOD AT HOREB

He said, "Go out and stand on the mountain before the Lord, for the Lord is about to pass by." Now there was a great wind, so strong that it was splitting mountains and breaking rocks in pieces before the Lord, but the Lord was not in the wind; and after the wind an earthquake, but the Lord was not in the earthquake; and after the earthquake a fire, but the Lord was not in the fire; and after the fire a sound of sheer silence. When Elijah heard it, he wrapped his face in his mantle and went out and stood at the entrance of the cave. Then there came a voice to him that said, "What are you doing here, Elijah?" He answered, "I have been very zealous for the Lord, the God of hosts; for the Israelites have forsaken your covenant, thrown down your altars, and killed your prophets with the sword. I alone am left, and they are seeking my life, to take it away." Then the Lord said to him, "Go, return on your way to the wilderness of Damascus; when you arrive, you shall anoint Hazael as king over Aram. Also you shall anoint Jehu son of Nimshi as king over Israel; and you shall anoint Elisha son of Shaphat of Abel-meholah as prophet in your place. Whoever escapes from the sword of Hazael, Jehu shall kill; and whoever escapes from the sword of Jehu, Elisha shall kill. Yet I will leave seven thousand in Israel, all the knees that have not bowed to Baal, and every mouth that has not kissed him."

Elijah did as God instructed him and continued to proclaim God's word to the kings of Israel, even though they ignored him. Elijah was faithful to God to the end. But Elijah's exit from this world did not come with mere death; God took Elijah up to heaven in a whirlwind, with a chariot of fire and horses of fire. Elijah's student, Elisha, took up Elijah's mantle as his successor, proclaiming God's word to the kings of Israel and the people, calling them to repent and return to God, and performing signs and miracles as Elijah had before him. Under Elisha, Elijah's prophecy against Ahab and Jezebel was fulfilled when Jehu was anointed king and called for the death of Jezebel and the destruction of the pagan altars. Yet shortly after, the people once again turned away from God, and the kingdom of Israel fell deeper and deeper into sin. Other prophets spoke out against the leaders of Israel. But their prophecies fell on deaf ears and hard hearts. Finally, the kingdom of Israel fell to Assyria and was led into captivity.

POINT OF INTEREST

Some of the most beautiful words in the Bible are spoken by the prophets who urge God's people to return their hearts to God. The prophet Amos begged the people of God to "let justice roll down like waters, and righteousness like an ever-flowing stream" (Amos 5:24). Micah reminds them that what God requires is for people "to do justice, and to love kindness, and to walk humbly with your God" (Micah 6:8b).

Meanwhile, in Judah, things did not fare much better. Though Rehoboam began with good intentions, he quickly abandoned the law of the Lord and led the people astray. Many of the succeeding kings also led the people into sin. So God sent prophets to the kings and the people of Judah as well, hoping against hope that some remnant of God's people remained faithful. One of those prophets was a man named Isaiah, who was called by God in a beautiful vision.

GOD CALLS ISAIAH

In the year that King Uzziah died, I saw the Lord sitting on a throne, high and lofty; and the hem of his robe filled the temple. Seraphs were in attendance above him; each had six wings: with two they covered their faces, and with two they covered their feet, and with two they flew. And one called to another and said:

> "Holy, holy, holy is the Lord of hosts;
> the whole earth is full of his glory."

The pivots on the thresholds shook at the voices of those who called, and the house filled with smoke. And I said: "Woe is me! I am lost, for I am a man of unclean lips, and I live among a people of unclean lips; yet my eyes have seen the King, the Lord of hosts!"

Then one of the seraphs flew to me, holding a live coal that had been taken from the altar with a pair of tongs. The seraph touched my mouth with it and said: "Now that this has touched your lips, your guilt has departed and your sin is blotted out." Then I heard the voice of the Lord saying, "Whom shall I send, and who will go for us?" And I said, "Here am I; send me!"

Isaiah was given a particular task: to warn the people of the consequences that would befall them if they continued to disobey the Lord. Isaiah took this commission seriously;

SCENIC VIEW
God often appears in the Bible in conjunction with fire. God appears to Moses in a burning bush (Exodus 3), sends a pillar of fire to guide the Israelites out of Egypt (Exodus 13:21-22), and shields Daniel's friends in the midst of a fiery furnace (Daniel 3:19-30). Here in Isaiah, we are reminded of fire's purifying power; the fiery coal touches Isaiah's lips and thereby cleanses his sin. The fire of God is often about purification, rather than punishment (Malachi 3:1-18, Psalm 66:10-12).

he spent three years walking around naked and barefoot in an attempt to draw attention to his message. Isaiah spoke prophecies of judgment against all of the nations: Assyria, Babylon, and Egypt. But God reserved his harshest words for his own people. God called Israel and Judah his beloved vineyard, which he tended and cared for lovingly. Yet they had not produced good fruit, they were instead unfaithful and unjust, ignoring God and abusing the poor in their midst, and Isaiah cried out to them in condemnation.

Ah, you who join house to house,
    who add field to field,
until there is room for no one but you,
    and you are left to live alone
    in the midst of the land!
The Lord of hosts has sworn in my hearing:
Surely many houses shall be desolate,
    large and beautiful houses, without inhabitant.

Ah, you who rise early in the morning
    in pursuit of strong drink,
who linger in the evening
    to be inflamed by wine,
whose feasts consist of lyre and harp,
    tambourine and flute and wine,
but who do not regard the deeds of the Lord,
    or see the work of his hands!
Ah, you who call evil good
    and good evil,
who put darkness for light
    and light for darkness,
who put bitter for sweet
    and sweet for bitter!
Ah, you who are wise in your own eyes,
    and shrewd in your own sight!
Ah, you who are heroes in drinking wine
    and valiant at mixing drink,

who acquit the guilty for a bribe,
  and deprive the innocent of their rights!
Therefore, as the tongue of fire devours the stubble,
  and as dry grass sinks down in the flame,
so their root will become rotten,
  and their blossom go up like dust;
for they have rejected the instruction of the Lord of hosts,
  and have despised the word of the Holy One of Israel.
Therefore the anger of the Lord was kindled against
    his people,
  and he stretched out his hand against them
    and struck them;
  the mountains quaked,
and their corpses were like refuse
  in the streets.
For all this his anger has not turned away,
  and his hand is stretched out still.

The people of God were not living as God called them to live, as a reflection of God's holiness in the world. The religious and political leaders were abusing their power and wealth, and all people were thinking of their own good, rather than serving and loving one another. As if their abuses and injustice were not enough, the people also failed in their worship of God and turned to idols. Isaiah was not alone in calling the people to repentance. God sent another prophet, Jeremiah, who was called as a young boy to speak to the people of Judah.

GOD CALLS JEREMIAH

 Now the word of the Lord came to me saying,

  "Before I formed you in the womb I knew you,
and before you were born I consecrated you;
I appointed you a prophet to the nations."

Then I said, "Ah, Lord God! Truly I do not know how to speak, for I am only a boy." But the Lord said to me, "Do not say, 'I am only a boy'; for you shall go to all to whom I send you, and you shall speak whatever I command you. Do not be afraid of them, for I am with you to deliver you, says the Lord."

TRAIL CROSSING
God says that he called Jeremiah even before he was born. In Luke we hear about another person who was called before he was born: John the Baptist. Read Luke 1:5-25, 39-45 to hear his story.

Then the Lord put out his hand and touched my mouth; and the Lord said to me,

"Now I have put my words in your
     mouth.
See, today I appoint you over nations
     and over kingdoms,
to pluck up and to pull down,
to destroy and to overthrow,
to build and to plant."

Like Isaiah, Jeremiah warned the people that they must repent and return to God in order to avoid complete destruction. Through Jeremiah, God tried yet another time to call the people back from the brink.

And when your people say, "Why has the Lord our God done all these things to us?" you shall say to them, "As you have forsaken me and served foreign gods in your land, so you shall serve strangers in a land that is not yours."

Declare this in the house of Jacob,
     proclaim it in Judah:
Hear this, O foolish and senseless people,
     who have eyes, but do not see,
     who have ears, but do not hear.
Do you not fear me? says the Lord;
     Do you not tremble before me?
I placed the sand as a boundary for the sea,
     a perpetual barrier that it cannot pass;
though the waves toss, they cannot prevail,
     though they roar, they cannot pass over it.

But this people has a stubborn and rebellious heart;
  they have turned aside and gone away.
They do not say in their hearts,
  "Let us fear the Lord our God,
who gives the rain in its season,
  the autumn rain and the spring rain,
and keeps for us
  the weeks appointed for the harvest."
Your iniquities have turned these away,
  and your sins have deprived you of good.
For scoundrels are found among my people;
  they take over the goods of others.
Like fowlers they set a trap;
  they catch human beings.
Like a cage full of birds,
  their houses are full of treachery;
therefore they have become great and rich,
  they have grown fat and sleek.
They know no limits in deeds of wickedness;
  they do not judge with justice
the cause of the orphan, to make it prosper,
  and they do not defend the rights of the needy.
Shall I not punish them for these things?
says the Lord,
  and shall I not bring retribution
  on a nation such as this?
An appalling and horrible thing
  has happened in the land:
the prophets prophesy falsely,
  and the priests rule as the prophets direct;
my people love to have it so,
  but what will you do when the end comes?

The word that came to Jeremiah from the Lord: Stand in the gate of the Lord's house, and proclaim there this word, and say, Hear the word of the Lord, all you people of Judah, you that enter these gates to worship the Lord. Thus says the Lord of hosts, the God of Israel: Amend your ways and your doings, and let me dwell with you in this place. Do not trust in these deceptive words: "This is the temple of the Lord, the temple of the Lord, the temple of the Lord."

For if you truly amend your ways and your doings, if you truly act justly one with another, if you do not oppress the alien, the orphan, and the widow, or shed innocent blood in this place, and if you do not go after other gods to your own hurt, then I will dwell with you in this place, in the land that I gave of old to your ancestors forever and ever.

Here you are, trusting in deceptive words to no avail. Will you steal, murder, commit adultery, swear falsely, make offerings to Baal, and go after other gods that you have not known, and then come and stand before me in this house, which is called by my name, and say, "We are safe!"—only to go on doing all these abominations? Has this house, which is called by my name, become a den of robbers in your sight? You know, I too am watching, says the Lord. Go now to my place that was in Shiloh, where I made my name dwell at first, and see what I did to it for the wickedness of my people Israel. And now, because you have done all these things, says the Lord, and when I spoke to you persistently, you did not listen, and when I called you, you did not answer, therefore I will do to the house that is called by my name, in which you trust, and to the place that I gave to you and to your ancestors, just what I did to Shiloh. And I will cast you out of my sight, just as I cast out all your kinsfolk, all the offspring of Ephraim. For the people of Judah have done evil in my sight, says the Lord; they have set their abominations in the house that is called by my name, defiling it.

TRAIL CROSSING
Jesus quotes this passage in Matthew 21:13. Like Jeremiah, Jesus has a big problem with the hypocrisy of people coming and worshiping God but acting unjustly in their daily lives.

God spoke through Isaiah and Jeremiah and other prophets again and again, warning the people of Judah that, if they continued their disobedience, they would be conquered by other nations and exiled, just as the people of Israel had been. But the people of Judah did not heed the prophets' calls. And so the prophecies of Jeremiah and Isaiah became a reality, and the calamity that God had warned of came to pass.

Judah became trapped between the armies of Egypt on one side, and the armies of Babylon on the other. The court of Judah was divided, with some wanting to unite with Egypt and others with Babylon, and only a few prophets crying in vain that the people should turn to the Lord, instead of earthly rulers. After Egypt was defeated by Babylon, the Babylonian army, led by King Nebuchadnezzar, laid siege to Jerusalem. Judah's king, Jehoiakim, was killed during the siege, and eventually the city fell. Jerusalem's wall and the temple were destroyed, and the people of Judah were scattered. Some fled to surrounding countries, and many were deported to Babylon by their captors.

By the rivers of Babylon—
   there we sat down and
     there we wept
   when we remembered Zion.
On the willows there
   we hung up our harps.
For there our captors
   asked us for songs,
and our tormentors asked for
     mirth, saying,
   "Sing us one of the songs of Zion!"
How could we sing the Lord's song
   in a foreign land?
If I forget you, O Jerusalem,
   let my right hand wither!
Let my tongue cling to the roof of my mouth,if I do not
   remember you,
   if I do not set Jerusalem
   above my highest joy.

SCENIC VIEW

This is Psalm 137, a psalm written during the exile. The psalmist is expressing deep grief and pain, yet turning that sadness into a conversation with God. The psalms express everything from joy to sadness, the full range of human emotion, reminding us that God is big enough for all of our emotions.

It was a dark time, indeed, for God's people. They were far from home, unable to worship God in their holy place, unable to observe their festivals, unsure of how to remain faithful in a foreign land. The people were in exile, distant not only from their home, but also from their God. But God was not finished with them yet; even in the midst of the people's faithlessness, God remained faithful, waiting to draw the people back in love.

Scripture Citations
1 KINGS 17:8-24 | 18:1-2, 17-40 | 19:9-18
ISAIAH 6:1-8 | 5:8-9, 11-12, 20-25
JEREMIAH 1:4-10 | 5:19-31 | 7:1-15, 30
PSALM 137:1-6

QUESTIONS FOR THE JOURNEY

1. Elijah, Isaiah, and Jeremiah each encounter and are called by God. How are their encounters with God similar? How are they different? What might we learn about God's presence from these stories?

2. Through the prophets, God speaks words of judgment about how the people of God are living. Which parts of the prophecies stand out to you? What seems to anger God the most? How can we hear the words of these prophets in our time?

3. The prophets often speak about the relationship between worship and living justly. What are some of the things that you notice from their words? How do you wrestle with the relationship between how you worship and how you live?

4. The prophets speak persistently to the people, calling them to return to God, but they refuse to hear. What might we learn about God from this persistence? What might we learn about ourselves?

5. What connections do you hear between this week's story and the stories of previous weeks?

NEXT STEPS

- Some of the most famous references to the words of the prophets are in the preaching of civil rights leader Martin Luther King Jr. Read his "Letter from a Birmingham Jail" or listen to his "I Have a Dream" speech. What connections does he make between the times of the prophets and his own time? What connections might we then make with our world today?

- The prophets proclaimed God's special concern for the poor, the outcast, the stranger, and the widow. How can you pray for these people? How do the words of the prophets call you beyond prayer to action? Resolve to act on one or two specific ways that you will do justice, welcome the stranger, or care for orphans and widows this month.

14
Daniel, Servant of the Living God

Driven into exile in Babylon, God's people began to wrestle with what faithfulness looked like in a foreign land. How could they worship God when the temple, the center for worship, was destroyed, and they were hundreds of miles away? How could they observe their festivals in a distant land? And, most importantly, how could they return to worshiping God, and only God, when the leaders of Babylon demanded otherwise?

Four young men, in particular, were faced with this dilemma: Shadrach, Meshach, Abednego, and Daniel. They had been taken into exile when Israel fell, and they were sent to serve in King Nebuchadnezzar's court. The four of them had great knowledge and wisdom, and God gave Daniel the ability to interpret dreams. Once, King Nebuchadnezzar had a very troubling dream, and no one in his court was able to interpret it. Daniel prayed to God for wisdom and insight and was able to interpret the dream for the king. So Daniel rose in the ranks of the king's court, and his three friends, Shadrach, Meshach, and Abednego were appointed overseers.

*Yet in spite of the favor that Daniel and his friends had garnered,
they were not exempt from the challenges that faced the Israelites in
exile. One day, King Nebuchadnezzar made a golden statue and
commanded all people to fall down and worship it every time they
heard the sound of music in the streets. If they did not worship
the statue, they would be thrown into a furnace of blazing fire.
But Shadrach, Meshach, and Abednego refused to do as King
Nebuchadnezzar commanded, and some of the king's followers
reported the infraction to him.*

"There are certain Jews whom you have appointed over
the affairs of the province of Babylon: Shadrach, Meshach,
and Abednego. These pay no heed to you, O king. They do not
serve your gods and they do not worship the golden statue that
you have set up."

Then Nebuchadnezzar in furious rage commanded that
Shadrach, Meshach, and Abednego be brought in; so they
brought those men before the king. Nebuchadnezzar said to
them, "Is it true, O Shadrach, Meshach, and Abednego, that
you do not serve my gods and you do not worship the golden
statue that I have set up? Now if you are ready when you hear
the sound of the horn, pipe, lyre, trigon, harp, drum, and entire
musical ensemble to fall down and worship the statue that I
have made, well and good. But if you do not worship, you shall
immediately be thrown into a furnace of blazing fire, and who
is the god that will deliver you out of my hands?"

Shadrach, Meshach, and Abednego answered the king, "O
Nebuchadnezzar, we have no need to present a defense to you
in this matter. If our God whom we serve is able to deliver us
from the furnace of blazing fire and out of your hand, O king,
let him deliver us. But if not, be it known to you, O king, that
we will not serve your gods and we will not worship the golden
statue that you have set up."

THE FIERY FURNACE

Then Nebuchadnezzar was so filled with rage against Shadrach, Meshach, and Abednego that his face was distorted. He ordered the furnace heated up seven times more than was customary, and ordered some of the strongest guards in his army to bind Shadrach, Meshach, and Abednego and to throw them into the furnace of blazing fire. So the men were bound, still wearing their tunics, their trousers, their hats, and their other garments, and they were thrown into the furnace of blazing fire. Because the king's command was urgent and the furnace was so overheated, the raging flames killed the men who lifted Shadrach, Meshach, and Abednego. But the three men, Shadrach, Meshach, and Abednego, fell down, bound, into the furnace of blazing fire.

Then King Nebuchadnezzar was astonished and rose up quickly. He said to his counselors, "Was it not three men that we threw bound into the fire?" They answered the king, "True, O king." He replied, "But I see four men unbound, walking in the middle of the fire, and they are not hurt; and the fourth has the appearance of a god." Nebuchadnezzar then approached the door of the furnace of blazing fire and said, "Shadrach, Meshach, and Abednego, servants of the Most High God, come out! Come here!" So Shadrach, Meshach, and Abednego came out from the fire. And the satraps, the prefects, the governors, and the king's counselors gathered together and saw that the fire had not had any power over the bodies of those men; the hair of their heads was not singed, their tunics were not harmed, and not even the smell of fire came from them. Nebuchadnezzar said, "Blessed be the God of Shadrach, Meshach, and Abednego, who has sent his angel and delivered his servants who trusted in him. They disobeyed the king's command and yielded up their bodies rather than serve and worship any god except their own God. Therefore I make a decree: Any people, nation, or language that utters blasphemy against the God of Shadrach,

SCENIC VIEW
King Nebuchadnezzar calls
God "the God of Shadrach,
Meshach, and Abednego."
The king meets the true God
through ordinary people who
are willing to serve and follow
God even in the face of danger
and death. In fact, God is
often named in relationship to
ordinary people reminding us
that the same God who made
the heavens and the earth
is the God of individuals,
the God of us. Check out
Exodus 3:6, 2 Kings 2:14,
and 2 Chronicles 21:12
for some other examples.

Meshach, and Abednego shall be torn limb from limb, and their houses laid in ruins; for there is no other god who is able to deliver in this way." Then the king promoted Shadrach, Meshach, and Abednego in the province of Babylon.

So God was at work in and through faithful people, even as they lived in exile. Daniel continued to serve King Nebuchadnezzar and to help him by interpreting his dreams. In time, King Nebuchadnezzar died, and his son, Belshazzar, ascended the throne. Daniel remained as a trusted advisor to Belshazzar as well.

King Belshazzar made a great festival for a thousand of his lords, and he was drinking wine in the presence of the thousand. Under the influence of the wine, Belshazzar commanded that they bring in the vessels of gold and silver that his father Nebuchadnezzar had taken out of the temple in Jerusalem, so that the king and his lords, his wives, and his concubines might drink from them. So they brought in the vessels of gold and silver that had been taken out of the temple, the house of God in Jerusalem, and the king and his lords, his wives, and his concubines drank from them. They drank the wine and praised the gods of gold and silver, bronze, iron, wood, and stone.

THE WRITING ON THE WALL

Immediately the fingers of a human hand appeared and began writing on the plaster of the wall of the royal palace, next to the lampstand. The king was watching the hand as it wrote. Then the king's face turned pale, and his thoughts terrified him. His limbs gave way, and his knees knocked together. The king cried aloud to bring in the enchanters, the

Chaldeans, and the diviners; and the king said to the wise men of Babylon, "Whoever can read this writing and tell me its interpretation shall be clothed in purple, have a chain of gold around his neck, and rank third in the kingdom." Then all the king's wise men came in, but they could not read the writing or tell the king the interpretation. Then King Belshazzar became greatly terrified and his face turned pale, and his lords were perplexed.

> **POINT OF INTEREST**
> This is where the phrase "the writing on the wall" comes from. Many of our colloquial phrases come from the Bible. "By the skin of my teeth" is from Job 19:20, "go the second mile" is from Matthew 5:41, and "a drop in the bucket" comes from Isaiah 40:15.

Then Daniel was brought in before the king. The king said to Daniel, "So you are Daniel, one of the exiles of Judah, whom my father the king brought from Judah? I have heard of you that a spirit of the gods is in you, and that enlightenment, understanding, and excellent wisdom are found in you. Now the wise men, the enchanters, have been brought in before me to read this writing and tell me its interpretation, but they were not able to give the interpretation of the matter. But I have heard that you can give interpretations and solve problems. Now if you are able to read the writing and tell me its interpretation, you shall be clothed in purple, have a chain of gold around your neck, and rank third in the kingdom."

Then Daniel answered in the presence of the king, "Let your gifts be for yourself, or give your rewards to someone else! Nevertheless I will read the writing to the king and let him know the interpretation.

You have exalted yourself against the Lord of heaven! The vessels of his temple have been brought in before you, and you and your lords, your wives and your concubines have been drinking wine from them. You have praised the gods of silver and gold, of bronze, iron, wood, and stone, which do not see or hear or know; but the God in whose power is your very breath, and to whom belong all your ways, you have not honored.

"So from his presence the hand was sent and this writing was inscribed. And this is the writing that was inscribed: mene, mene, tekel, and parsin. This is the interpretation of the matter: mene, God has numbered the days of your kingdom and brought it to an end; tekel, you have been weighed on the scales and found wanting; peres, your kingdom is divided and given to the Medes and Persians."

Then Belshazzar gave the command, and Daniel was clothed in purple, a chain of gold was put around his neck, and a proclamation was made concerning him that he should rank third in the kingdom. That very night Belshazzar, the Chaldean king, was killed. And Darius the Mede received the kingdom, being about sixty-two years old.

It pleased Darius to set over the kingdom one hundred twenty satraps, stationed throughout the whole kingdom, and over them three presidents, including Daniel; to these the satraps gave account, so that the king might suffer no loss. Soon Daniel distinguished himself above all the other presidents and satraps because an excellent spirit was in him, and the king planned to appoint him over the whole kingdom. So the presidents and the satraps tried to find grounds for complaint against Daniel in connection with the kingdom. But they could find no grounds for complaint or any corruption, because he was faithful, and no negligence or corruption could be found in him. The men said, "We shall not find any ground for complaint against this Daniel unless we find it in connection with the law of his God."

So the presidents and satraps conspired and came to the king and said to him, "O King Darius, live forever! All the presidents of the kingdom, the prefects and the satraps, the counselors and the governors are agreed that the king should establish an ordinance and enforce an interdict, that whoever prays to anyone, divine or human, for thirty days, except to you, O king, shall be thrown into a den of lions. Now, O king, establish the interdict and sign the document, so that it cannot be changed, according to the law of the Medes and the Persians, which cannot be revoked." Therefore King Darius signed the document and interdict.

DANIEL IN THE LIONS' DEN

Although Daniel knew that the document had been signed, he continued to go to his house, which had windows in its upper room open toward Jerusalem, and to get down on his knees three times a day to pray to his God and praise him, just as he had done previously. The conspirators came and found Daniel praying and seeking mercy before his God. Then they approached the king and said concerning the interdict, "O king! Did you not sign an interdict, that anyone who prays to anyone, divine or human, within thirty days except to you, O king, shall be thrown into a den of lions?" The king answered, "The thing stands fast, according to the law of the Medes and Persians, which cannot be revoked." Then they responded to the king, "Daniel, one of the exiles from Judah, pays no attention to you, O king, or to the interdict you have signed, but he is saying his prayers three times a day."

When the king heard the charge, he was very much distressed. He was determined to save Daniel, and until the sun went down he made every effort to rescue him. Then the conspirators came to the king and said to him, "Know, O king, that it is a law of the Medes and Persians that no interdict or ordinance that the king establishes can be changed."

Then the king gave the command, and Daniel was brought and thrown into the den of lions. The king said to Daniel, "May your God, whom you faithfully serve, deliver you!" A stone was brought and laid on the mouth of the den, and the king sealed it with his own signet and with the signet of his lords, so that nothing might be changed concerning Daniel. Then the

> **TRAIL CROSSING**
> Later in the Bible, we will hear another story about a stone rolled in front of a cave. Check out Matthew 27:57—28:10 to see what happens in that story.

king went to his palace and spent the night fasting; no food was brought to him, and sleep fled from him.

DANIEL SAVED FROM THE LIONS

Then, at break of day, the king got up and hurried to the den of lions. When he came near the den where Daniel was, he cried out anxiously to Daniel, "O Daniel, servant of the living God, has your God whom you faithfully serve been able to deliver you from the lions?" Daniel then said to the king, "O king, live forever! My God sent his angel and shut the lions' mouths so that they would not hurt me, because I was found blameless before him; and also before you, O king, I have done no wrong." Then the king was exceedingly glad and commanded that Daniel be taken up out of the den. So Daniel was taken up out of the den, and no kind of harm was found on him, because he had trusted in his God. The king gave a command, and those who had accused Daniel were brought and thrown into the den of lions—they, their children, and their wives. Before they reached the bottom of the den the lions overpowered them and broke all their bones in pieces.

Then King Darius wrote to all peoples and nations of every language throughout the whole world: "May you have abundant prosperity! I make a decree, that in all my royal dominion people should tremble and fear before the God of Daniel:

> For he is the living God,
>   enduring forever.
> His kingdom shall never be destroyed,
>   and his dominion has no end.
> He delivers and rescues,
>   he works signs and wonders in heaven and on earth;
> for he has saved Daniel
>   from the power of the lions."

So this Daniel prospered during the reign of Darius and the reign of Cyrus the Persian.

And thus it is that even when the people were in exile, God was at work, in surprising ways and through surprising people. In the court of Darius and through the reign of Cyrus the Persian, God's deliverance of the people came. The destruction that Isaiah and Jeremiah had prophesied came to pass, and the people were driven into exile just as the prophets had foretold. But Isaiah and Jeremiah were not only prophets of doom and gloom. In the midst of Isaiah's prophecies of judgment and warning, he also spoke to the people of God's promise of hope, which stood firm even in the face of their failures and disobedience. Though their disobedience had taken them far from God, God did not abandon the people.

So Isaiah spoke again, declaring God's promise that the people's exile would not be forever and that someday in the future they would be comforted.

> The spirit of the Lord God is
>   upon me,
> because the Lord has
>   anointed me;
> he has sent me to bring good news
>   to the oppressed,
>   to bind up the brokenhearted,
> to proclaim liberty to the captives,
>   and release to the prisoners;
> to proclaim the year of the Lord's favor,
>   and the day of vengeance of our God;
>   to comfort all who mourn;
> to provide for those who mourn in Zion—
>   to give them a garland instead of ashes,
> the oil of gladness instead of mourning,
>   the mantle of praise instead of a faint spirit.
> They will be called oaks of righteousness,
>   the planting of the Lord, to display his glory.

TRAIL CROSSING
One of the first things Jesus does in his adult ministry is read and interpret this portion of Isaiah 61 in the synagogue. Read Luke 4:14-30 to hear what Jesus said and how the people responded.

They shall build up the ancient ruins,
    they shall raise up the former devastations;
they shall repair the ruined cities,
    the devastations of many generations.

Comfort, O comfort my people,
    says your God.
Speak tenderly to Jerusalem,
    and cry to her
that she has served her term,
    that her penalty is paid,
that she has received from the Lord's hand
    double for all her sins.
A voice cries out:
"In the wilderness prepare the way of the Lord,
    make straight in the desert a highway for our God.
Every valley shall be lifted up,
    and every mountain and hill be made low;
the uneven ground shall become level,
    and the rough places a plain.
Then the glory of the Lord shall be revealed,
    and all people shall see it together,
    for the mouth of the Lord has spoken."
A voice says, "Cry out!"
    And I said, "What shall I cry?"
All people are grass,
    their constancy is like the flower of the field.
The grass withers, the flower fades,
    when the breath of the Lord blows upon it;
    surely the people are grass.
The grass withers, the flower fades;
    but the word of our God will stand forever.
Get you up to a high mountain,
    O Zion, herald of good tidings;
lift up your voice with strength,

O Jerusalem, herald of good tidings,
lift it up, do not fear;
say to the cities of Judah,
"Here is your God!"
See, the Lord God comes with might,
and his arm rules for him;
his reward is with him,
and his recompense before him.
He will feed his flock like a shepherd;
he will gather the lambs in his arms,
and carry them in his bosom,
and gently lead the mother sheep.

Much sadness and pain came before the people would experience the joy that God promised. In exile, the people suffered the consequences of their disobedience and injustice before they felt the holy comfort of God. Yet the words of Isaiah were something for the exiled people of Israel and Judah to treasure in their hearts on the most difficult of days. God promised that, when the time was ready, he would send a deliverer.

The people who walked in darkness
have seen a great light;
those who lived in a land of deep darkness—
on them light has shined.
You have multiplied the nation,
you have increased its joy;
they rejoice before you
as with joy at the harvest,
as people exult when dividing plunder.
For the yoke of their burden,
and the bar across their shoulders,
the rod of their oppressor,
you have broken as on the day of Midian.
For all the boots of the tramping warriors
and all the garments rolled in blood
shall be burned as fuel for the fire.

SCENIC VIEW
This is one of Isaiah's prophecies about a Messiah, a deliverer, who will come to save God's people. Isaiah 11:1 5, 42:1 9, and 53:1-12 tell us more about this servant who will come to free the people. Read those passages and notice some of the surprising characteristics this Messiah will have.

For a child has been born for us,
     a son given to us;
authority rests upon his shoulders;
     and he is named
Wonderful Counselor, Mighty God,
     Everlasting Father, Prince of Peace.
His authority shall grow continually,
     and there shall be endless peace
for the throne of David and
     his kingdom.
He will establish and uphold it
with justice and with righteousness
from this time onward and forevermore.
The zeal of the Lord of hosts will do this.

When that deliverer comes, God promised not only that Jerusalem would be restored but also that all things would be made new.

For I am about to create new heavens
     and a new earth;
the former things shall not be remembered
     or come to mind.
But be glad and rejoice forever
     in what I am creating;
for I am about to create Jerusalem as a joy,
     and its people as a delight.
I will rejoice in Jerusalem,
     and delight in my people;
no more shall the sound of weeping be heard in it,
     or the cry of distress.
No more shall there be in it
     an infant that lives but a few days,
     or an old person who does not live out a lifetime;
for one who dies at a hundred years will be considered
     a youth,
     and one who falls short of a hundred will be
          considered accursed.

They shall build houses and inhabit them;
  they shall plant vineyards and eat their fruit.
They shall not build and another inhabit;
  they shall not plant and another eat;
for like the days of a tree shall the days of my people be,
    and my chosen shall long enjoy the work of
      their hands.
They shall not labor in vain,
  or bear children for calamity;
for they shall be offspring blessed by the Lord—
  and their descendants as well.
Before they call I will answer,
  while they are yet speaking I will hear.
The wolf and the lamb shall feed together,
  the lion shall eat straw like the ox;
  but the serpent—its food shall be dust!
They shall not hurt or destroy
  on all my holy mountain,
says the Lord.

It was a beautiful vision, a promise, that Isaiah offered to the people of God in their darkest hour. And Isaiah was not alone in proclaiming the good news, even during a time of deep darkness. In the midst of exile, God called Ezekiel, a priest and prophet, to reiterate many of the themes of Isaiah and Jeremiah. Ezekiel, like Jeremiah and Isaiah before him, was given a glorious, mystical vision of God, and called by God to speak both judgment and hope to the people. In an astonishing vision, Ezekiel prophesied not only that Jerusalem would be restored and the city and temple renewed but also that the people would be brought to new life.

> **SCENIC VIEW**
> The story of Ezekiel's call and commissioning by God is both beautiful and strange. Read Ezekiel 1:1—3:11 to hear about his vision of God's glory.

The hand of the Lord came upon me, and he brought me out by the spirit of the Lord and set me down in the middle of a valley; it was full of bones. He led me all around them; there were very many lying in the valley, and they were very dry. He said to me, "Mortal, can these bones live?" I answered, "O Lord God, you know." Then he said to me, "Prophesy to these bones, and say to them: O dry bones, hear the word of the Lord. Thus says the Lord God to these bones: I will cause breath to enter you, and you shall live. I will lay sinews on you, and will cause flesh to come upon you, and cover you with skin, and put breath in you, and you shall live; and you shall know that I am the Lord."

So I prophesied as I had been commanded; and as I prophesied, suddenly there was a noise, a rattling, and the bones came together, bone to its bone. I looked, and there were sinews on them, and flesh had come upon them, and skin had covered them; but there was no breath in them. Then he said to me, "Prophesy to the breath, prophesy, mortal, and say to the breath: Thus says the Lord God: Come from the four winds, O breath, and breathe upon these slain, that they may live." I prophesied as he commanded me, and the breath came into them, and they lived, and stood on their feet, a vast multitude.

Then he said to me, "Mortal, these bones are the whole house of Israel. They say, 'Our bones are dried up, and our hope is lost; we are cut off completely.' Therefore prophesy, and say to them, Thus says the Lord God: I am going to open your graves, and bring you up from your graves, O my people; and I will bring you back to the land of Israel. And you shall know that I am the Lord, when I open your graves, and bring you up from your graves, O my people. I will put my spirit within you, and you shall live, and I will place you on your own soil; then you shall know that I, the Lord, have spoken and will act, says the Lord."

POINT OF INTEREST
This startling vision of Ezekiel is one of the stories that is historically read at the Easter Vigil as we wait in darkness for light to dawn on Easter morning.

As they lived in exile, the people remembered and repeated the words of the prophets Isaiah and Ezekiel, believing that, in spite of their sin, God would remain faithful to them. And, of course, God was faithful, and deliverance did come. After their seventy years in exile, God would work through surprising people: foreign kings in a foreign land to bring his people home once again.

Scripture Citations
DANIEL 3:12-30 | 5:1-9, 13-17, 23-31 | 6:1-28
ISAIAH 61:1-4 | 40:1-11 | 9:2-7 | 65:17-25
EZEKIEL 37:1-14

QUESTIONS FOR THE JOURNEY

1. Shadrach, Meshach, Abednego, and Daniel all have to make difficult choices about obeying God instead of worldly authorities. When have you had to make a choice about following God, even when it might have brought you into conflict with others? What were the consequences of that choice? How did you experience God's presence during that time?

2. Ezekiel, Isaiah, and Daniel each have visions of the salvation of God. How do those visions compare to one another? What might we learn about God and God's salvation from each vision? What about these visions do you find challenging? What do you find comforting?

3. The prophet Isaiah writes about "the way of the Lord…a highway for our God." Look carefully at that portion of today's chapter. What does God's pathway look like? What implication does this have for our walk with God?

4. The prophets alternate words of judgment with words of comfort. What is the relationship between these two different kinds of speech? What does each of them teach us about God?

5. In their darkest hour, the people of Israel cling to the promises of God and repeat the verses of their holy scriptures to find comfort and hope. What verses from the Bible have brought you comfort and hope in difficult times? How might some of these comforting words speak to you today?

NEXT STEPS

- In this chapter we hear the stories of some extraordinary prophets: Isaiah, Ezekiel, and Daniel. Unfortunately, though they speak passionately and live faithful, dedicated lives, these prophets are largely unsuccessful; the people do not heed their calls to change and repent. In fact, there is only one story in the Hebrew Bible of a successful prophet, whose prophecies cause the people to turn from their evil ways: Jonah. Read the book of Jonah (it's only a few pages long). What do you notice about Jonah's story? How is he like the other prophets we hear about? How does he differ? What is his reaction to the "success" of his prophecy?

- Ezekiel, Isaiah, and many of the other prophets had beautiful, intricate visions of God. Close your eyes and imagine God. What does God look like? Smell like? Sound like? Draw, paint, or write about your vision of God and God's glory.

15
Go Up and Rebuild

In the first year of King Cyrus of Persia, in order that the word of the Lord by the mouth of Jeremiah might be accomplished, the Lord stirred up the spirit of King Cyrus of Persia so that he sent a herald throughout all his kingdom, and also in a written edict declared:

"Thus says King Cyrus of Persia: The Lord, the God of heaven, has given me all the kingdoms of the earth, and he has charged me to build him a house at Jerusalem in Judah. Any of those among you who are of his people—may their God be with them!—are now permitted to go up to Jerusalem in Judah, and rebuild the house of the Lord, the God of Israel—he is the God who is in Jerusalem; and let all survivors, in whatever place they reside, be assisted by the people of their place with silver and gold, with goods and with animals, besides freewill offerings for the house of God in Jerusalem."

The heads of the families of Judah and Benjamin, and the priests and the Levites—everyone whose spirit God had stirred—got ready to go up and rebuild the house of the Lord in Jerusalem.

All their neighbors aided them with silver vessels, with gold, with goods, with animals, and with valuable gifts, besides all that was freely offered. King Cyrus himself brought out the vessels of the house of the Lord that Nebuchadnezzar had carried away from Jerusalem and placed in the house of his gods.

So a small group of people, only a portion of those who had gone into exile, returned to Jerusalem, bringing with them the gifts of their neighbors and of King Cyrus. The city was in utter destruction and ruin—the temple had been completely obliterated. Seven months after their return, the people gathered in Jerusalem, and the priests and Levites constructed an altar on the ruins of the old one and began offering sacrifices according to the rules passed down from Moses. After months of offering sacrifices and gathering supplies, they began to lay the foundation for a new temple.

SCENIC VIEW

Here we get a glimpse of what worship looked like in the temple. There are vestments and music, and people are singing a responsive psalm. This same phrase of praise is repeated throughout the Bible, especially in the psalms (Psalm 107:1 and 118:1). It is the psalm that David sang when the Ark of the covenant was brought into Jerusalem (1 Chronicles 16:7-36), and the psalm everyone sang when Solomon dedicated the temple the first time (2 Chronicles 5:13).

When the builders laid the foundation of the temple of the Lord, the priests in their vestments were stationed to praise the Lord with trumpets, and the Levites, the sons of Asaph, with cymbals, according to the directions of King David of Israel; and they sang responsively, praising and giving thanks to the Lord,

> "For he is good,
> for his steadfast love endures
>   forever toward Israel."

And all the people responded with a great shout when they praised the Lord, because the foundation of the house of the Lord was laid. But many of the priests and Levites and heads of families, old people who had seen the first house on its foundations, wept with a loud voice when they saw this house, though many shouted aloud for joy, so that the people could not distinguish the sound of the joyful shout from the sound of the people's weeping, for the people shouted so loudly that the sound was heard far away.

Though they had returned to Jerusalem, the people of Israel still had overseers from Persia. Some of the local officials were upset about the reconstruction of the temple and wrote a letter of complaint to King Artaxerxes of Persia, telling him that the city of Jerusalem was a rebellious and wicked city and should not be rebuilt. Artaxerxes believed them and sent officials to stop the reconstruction of the temple. For sixteen years, the Israelites stopped construction on God's house and focused instead on building their own houses and settling back into the land around Jerusalem.

But God sent two prophets, Haggai and Zechariah, to prophesy to the people of Judah and Jerusalem and call them to return to the work of rebuilding the temple.

In the second year of King Darius, in the sixth month, on the first day of the month, the word of the Lord came by the prophet Haggai to Zerubbabel son of Shealtiel, governor of Judah, and to Joshua son of Jehozadak, the high priest: Thus says the Lord of hosts: These people say the time has not yet come to rebuild the Lord's house. Then the word of the Lord came by the prophet Haggai, saying: Is it a time for you yourselves to live in your paneled houses, while this house lies in ruins? Now therefore thus says the Lord of hosts: Consider how you have fared. You have sown much, and harvested little; you eat, but you never have enough;

> **POINT OF INTEREST**
>
> God has some harsh words for people who live in fancy houses while neglecting God's house of worship. Other prophets will similarly condemn leaders who live in extravagant houses while the poor suffer (Micah 2:1-3).

you drink, but you never have your fill; you clothe yourselves, but no one is warm; and you that earn wages earn wages to put them into a bag with holes. Thus says the Lord of hosts: Consider how you have fared. Go up to the hills and bring wood and build the house, so that I may take pleasure in it and be honored, says the Lord. You have looked for much, and, lo, it came to little; and when you brought it home, I blew it away. Why? says the Lord of hosts. Because my house lies in ruins, while all of you hurry off to your own houses.

The people began once more to build the temple. Yet again, the governor of the region complained to the king. But the new king, King Darius, found record of King Cyrus' decree, allowing the Israelites to reconstruct the temple. King Darius instructed the governor to let the people rebuild the house of God—and even paid for it out of the royal treasury.

THE TEMPLE IS REBUILT

So the elders of the Jews built and prospered, through the prophesying of the prophet Haggai and Zechariah son of Iddo. They finished their building by command of the God of Israel and by decree of Cyrus, Darius, and King Artaxerxes of Persia; and this house was finished on the third day of the month of Adar, in the sixth year of the reign of King Darius.

The people of Israel, the priests and the Levites, and the rest of the returned exiles, celebrated the dedication of this house of God with joy. They offered at the dedication of this house of God one hundred bulls, two hundred rams, four hundred lambs, and as a sin offering for all Israel, twelve male goats, according to the number of the tribes of Israel. Then they set the priests in their divisions and the Levites in their courses for the service of God at Jerusalem, as it is written in the book of Moses.

POINT OF INTEREST
One of the first things the Israelites do after returning to Jerusalem and rebuilding the temple is to celebrate the Passover, as Moses instructed the people in Exodus 12:43-49. This is a sign that the worship God asks for is being observed once more, and the people are recommitting themselves to faithfulness.

On the fourteenth day of the first month the returned exiles kept the passover. For both the priests and the Levites had purified themselves; all of them were clean. So they killed the passover lamb for all the returned exiles, for their fellow priests, and for themselves. It was eaten by the people of Israel who had returned from exile, and also by all who had joined them and separated themselves from the pollutions of the nations of the land to worship the Lord, the God of Israel. With joy they celebrated the festival of unleavened bread seven days; for the Lord had made them joyful, and had turned the heart of the king of Assyria to them, so that he aided them in the work on the house of God, the God of Israel.

At first, only some of the Israelites had returned, but now Ezra led the rest of the Israelites from the land of their exile back to Jerusalem. King Artaxerxes gave Ezra authority to take any Israelites who wished to return back to Jerusalem, and gave him power to appoint judges and magistrates in that region. So Ezra returned, bringing with him the descendants of those who had been exiled. Though the temple had been rebuilt, the wall surrounding Jerusalem was still in ruins. Nehemiah, cupbearer to King Artaxerxes, asked the king for permission to rebuild the wall. King Artaxerxes granted permission and sent Nehemiah to Jerusalem as governor of the region with a mission to rebuild. In the face of opposition from leaders in the area, Nehemiah returned and joined with Ezra to exhort the people and support them in their efforts to rebuild. After years of labor, the wall surrounding Jerusalem was completed along with the gates, and the people of Israel resettled in their land.

THE BOOK OF THE LAW

When the seventh month came—the people of Israel being settled in their towns—all the people gathered together into the square before the Water Gate. They told the scribe Ezra to bring the book of the law of Moses, which the Lord had given to Israel. Accordingly, the priest Ezra brought the law before the assembly, both men and women and all who could hear with understanding. This was on the first day of the seventh month. He read from it facing the square before the Water Gate from early morning until midday, in the presence of the men and the women and those who could understand; and the ears of all the people were attentive to the book of the law.

And Ezra opened the book in the sight of all the people, for he was standing above all the people; and when he opened it, all the people stood up. Then Ezra blessed the Lord, the great God, and all the people answered, "Amen, Amen," lifting up their hands. Then they bowed their heads and worshiped the Lord with their faces to the ground.

The Levites helped the people to understand the law, while the people remained in their places. So they read from the book, from the law of God, with interpretation. They gave the sense, so that the people understood the reading.

And Nehemiah, who was the governor, and Ezra the priest and scribe, and the Levites who taught the people said to all the people, "This day is holy to the Lord your God; do not mourn or weep." For all the people wept when they heard the words of the law. Then he said to them, "Go your way, eat the fat and drink sweet wine and send portions of them to those for whom nothing is prepared, for this day is holy to our Lord; and do not be grieved, for the joy of the Lord is your strength." So the Levites stilled all the people, saying, "Be quiet, for this day is holy; do not be grieved." And all the people went their way to eat and drink and to send portions and to make great rejoicing, because they had understood the words that were declared to them.

> **YOU ARE HERE**
>
> Ezra and the Levites not only read the scriptures aloud but also helped people interpret and understand the holy words. If we sometimes need help reading and understanding the Bible, we are in good company!

THE FESTIVAL OF BOOTHS CELEBRATED

On the second day the heads of ancestral houses of all the people, with the priests and the Levites, came together to the scribe Ezra in order to study the words of the law. And they found it written in the law, which the Lord had commanded by Moses, that the people of Israel should live in booths during the festival of the seventh month, and that they should publish and proclaim in all their towns and in Jerusalem as follows, "Go out to the hills and bring branches of olive, wild olive, myrtle, palm, and other leafy trees to make booths, as it is written." So the people went out and brought them, and made booths for themselves, each on the roofs of their houses, and in their courts

SCENIC VIEW
As soon as they learned of the Festival of Booths (Leviticus 23:33-44), the people immediately wanted to fulfill the scriptures by celebrating it. Jewish people today still celebrate this biblical festival, also called Sukkot, in early fall.

and in the courts of the house of God, and in the square at the Water Gate and in the square at the Gate of Ephraim. And all the assembly of those who had returned from the captivity made booths and lived in them; for from the days of Jeshua son of Nun to that day the people of Israel had not done so. And there was very great rejoicing. And day by day, from the first day to the last day, he read from the book of the law of God. They kept the festival seven days; and on the eighth day there was a solemn assembly, according to the ordinance.

The people of Israel engaged in a time of fasting and prayer, confessing their sins, reading from the book of the law, and worshiping and praising God. When they were finished, Ezra stood before them and recounted the whole story of God to the gathered people, from the beginning of creation to that moment.

THE STORY OF GOD'S PEOPLE

And Ezra said: "You are the Lord, you alone; you have made heaven, the heaven of heavens, with all their host, the earth and all that is on it, the seas and all that is in them. To all of them you give life, and the host of heaven worships you. You are the Lord, the God who chose Abram and brought him out of Ur of the Chaldeans and gave him the name Abraham; and you found his heart faithful before you, and made with him a covenant to give to his descendants the land of the Canaanite, the Hittite, the Amorite, the Perizzite, the Jebusite, and the Girgashite; and you have fulfilled your promise, for you are righteous.

TRAIL CROSSING

Ezra knew his Bible; he was able to tell the whole story of God's love and salvation from memory. Throughout the Bible, we have these beautiful summaries of the faith; compare this one to the version in 1 Corinthians 15:1-11.

"And you saw the distress of our ancestors in Egypt and heard their cry at the Red Sea. You performed signs and wonders against Pharaoh and all his servants and all the people of his land, for you knew that they acted insolently against our ancestors. You made a name for yourself, which remains to this day. And you divided the sea before them, so that they passed through the sea on dry land, but you threw their pursuers into the depths, like a stone into mighty waters. Moreover, you led them by day with a pillar of cloud, and by night with a pillar of fire, to give them light on the way in which they should go. You came down also upon Mount Sinai, and spoke with them from heaven, and gave them right ordinances and true laws, good statutes and commandments, and you made known your holy sabbath to them and gave them commandments and statutes and a law through your servant Moses. For their hunger you gave them bread from heaven, and for their thirst you brought water for them out of the rock, and you told them to go in to possess the land that you swore to give them.

"But they and our ancestors acted presumptuously and stiffened their necks and did not obey your commandments; they refused to obey, and were not mindful of the wonders that you performed among them; but they stiffened their necks and determined to return to their slavery in Egypt. But you are a God ready to forgive, gracious and merciful, slow to anger and abounding in steadfast love, and you did not forsake them. Even when they had cast an image of a calf for themselves and said, 'This is your God who brought you up out of Egypt,' and had committed great blasphemies, you in your great mercies did not forsake them in the wilderness; the pillar of cloud that led them in the way did not leave them by day, nor the pillar of fire by night that gave them light on the way by which they should go. You gave your good spirit to instruct them, and did not withhold your manna from their mouths, and gave them water for their thirst. Forty years you sustained them in the wilderness so that they lacked nothing; their clothes did not wear out and their feet did not swell. And you gave them kingdoms and peoples, and allotted to them every corner, so they took possession of the land of King Sihon of Heshbon and the land of King Og of Bashan. You multiplied their descendants like the stars of heaven, and brought them into the land that you had told their ancestors to enter and possess. So the descendants went in and possessed the land, and you subdued before them the inhabitants of the land, the Canaanites, and gave them into their hands, with their kings and the peoples of the land, to do with them as they pleased. And they captured fortress cities and a rich land, and took possession of houses filled with all sorts of goods, hewn cisterns, vineyards, olive orchards, and fruit trees in abundance; so they ate, and were filled and became fat, and delighted themselves in your great goodness.

"Nevertheless they were disobedient and rebelled against you and cast your law behind their backs and killed your prophets, who had warned them in order to turn them back to you, and they committed great blasphemies. Therefore you gave them into the hands of their enemies, who made them suffer. Then in the time of their suffering they cried out to you and you heard them from heaven, and according to your great mercies you gave them saviors who saved them from the hands of their enemies. But after they had rest, they again did evil before you, and you abandoned them to the hands of their enemies, so that they had dominion over them; yet when they turned and cried to you, you heard from heaven, and many times you rescued them according to your mercies. And you warned them in order to turn them back to your law. Yet they acted presumptuously and did not obey your commandments, but sinned against your ordinances, by the observance of which a person shall live. They turned a stubborn shoulder and stiffened their neck and would not obey.

Many years you were patient with them, and warned them by your spirit through your prophets; yet they would not listen. Therefore you handed them over to the peoples of the lands. Nevertheless, in your great mercies you did not make an end of them or forsake them, for you are a gracious and merciful God.

"Now therefore, our God—the great and mighty and awesome God, keeping covenant and steadfast love—do not treat lightly all the hardship that has come upon us, upon our kings, our officials, our priests, our prophets, our ancestors, and all your people, since the time of the kings of Assyria until today.

Ezra pleaded with God to remember the people and urged the people to repent and return to the Lord. So the people of Israel recommitted themselves to God, vowing to walk in God's law and observe God's commandments. They promised to bring their first fruits to God, to tithe, and to not neglect the house of God.

Though many of the exiled Israelites returned with Ezra to Jerusalem, others remained in the lands of their exile. While God was powerfully present in the rebuilt temple and with those who returned to Jerusalem, God did not abandon those who were scattered abroad.

QUEEN ESTHER SAVES HER PEOPLE

In Persia, King Ahasuerus became angry with his wife, Queen Vashti, and deposed her, then began the search for a new queen. A young Jewish woman named Esther, niece of Mordecai, gained the attention and favor of the king. The king loved Esther, and she won his favor and devotion, but she did not tell the king about her Jewish ancestry. Mordecai, Esther's uncle, discovered an assassination plot and warned the king, further gaining favor for both Mordecai and

Esther. But one of the king's officials, Haman, became jealous of the honors the king bestowed on Mordecai.

When Haman saw that Mordecai did not bow down or do obeisance to him, Haman was infuriated. But he thought it beneath him to lay hands on Mordecai alone. So, having been told who Mordecai's people were, Haman plotted to destroy all the Jews, the people of Mordecai, throughout the whole kingdom of Ahasuerus.

Then Haman said to King Ahasuerus, "There is a certain people scattered and separated among the peoples in all the provinces of your kingdom; their laws are different from those of every other people, and they do not keep the king's laws, so that it is not appropriate for the king to tolerate them. If it pleases the king, let a decree be issued for their destruction, and I will pay ten thousand talents of silver into the hands of those who have charge of the king's business, so that they may put it into the king's treasuries." So the king took his signet ring from his hand and gave it to Haman son of Hammedatha the Agagite, the enemy of the Jews. The king said to Haman, "The money is given to you, and the people as well, to do with them as it seems good to you."

When Mordecai learned all that had been done, Mordecai tore his clothes and put on sackcloth and ashes, and went through the city, wailing with a loud and bitter cry; In every province, wherever the king's command and his decree came, there was great mourning among the Jews, with fasting and weeping and lamenting, and most of them lay in sackcloth and ashes.

POINT OF INTEREST
In the Bible, when people grieve, they do so loudly and visibly; they put ashes on their heads, wear special clothes, and often wail aloud. These are outward, visible signs of how they are feeling on the inside, much like the tradition of people wearing black while in mourning.

Mordecai sent word to Esther, begging her to go speak to the king on behalf of the Jewish people. Esther hesitated because the law allowed the king to put to death anyone who approached him uninvited, and she had not been invited to speak to the king.

Mordecai told them to reply to Esther, "Do not think that in the king's palace you will escape any more than all the other Jews. For if you keep silence at such a time as this, relief and deliverance will rise for the Jews from another quarter, but you and your father's family will perish. Who knows? Perhaps you have come to royal dignity for just such a time as this." Then Esther said in reply to Mordecai, "Go, gather all the Jews to be found in Susa, and hold a fast on my behalf, and neither eat nor drink for three days, night or day. I and my maids will also fast as you do. After that I will go to the king, though it is against the law; and if I perish, I perish." Mordecai then went away and did everything as Esther had ordered him.

Risking her life, Esther agreed to approach the king and intercede for God's people. First, she prepared a series of lavish banquets to honor and appease the king. Then the king asked her what she wanted.

Then Queen Esther answered, "If I have won your favor, O king, and if it pleases the king, let my life be given me—that is my petition—and the lives of my people—that is my request. For we have been sold, I and my people, to be destroyed, to be killed, and to be annihilated. If we had been sold merely as slaves, men and women, I would have held my peace; but no enemy can compensate for this damage to the king." Then King Ahasuerus said to Queen Esther, "Who is he, and where is he, who has presumed to do this?" Esther said, "A foe and enemy, this wicked Haman!" Then Haman was terrified before the king and the queen.

King Ahasuerus granted Esther's request; the slaughter of the Jews was called off, and Haman instead was hanged on the gallows he had constructed to execute others. God was present once again, through unexpected people in unexpected places.

Thus it was that many Jews had returned to Jerusalem, but others were still scattered abroad. The descendants of Israel and Judah had recommitted themselves to following God and worshiping God, yet they still fell short of being the people God was calling them to be. They were settled back in the land that God had promised to them, but they were not alone there. They lived in the midst of Samaritans, Gentiles, and others who did not believe in or follow their God. And they wrestled with how they were called to live among and intermingled with other people, rather than set apart from them. In the years to come, divisions would arise, even among the Jews; there would be Pharisees and Sadducees, different sects within Judaism, who disagreed about the interpretation of the Torah, or about where emphasis should be placed in living according to God's laws.

The story of the people of God continued—flawed, broken, and ordinary people, trying imperfectly to follow the extraordinary God who loved them more than anything.

Scripture Citations
EZRA 1:1-7 | 3:10-13 | 6:14-22
HAGGAI 1:1-9
NEHEMIAH 7:73b—8:1-3, 5-6, 9-18 | 9:6-32
ESTHER 3:5-6, 8-11 | 4: 1-3, 13-17 | 7: 3-6

QUESTIONS FOR THE JOURNEY

1. King Cyrus, King Darius, and King Artaxerxes are outsiders. They are not Israelites, yet they help the Israelites fulfill what God asks of them. Who are some of the other "outsiders" that we have heard about in the biblical story? What might their presence and action tell us about God's salvation?

2. The people of Israel face numerous obstacles to rebuilding the temple and the wall around Jerusalem, yet they persevere over many years. When have you faced obstacles in what God was calling you to do? How have you found the strength to persevere?

3. Ezra, Nehemiah, Haggai, and Zechariah speak the truth to the people, even when it is hard for them to hear. Who are some people in your life who have spoken truth to you, even when it was hard? When have you been the person speaking truth, even when it was hard?

4. When Ezra reads the people the scriptures for the first time, they are overcome with both joy and conviction. Have you ever been deeply touched by a passage of the Bible? What was the passage, and what has it meant to you?

5. Esther is one among many of the female leaders we have read about in the Hebrew Bible. How does her story and kind of leadership compare to some of the other biblical women we have encountered (Miriam, Sarah, Deborah, Ruth, etc.)?

6. The journey of the people of God has involved a great detour: a time of strife and conflict followed by years of exile. They have finally made their way back home, home to their holy land, but also home to the heart of God. What detours have you experienced in your life's journey? Have you made your way back home yet? If so, what was that homecoming like? If you're not home, what steps might you take to return?

NEXT STEPS

- Ezra is able to retell the story of God's salvation so that people gain a sense of the continuity of God's presence with them, even in the midst of struggle and in spite of their sin. How would you tell the story of God's salvation, if someone asked you? Take time to think it over or even write it down.

- Before Esther goes to the king, she asks Mordecai and the other Jews to fast and pray on her behalf; even though she goes before the king by herself, she is not alone but is supported by a community. Make a list of some of the communities that have supported you at critical times in your life and what that support looked like. Then make a list of some ways that you can support others, both in your family and in your wider community of faith.

16
Good News of Great Joy

Nearly four hundred years passed. The people of God resettled and rebuilt in the land that God promised them. It was a time of relative peace and prosperity, as the people reestablished their lives and their worship. In the political arena, the Persians were replaced by the Greeks after the conquest of Alexander the Great, and first the Ptolemies of Egypt and then Seleucids of Syria were given governance over the land where the Jewish people lived. Then, in 63 BCE, General Pompey conquered Palestine, and Roman rule began.

As political leadership changed, so too did the religious establishment. The high priest and the scribes began to exercise a great deal of religious and political power. Sometimes religious leaders exercised their power well, but other times they abused their power for wealth and personal gain. Divisions between the Pharisees and the Sadducees became deeper, as each group became more and more convinced that they had the right understanding of God. Even in the midst of relative peace, the people strayed from God. Even as they observed the right festivals and said the right prayers, people *were not living the lives of love and mercy and kindness that God called them to live.*

And so, once again, the God who has loved the people from the beginning of creation, who has pursued them even as they wandered afar, who has been faithful to them even when they were faithless, spoke to the people. But this time God spoke in a different way. It was a way that was both new and unique and as old as time itself. It was the way that God had been speaking since before time and forever, if only people had ears to hear.

HYMN TO THE PREEXISTENT CHRIST

In the beginning was the Word, and the Word was with God, and the Word was God. He was in the beginning with God. All things came into being through him, and without him not one thing came into being. What has come into being in him was life, and the life was the light of all people. The light shines in the darkness, and the darkness did not overcome it.

He was in the world, and the world came into being through him; yet the world did not know him. He came to what was his own, and his own people did not accept him. But to all who received him, who believed in his name, he gave power to become children of God, who were born, not of blood or of the will of the flesh or of the will of man, but of God.

And the Word became flesh and lived among us, and we have seen his glory, the glory as of a father's only son, full of grace and truth. From his fullness we have all received, grace upon grace. The law indeed was given through Moses; grace and truth came through Jesus Christ. No one has ever seen God. It is God the only Son, who is close to the Father's heart, who has made him known.

THE BIRTH OF JESUS FORETOLD

The angel Gabriel was sent by God to a town in Galilee called Nazareth, to a virgin engaged to a man whose name was Joseph, of the house of David. The virgin's name was Mary. And he came to her and said, "Greetings, favored one! The Lord is with you." But she was much perplexed by his words and pondered what sort of greeting this might be. The angel said to her, "Do not be afraid, Mary, for you have found favor with God. And now, you will conceive in your womb and bear a son, and you will name him Jesus. He will be great, and will be called the Son of the Most High, and the Lord God will give to him the throne of his ancestor David. He will reign over the house of Jacob forever, and of his kingdom there will be no end." Mary said to the angel, "How can this be, since I am a virgin?" The angel said to her, "The Holy Spirit will come upon you, and the power of the Most High will overshadow you; therefore the child to be born will be holy; he will be called Son of God. And now, your relative Elizabeth in her old age has also conceived a son; and this is the sixth month for her who was said to be barren. For nothing will be impossible with God." Then Mary said, "Here am I, the servant of the Lord; let it be with me according to your word." Then the angel departed from her.

TRAIL CROSSING

When the angel Gabriel appears to Mary, one of the first things he says is "Do not be afraid." This might seem strange, because we often see angels depicted in art as beautiful women or chubby babies. But in the Bible, angels are described as both beautiful and terrifying, with many wings and eyes, or faces like lightning (Isaiah 6:2-6, Daniel 10:5-6). Yet throughout the Bible, God has told people they do not need to be afraid, even in the face of scary things (Psalm 27:1, Isaiah 41:10, Deuteronomy 31:6). And Jesus often told people not to be afraid (John 14:27, Mark 6:50).

SCENIC VIEW
This song by Mary is called
the *Magnificat* and is often
sung or said in churches to this
day. This might remind you of
another song in the Bible,
1 Samuel 2:1-10. Reread both
songs. What are they saying
about how the world works?
Do you think it is true?

In those days Mary set out and went with haste to a Judean town in the hill country, where she entered the house of Zechariah and greeted Elizabeth. When Elizabeth heard Mary's greeting, the child leaped in her womb. And Elizabeth was filled with the Holy Spirit and exclaimed with a loud cry, "Blessed are you among women, and blessed is the fruit of your womb. And why has this happened to me, that the mother of my Lord comes to me? For as soon as I heard the sound of your greeting, the child in my womb leaped for joy. And blessed is she who believed that there would be a fulfillment of what was spoken to her by the Lord."
And Mary said,

"My soul magnifies the Lord,
    and my spirit rejoices in God my Savior,
for he has looked with favor on the lowliness
        of his servant.
Surely, from now on all generations will call me blessed;
for the Mighty One has done great things for me,
    and holy is his name.
His mercy is for those who fear him
    from generation to generation.
He has shown strength with his arm;
    he has scattered the proud in the thoughts
        of their hearts.
He has brought down the powerful from their thrones,
    and lifted up the lowly;
he has filled the hungry with good things,
    and sent the rich away empty.
He has helped his servant Israel,
    in remembrance of his mercy,
according to the promise he made to our ancestors, to
    Abraham and to his descendants forever."

And Mary remained with her about three months and then returned to her home.

THE BIRTH OF JESUS THE MESSIAH

Now the birth of Jesus the Messiah took place in this way. When his mother Mary had been engaged to Joseph, but before they lived together, she was found to be with child from the Holy Spirit. Her husband Joseph, being a righteous man and unwilling to expose her to public disgrace, planned to dismiss her quietly. But just when he had resolved to do this, an angel of the Lord appeared to him in a dream and said, "Joseph, son of David, do not be afraid to take Mary as your wife, for the child conceived in her is from the Holy Spirit. She will bear a son, and you are to name him Jesus, for he will save his people from their sins." All this took place to fulfill what had been spoken by the Lord through the prophet: "Look, the virgin shall conceive and bear a son, and they shall name him Emmanuel," which means, "God is with us." When Joseph awoke from sleep, he did as the angel of the Lord commanded him; he took her as his wife, but had no marital relations with her until she had borne a son; and he named him Jesus.

> **POINT OF INTEREST**
> The census under Quirinius took place about ten to twelve years after the death of Herod. The exact date of Jesus' birth is therefore a bit fuzzy.

In those days a decree went out from Emperor Augustus that all the world should be registered. This was the first registration and was taken while Quirinius was governor of Syria. All went to their own towns to be registered. Joseph also went from the town of Nazareth in Galilee to Judea, to the city of David called Bethlehem, because he was descended from the house and family of David. He went to be registered with Mary, to whom he was engaged and who was expecting a child. While they were there, the time came for her to deliver her child. And she gave birth to her firstborn son and wrapped him in bands of cloth, and laid him in a manger, because there was no place for them in the inn.

THE SHEPHERDS AND THE ANGELS

In that region there were shepherds living in the fields, keeping watch over their flock by night. Then an angel of the Lord stood before them, and the glory of the Lord shone around them, and they were terrified. But the angel said to them, "Do not be afraid; for see—I am bringing you good news of great joy for all the people: to you is born this day in the city of David a Savior, who is the Messiah, the Lord. This will be a sign for you: you will find a child wrapped in bands of cloth and lying in a manger." And suddenly there was with the angel a multitude of the heavenly host, praising God and saying, "Glory to God in the highest heaven, and on earth peace among those whom he favors!" When the angels had left them and gone into heaven, the shepherds said to one another, "Let us go now to Bethlehem and see this thing that has taken place, which the Lord has made known to us." So they went with haste and found Mary and Joseph, and the child lying in the manger. When they saw this, they made known what had been told them about this child; and all who heard it were amazed at what the shepherds told them. But Mary treasured all these words and pondered them in her heart. The shepherds returned, glorifying and praising God for all they had heard and seen, as it had been told them.

After eight days had passed, it was time to circumcise the child; and he was called Jesus, the name given by the angel before he was conceived in the womb.

> **POINT OF INTEREST**
> These words form the basis of another important Christian hymn, the *Gloria*. One of the ways that prayers were remembered and passed down through the centuries was by setting them to music and singing them.

JESUS IS PRESENTED IN THE TEMPLE

When the time came for their purification according to the law of Moses, they brought him up to Jerusalem to present him to the Lord (as it is written in the law of the Lord, "Every firstborn male shall be designated as holy to the Lord"), and they offered a sacrifice according to what is stated in the law of the Lord, "a pair of turtledoves or two young pigeons."

Now there was a man in Jerusalem whose name was Simeon; this man was righteous and devout, looking forward to the consolation of Israel, and the Holy Spirit rested on him. It had been revealed to him by the Holy Spirit that he would not see death before he had seen the Lord's Messiah. Guided by the Spirit, Simeon came into the temple; and when the parents brought in the child Jesus, to do for him what was customary under the law, Simeon took him in his arms and praised God, saying, "Master, now you are dismissing your servant in peace, according to your word; for my eyes have seen your salvation, which you have prepared in the presence of all peoples, a light for revelation to the Gentiles and for glory to your people Israel."

> **POINT OF INTEREST**
> Simeon's words are often called the Song of Simeon, or the *Nunc Dimittis*, from the Latin for "Now you dismiss..." This beautiful prayer has been sung or said by Christians around the world for centuries, usually in nighttime services like Compline or Evening Prayer.

And the child's father and mother were amazed at what was being said about him. Then Simeon blessed them and said to his mother Mary, "This child is destined for the falling and the rising of many in Israel, and to be a sign that will be opposed so that the inner thoughts of many will be revealed—and a sword will pierce your own soul too."

There was also a prophet, Anna the daughter of Phanuel, of the tribe of Asher. She was of a great age, having lived with her husband seven years after her marriage, then as a widow to the age of eighty-four. She never left the temple but worshiped there with fasting and prayer night and day. At that moment she came, and began to praise God and to speak about the child to all who were looking for the redemption of Jerusalem. When they had finished everything required by the law of the Lord, they returned to Galilee, to their own town of Nazareth. The child grew and became strong, filled with wisdom; and the favor of God was upon him.

THE VISIT OF THE WISE MEN

 In the time of King Herod, after Jesus was born in Bethlehem of Judea, wise men from the East came to Jerusalem, asking, "Where is the child who has been born king of the Jews? For we observed his star at its rising, and have come to pay him homage." When King Herod heard this, he was frightened, and all Jerusalem with him; and calling together all the chief priests and scribes of the people, he inquired of them where the Messiah was to be born. They told him, "In Bethlehem of Judea; for so it has been written by the prophet: 'And you, Bethlehem, in the land of Judah, are by no means least among the rulers of Judah; for from you shall come a ruler who is to shepherd my people Israel.'" Then Herod secretly called for the wise men and learned from them the exact time when the star had appeared. Then he sent them to Bethlehem, saying, "Go and search diligently for the child; and when you have found him, bring me word so that I may also go and pay him homage."

When they had heard the king, they set out; and there, ahead of them, went the

TRAIL CROSSING
Notice that the story doesn't say how many wise men there were. It only says that they brought three gifts: gold, frankincense, and myrrh. These items are the kind of extravagant gifts one would give to a king, a reminder that Jesus is king of heaven and earth. But these are also items that God commands Moses to use in worship: Gold decorates the ark of the covenant and holy vessels, myrrh is used in anointing oil, and frankincense is used in incense (Exodus 30:23-34). The wise men's act of offering is also an act of worship. And myrrh was specifically used in anointing bodies for burial; Jesus' death is pre-figured even at his birth (John 19:39).

star that they had seen at its rising, until it stopped over the place where the child was. When they saw that the star had stopped, they were overwhelmed with joy. On entering the house, they saw the child with Mary his mother; and they knelt down and paid him homage. Then, opening their treasure chests, they offered him gifts of gold, frankincense, and myrrh. And having been warned in a dream not to return to Herod, they left for their own country by another road.

THE ESCAPE TO EGYPT

Now after they had left, an angel of the Lord appeared to Joseph in a dream and said, "Get up, take the child and his mother, and flee to Egypt, and remain there until I tell you; for Herod is about to search for the child, to destroy him." Then Joseph got up, took the child and his mother by night, and went to Egypt, and remained there until the death of Herod. This was to fulfill what had been spoken by the Lord through the prophet, "Out of Egypt I have called my son."

THE MASSACRE OF THE INFANTS

When Herod saw that he had been tricked by the wise men, he was infuriated, and he sent and killed all the children in and around Bethlehem who were two years old or under, according to the time that he had learned from the wise men. Then was fulfilled what had been spoken through the prophet Jeremiah:

> **POINT OF INTEREST**
> Herod was a brutal and paranoid dictator. This story is not recounted in any other histories, but it is consistent with Herod's vicious tendencies.

"A voice was heard in Ramah, wailing and loud lamentation, Rachel weeping for her children; she refused to be consoled, because they are no more."

THE RETURN FROM EGYPT

When Herod died, an angel of the Lord suddenly appeared in a dream to Joseph in Egypt and said, "Get up, take the child and his mother, and go to the land of Israel, for those who were seeking the child's life are dead." Then Joseph got up, took the child and his mother, and went to the land of Israel. But when he heard that Archelaus was ruling over Judea in place of his father Herod, he was afraid to go there. And after being warned in a dream, he went away to the district of Galilee. There he made his home in a town called Nazareth, so that what had been spoken through the prophets might be fulfilled, "He will be called a Nazorean."

THE BOY JESUS IN THE TEMPLE

Now every year his parents went to Jerusalem for the festival of the Passover. And when he was twelve years old, they went up as usual for the festival. When the festival was ended and they started to return, the boy Jesus stayed behind in Jerusalem, but his parents did not know it. Assuming that he was in the group of travelers, they went a day's journey. Then they started to look for him among their relatives and friends. When they did not find him, they returned to Jerusalem to search for him. After three days they found him in the temple, sitting among the teachers, listening to them and asking them questions. And all who heard him were amazed at his understanding and his answers. When his parents saw him they were astonished; and his mother said to him, "Child, why have you treated us like this? Look, your father and I have been searching for you in great anxiety." He said to them, "Why were you searching for me? Did you not know that I must be in my Father's house?" But they did not understand what he said to them. Then he went down with them and came to Nazareth, and was obedient

POINT OF INTEREST
This is the only story in the Bible we have about Jesus' childhood.

to them. His mother treasured all these things in her heart. And Jesus increased in wisdom and in years, and in divine and human favor.

Scripture Citations
JOHN 1.1-3, 10-14, 16-18
LUKE 1:26-56 | 2:1-40 | 2:41-52
MATTHEW 1:18-25 | 2:1-23

QUESTIONS FOR THE JOURNEY

1. Dreams and fulfillment of prophecy loom large in stories about Jesus' birth. Why do you think the gospel writers tell the stories in this way?

2. How is God doing a new thing in Christ? How is God doing the same thing?

3. How does Mary model faithfulness for us? What can we learn from her story?

4. How does Joseph model faithfulness? What can we learn from his story?

5. The early stories of Jesus are full of hymns; in this chapter we hear the *Magnificat*, the *Gloria*, and the *Nunc Dimittis*. How can music help us remember prayers and worship God? What hymns or prayers have been important in your life of faith?

6. In this chapter, we hear many different people respond to the news of Jesus' birth: Mary and Joseph, the shepherds and wise men, Simeon and Anna, and King Herod. What do we learn from each person's response? Which response resonates most deeply with you, and why?

NEXT STEPS

- Read Matthew 1:18-2:23, then read Luke 1:5-2:52. How are the stories different from one another? How are they the same? How are they different than what you read in this chapter?

- Read Exodus 1:18-2:10. How is it like Matthew's birth narrative? Why do you think Matthew tells his story in this way?

17
Follow Me

JESUS IS BAPTIZED

The word of God came to John son of Zechariah in the wilderness. He went into all the region around the Jordan, proclaiming a baptism of repentance for the forgiveness of sins, as it is written in the book of the words of the prophet Isaiah, "The voice of one crying out in the wilderness: 'Prepare the way of the Lord, make his paths straight. Every valley shall be filled, and every mountain and hill shall be made low, and the crooked shall be made straight, and the rough ways made smooth; and all flesh shall see the salvation of God.'"

In those days Jesus came from Nazareth of Galilee and was baptized by John in the Jordan. And just as he was coming up out of the water, he saw the heavens torn apart and the Spirit descending like a dove on him. And a voice came from heaven, "You

> **TRAIL CROSSING**
> The Gospel of Mark does not depict Jesus' encounter with Satan. Jesus is just said to be with wild beasts, leaving the reader to imagine what that might have looked like. If you want to compare them, the other temptation narratives are found in Matthew 4:1-11 and Luke 4:1-13.

are my Son, the Beloved; with you I am well pleased." And the Spirit immediately drove him out into the wilderness. He was in the wilderness forty days, tempted by Satan; and he was with the wild beasts; and the angels waited on him.

JESUS BEGINS HIS MINISTRY

Then Jesus, filled with the power of the Spirit, returned to Galilee, and a report about him spread through all the surrounding country. He began to teach in their synagogues and was praised by everyone.

When he came to Nazareth, where he had been brought up, he went to the synagogue on the sabbath day, as was his custom. He stood up to read, and the scroll of the prophet Isaiah was given to him. He unrolled the scroll and found the place where it was written:

> "The Spirit of the Lord is upon me,
>   because he has anointed me
>   to bring good news to the poor.
> He has sent me to proclaim release to the captives
>   and recovery of sight to the blind,
>   to let the oppressed go free,
> to proclaim the year of the Lord's favor."

And he rolled up the scroll, gave it back to the attendant, and sat down. The eyes of all in the synagogue were fixed on him. Then he began to say to them, "Today this scripture has been fulfilled in your hearing." All spoke well of him and were amazed at the gracious words that came from his mouth.

JESUS CALLS DISCIPLES

As Jesus passed along the Sea of Galilee, he saw Simon and his brother Andrew casting a net into the sea—for they were fishermen. And Jesus said to them, "Follow me and I will make you fish for people." And immediately they left their nets and followed him. As he went a little farther, he saw James son of Zebedee and his brother John, who were in their boat mending the nets. Immediately he called them; and they left their father Zebedee in the boat with the hired men, and followed him.

The next day Jesus decided to go to Galilee. He found Philip and said to him, "Follow me." Now Philip was from Bethsaida, the city of Andrew and Peter. Philip found Nathanael and said to him, "We have found him about whom Moses in the law and also the prophets wrote, Jesus son of Joseph from Nazareth." Nathanael said to him, "Can anything good come out of Nazareth?" Philip said to him, "Come and see." When Jesus saw Nathanael coming toward him, he said of him, "Here is truly an Israelite in whom there is no deceit!" Nathanael asked him, "Where did you get to know me?" Jesus answered, "I saw you under the fig

> **POINT OF INTEREST**
> Nazareth was a tiny town in Galilee. One of the surest things that we know about the Jesus of history is that he was from Nazareth. No one would have made up that detail.

tree before Philip called you." Nathanael replied, "Rabbi, you are the Son of God! You are the King of Israel!" Jesus answered, "Do you believe because I told you that I saw you under the fig tree? You will see greater things than these." And he said to him, "Very truly, I tell you, you will see heaven opened and the angels of God ascending and descending upon the Son of Man."

JESUS CREATES CONTROVERSY AND GARNERS FAME

One sabbath he was going through the grainfields; and as they made their way his disciples began to pluck heads of grain. The Pharisees said to him, "Look, why are they doing what is not lawful on the sabbath?" And he said to them, "Have you never read what David did when he and his companions were hungry and in need of food? He entered the house of God, when Abiathar was high priest, and ate the bread of the Presence, which it is not lawful for any but the priests to eat, and he gave some to his companions." Then he said to them, "The sabbath was made for humankind, and not humankind for the sabbath; so the Son of Man is lord even of the sabbath."

Again he entered the synagogue, and a man was there who had a withered hand. They watched him to see whether he would cure him on the sabbath, so that they might accuse him. And he said to the man who had the withered hand, "Come forward." Then he said to them, "Is it lawful to do good or to do harm on the sabbath, to save life or to kill?" But they were silent. He looked around at them with anger; he was grieved at their hardness of heart and said to the man, "Stretch out your hand." He stretched it out, and his hand was restored. The Pharisees went out and immediately conspired with the Herodians against him, how to destroy him.

Jesus went throughout Galilee, teaching in their synagogues and proclaiming the good news of the kingdom and curing every disease and every sickness among the people. So his fame spread throughout all Syria, and they brought to him all the sick, those who were afflicted with various diseases and pains, demoniacs, epileptics, and paralytics, and he cured them. And great crowds followed him from Galilee, the Decapolis, Jerusalem, Judea, and from beyond the Jordan.

TRAIL CROSSING

This passage, commonly called Sermon on the Mount, is found only in the Gospel of Matthew. The Gospel of Luke contains many of the same teachings but in a much shorter form. For a fun exercise, compare this section to Luke 6:17-49, commonly called the Sermon on the Plain.

SERMON ON THE MOUNT

When Jesus saw the crowds, he went up the mountain; and after he sat down, his disciples came to him. Then he began to speak, and taught them, saying:

"Blessed are the poor in spirit, for theirs is the kingdom of heaven. Blessed are those who mourn, for they will be comforted. Blessed are the meek, for they will inherit the earth. Blessed are those who hunger and thirst for righteousness, for they will be filled. Blessed are the merciful, for they will receive mercy. Blessed are the pure in heart, for they will see God. Blessed are the peacemakers, for they will be called children of God. Blessed are those who are persecuted for righteousness' sake, for theirs is the kingdom of heaven. Blessed are you when people revile you and persecute you and utter all kinds of evil against you falsely on my account. Rejoice and be glad, for your reward is great in heaven, for in the same way they persecuted the prophets who were before you.

"You are the salt of the earth; but if salt has lost its taste, how can its saltiness be restored? It is no longer good for anything, but is thrown out and trampled under foot. You are the light of the world. A city built on a hill cannot be hid. No one after lighting a lamp puts it under the bushel basket, but on the lampstand, and it gives light to all in the house. In the same way, let your light shine before others, so that they may see your good works and give glory to your Father in heaven.

"Do not think that I have come to abolish the law or the prophets; I have come not to abolish but to fulfill. For truly I tell you, until heaven and earth pass away, not one letter, not one stroke of a letter, will pass from the law until all is accomplished. Therefore, whoever breaks one of the least of these commandments, and teaches others to do the same, will be called least

> **SCENIC VIEW**
> Jesus repeatedly reaffirms Mosaic law in the Gospel of Matthew, and he frequently quotes the Old Testament. Jesus is clear that he did not come to replace or throw out the Old Testament but to build on and fulfill it.

in the kingdom of heaven; but whoever does them and teaches them will be called great in the kingdom of heaven. For I tell you, unless your righteousness exceeds that of the scribes and Pharisees, you will never enter the kingdom of heaven.

"You have heard that it was said to those of ancient times, 'You shall not murder'; and 'whoever murders shall be liable to judgment.' But I say to you that if you are angry with a brother or sister, you will be liable to judgment; and if you insult a brother or sister, you will be liable to the council; and if you say, 'You fool,' you will be liable to the hell of fire. So when you are offering your gift at the altar, if you remember that your brother or sister has something against you, leave your gift there before the altar and go; first be reconciled to your brother or sister, and then come and offer your gift

"You have heard that it was said, 'You shall not commit adultery.' But I say to you that everyone who looks at a woman with lust has already committed adultery with her in his heart. If your right eye causes you to sin, tear it out and throw it away; it is better for you to lose one of your members than for your whole body to be thrown into hell. And if your right hand causes you to sin, cut it off and throw it away; it is better for you to lose one of your members than for your whole body to go into hell.

"It was also said, 'Whoever divorces his wife, let him give her a certificate of divorce.' But I say to you that anyone who divorces his wife, except on the ground of unchastity, causes her to commit adultery; and whoever marries a divorced woman commits adultery.

"You have heard that it was said, 'An eye for an eye and a tooth for a tooth.' But I say to you, Do not resist an evildoer. But if anyone strikes you on the right cheek, turn the other also; and if anyone wants to sue you and take your coat, give your cloak as well; and if anyone forces you to go one mile, go also the second mile. Give to everyone who begs from you, and do not refuse anyone who wants to borrow from you.

"You have heard that it was said, 'You shall love your neighbor and hate your enemy.' But I say to you, Love your enemies and pray for those who persecute you, so that you may be children of your Father in heaven; for he makes his sun rise on the evil and on the good, and sends rain on the righteous and on the unrighteous. For if you love those who love you, what reward do you have? Do not even the tax collectors do the same? And if you greet only your brothers and sisters, what more are you doing than others? Do not even the Gentiles do the same? Be perfect, therefore, as your heavenly Father is perfect.

POINT OF INTEREST
Luke 6:36 records this thought: "Be merciful, just as your Father is merciful." How are mercy and perfection related?

"Do not store up for yourselves treasures on earth, where moth and rust consume and where thieves break in and steal; but store up for yourselves treasures in heaven, where neither moth nor rust consumes and where thieves do not break in and steal. For where your treasure is, there your heart will be also. The eye is the lamp of the body. So, if your eye is healthy, your whole body will be full of light; but if your eye is unhealthy, your whole body will be full of darkness. If then the light in you is darkness, how great is the darkness! No one can serve two masters; for a slave will either hate the one and love the other, or be devoted to the one and despise the other. You cannot serve God and wealth.

"Therefore I tell you, do not worry about your life, what you will eat or what you will drink, or about your body, what you will wear. Is not life more than food, and the body more than clothing? Look at the birds of the air; they neither sow nor reap nor gather into barns, and yet your heavenly Father feeds them. Are you not of more value than they? And can any of you by worrying add a single hour to your span of life? And why do you worry about clothing? Consider the lilies of the field, how they grow; they neither toil nor spin, yet I tell you, even Solomon in all his glory was not clothed like one of these. But if God so clothes the grass of the field, which is alive today and tomorrow is thrown into the oven, will he not much more clothe you— you of little faith? Therefore do not worry, saying, 'What will we eat?' or 'What will we drink?' or 'What will we wear?' For it is the Gentiles who strive for all these things; and indeed your heavenly Father knows that you need all these things. But strive first for the kingdom of God and his righteousness, and all these things will be given to you as well. So do not worry about tomorrow, for tomorrow will bring worries of its own. Today's trouble is enough for today.

"Everyone then who hears these words of mine and acts on them will be like a wise man who built his house on rock. The rain fell, the floods came, and the winds blew and beat on that house, but it did not fall, because it had been founded on rock. And everyone who hears these words of mine and does not act on them will be like a foolish man who built his house on sand. The rain fell, and the floods came, and the winds blew and beat against that house, and it fell—and great was its fall!" Now when Jesus had finished saying these things, the crowds were astounded at his teaching, for he taught them as one having authority, and not as their scribes.

JESUS TEACHES THROUGH PARABLES

As is well known, Jesus did not just teach with sayings and aphorisms. His preferred teaching tool was the parable, a story that often had twists and turns and surprises for the audience.

THE SOWER

Again [Jesus] began to teach beside the sea. Such a very large crowd gathered around him that he got into a boat on the sea and sat there, while the whole crowd was beside the sea on the land. He began to teach them many things in parables, and in his teaching he said to them: "Listen! A sower went out to sow. And as he sowed, some seed fell on the path, and the birds came and ate it up. Other seed fell on rocky ground, where it did not have much soil, and it sprang up quickly, since it had no depth of soil. And when the sun rose, it was scorched; and since it had no root, it withered away. Other seed fell among thorns, and the thorns grew up and choked it, and it yielded no grain. Other seed fell into good soil and brought forth grain, growing up and increasing and yielding thirty and sixty and a hundredfold." And he said, "Let anyone with ears to hear listen!"

When he was alone, those who were around him along with the twelve asked him about the parables. And he said to them, "To you has been given the secret of the kingdom of God, but for those outside, everything comes in parables; in order that

> 'they may indeed look, but not perceive,
> and may indeed listen, but not understand;
> so that they may not turn again and be forgiven.'"

And he said to them, "Do you not understand this parable? Then how will you understand all the parables? The sower sows the word. These are the ones on the path where the word is sown: when they hear, Satan immediately comes and takes away the word that is sown in them. And these are the ones sown on rocky ground: when they hear the word, they immediately receive it with joy. But they have no root, and endure only for a while; then, when trouble or persecution arises on account of the word, immediately they fall away. And others are those sown among the thorns: these are the ones who hear the word, but the cares of the world, and the lure of wealth, and the desire for other things come in and choke the word, and it yields nothing. And these are the ones sown on the good soil: they hear the word and accept it and bear fruit, thirty and sixty and a hundredfold."

> **SCENIC VIEW**
> Many scholars think that this explanation of the meaning of the parable is a later interpretation. The original parable would have been told without any explanation, leading to the puzzlement expressed by the disciples. What other explanations could be given for the meaning of the various soils in the parable?

THE GOOD SAMARITAN

Just then a lawyer stood up to test Jesus. "Teacher," he said, "what must I do to inherit eternal life?" He said to him, "What is written in the law? What do you read there?" He answered, "You shall love the Lord your God with all your heart, and with all your soul, and with all your strength, and with all your mind; and your neighbor as yourself." And he said to him, "You have given the right answer; do this, and you will live."

But wanting to justify himself, he asked Jesus, "And who is my neighbor?" Jesus replied, "A man was going down from Jerusalem to Jericho, and fell into the hands of robbers, who stripped him, beat him, and went away, leaving him half dead. Now by chance a priest was going down that road; and when he saw him, he passed by on the other side. So likewise a Levite, when he came to the place and saw him, passed by on the other side. But a Samaritan while traveling came near him; and when he saw him, he was moved with pity. He went to him and bandaged his wounds, having poured oil and wine on them. Then he put him on his own animal, brought him to an inn, and took care of him. The next day he took out two denarii, gave them to the innkeeper, and said, 'Take care of him; and when I come back, I will repay you whatever more you spend.' Which of these three, do you think, was a neighbor to the man who fell into the hands of the robbers?" He said, "The one who showed him mercy." Jesus said to him, "Go and do likewise."

> **POINT OF INTEREST**
> The lawyer asks Jesus who to love. Jesus replies with how to love.

THE PARABLE OF TWO SONS

Now all the tax collectors and sinners were coming near to listen to him. And the Pharisees and the scribes were grumbling and saying, "This fellow welcomes sinners and eats with them."

Then Jesus said, "There was a man who had two sons. The younger of them said to his father, 'Father, give me the share of the property that will belong to me.' So he divided his property between them. A few days later the younger son gathered all he had and traveled to a distant country, and there he squandered his property in dissolute living. When he had spent everything, a severe famine took place throughout that country, and he began to be in need. So he went and hired himself out to one of the citizens of that country, who sent him to his fields to feed the pigs. He would gladly have filled himself with the pods that the pigs were eating; and no one gave him anything. But when he came to himself he said, 'How many of my father's hired hands have bread enough and to spare, but here I am dying of hunger! I will get up and go to my father, and I will say to him, "Father, I have sinned against heaven and before you; I am no longer worthy to be called your son; treat me like one of your hired hands."' So he set off and went to his father. But while he was still far off, his father saw him and was filled with compassion; he ran and put his arms around him and kissed him. Then the son said to him, 'Father, I have sinned against heaven and before you; I am no longer worthy to be called your son.' But the father said to his slaves, 'Quickly, bring out a robe—the best one—and put it on him; put a ring on his finger and sandals on his feet. And get the fatted calf and kill it, and let us eat and celebrate; for this son of mine was dead and is alive again; he was lost and is found!' And they began to celebrate.

"Now his elder son was in the field; and when he came and approached the house, he heard music and dancing. He called one of the slaves and asked what was going on. He replied, 'Your brother has come, and your father has killed the fatted calf, because he has got him back safe and sound.' Then he became angry and refused to go in. His father came out and began to plead with him. But he answered his father, 'Listen! For all these years I have been working like a slave for you, and I have never disobeyed your command; yet you have never given me even a young goat so that I might celebrate with my friends. But when this son of yours came back, who has devoured your property with prostitutes, you killed the fatted calf for him!' Then the father said to him, 'Son, you are always with me, and all that is mine is yours. But we had to celebrate and rejoice, because this brother of yours was dead and has come to life; he was lost and has been found.'"

THE RICH MAN AND LAZARUS

One day the Pharisees ridiculed Jesus, and Jesus told them this story.

"There was a rich man who was dressed in purple and fine linen and who feasted sumptuously every day. And at his gate lay a poor man named Lazarus, covered with sores, who longed to satisfy his hunger with what fell from the rich man's table; even the dogs would come and lick his sores. The poor man died and was carried away by the angels to be with Abraham. The rich man also died and was buried. In Hades, where he was being tormented, he looked up and saw Abraham far away with Lazarus by his side. He called out, 'Father Abraham, have mercy on me, and send Lazarus to dip the tip of his finger in water and cool my tongue; for I am in agony in these flames.' But Abraham said, 'Child, remember that during your lifetime you received your good things, and Lazarus in like manner evil things; but now he is comforted here, and you are in agony. Besides all this, between you and us a great chasm has been fixed, so that those who might want to pass from here to you cannot do so, and no one can cross from there to us.' He said, 'Then, father, I beg you to send him to my father's house— for I have five brothers—that he may warn them, so that they will not also come into this place of torment.' Abraham replied, 'They have Moses and the prophets; they should listen to them.' He said, 'No, father Abraham; but if someone goes to them from the dead, they will repent.' He said to him, 'If they do not listen to Moses and the prophets, neither will they be convinced even if someone rises from the dead.'"

> **SCENIC VIEW**
>
> Here Jesus tells a parable, a story, about a rich man and a poor person named Lazarus. This is not the same Lazarus that Jesus raises from the dead. For that story, read John 11:1-44.

THE SHEEP AND THE GOATS

Later Jesus was sitting on the Mount of Olives, teaching his disciples, and he said,

"When the Son of Man comes in his glory, and all the angels with him, then he will sit on the throne of his glory. All the nations will be gathered before him, and he will separate people one from another as a shepherd separates the sheep from the goats, and he will put the sheep at his right hand and the goats at the left. Then the king will say to those at his right hand, 'Come, you that are blessed by my Father, inherit the kingdom prepared for you from the foundation of the world; for I was hungry and you gave me food, I was thirsty and you gave me something to drink, I was a stranger and you welcomed me, I was naked and you gave me clothing, I was sick and you took care of me, I was in prison and you visited me.' Then the righteous will answer him, 'Lord, when was it that we saw you hungry and gave you food, or thirsty and gave you something to drink? And when was it that we saw you a stranger and welcomed you, or naked and gave you clothing? And when was it that we saw you sick or in prison and visited you?' And the king will answer them, 'Truly I tell you, just as you did it to one of the least of these who are members of my family, you did it to me.'"

> **SCENIC VIEW**
> John's Gospel does not contain many parables. These fabulous stories come from Matthew, Mark, and Luke.

Scripture Citations

Luke 3:2b-6 | 4:14-22a | 10:25-37 | 15:1-2,11-32 | 16:19-31
Mark 1:9-13, 16-20 | 2:23-3:6 | 4:1-20
John 1:43-51
Matthew 4:23—5:24, 27-32, 38-48 | 6:19-34 | 7:24-39 | 25:31-40

QUESTIONS FOR THE JOURNEY

1. What common themes emerge in this selection of Jesus' teachings? How are they different from what you remember? How are they the same?

2. Jesus' actions and teaching led to a lot of conflict with the religious authorities of the day. What is at the heart of their disagreement in these texts?

3. Do you think Jesus focuses more on behavior or belief? Which do you think is more important? Why?

4. The last two parables depict scenes of judgment. Many are surprised to learn that Jesus spoke more about hell than Paul the Apostle. Does this surprise you? Why or why not?

5. The interpretation of the parable of the sower seems to suggest that Jesus sometimes taught in parables so that people would NOT understand. What do you think of this explanation? Do you find it problematic? Why or why not?

6. In response to questions or criticism, Jesus often tells stories. Why do you think Jesus teaches in this way? What stories (biblical or otherwise) have been important in your life of faith?

NEXT STEPS

*   Read Luke's version of the sermon on the mount (6:17-49). How is it different from Matthew's version (5-7)? Which do you like more? Why?

*   This is just a small selection of teachings that Jesus gave. What important ones are missing? What important ideas about Jesus are not present here?

18
Proclaiming the Good News of the Kingdom

THE HEALING OF A PARALYTIC

One day, while [Jesus] was teaching, Pharisees and teachers of the law were sitting nearby (they had come from every village of Galilee and Judea and from Jerusalem); and the power of the Lord was with him to heal. Just then some men came, carrying a paralyzed man on a bed. They were trying to bring him in and lay him before Jesus; but finding no way to bring him in because of the crowd, they went up on the roof and let him down with his bed through the tiles into the middle of the crowd in front of Jesus. When he saw their faith, he said, "Friend, your sins are forgiven you." Then the scribes and the Pharisees began to question, "Who is this who is speaking blasphemies? Who can forgive sins but God alone?" When Jesus perceived their questionings, he answered them, "Why do you raise such questions in your hearts? Which is easier, to say, 'Your sins are forgiven you,' or to say, 'Stand up and walk'? But so that you may know that the Son of Man has authority on earth to forgive sins"—he said to the one who was paralyzed—"I say to you, stand up and take your bed and go to your home." Immediately he stood up before them, took what he had been lying on, and went to his home, glorifying God. Amazement seized all of them, and they glorified God and were filled with awe, saying, "We have seen strange things today."

THE GERASENE DEMONIAC

Then they arrived at the country of the Gerasenes, which is opposite Galilee. As he stepped out on land, a man of the city who had demons met him. For a long time he had worn no clothes, and he did not live in a house but in the tombs. When he saw Jesus, he fell down before him and shouted at the top of his voice, "What have you to do with me, Jesus, Son of the Most High God? I beg you, do not torment me"—for Jesus had commanded the unclean spirit to come out of the man. (For many times it had seized him; he was kept under guard and bound with chains and shackles, but he would break the bonds and be driven by the demon into the wilds.) Jesus then asked him, "What is your name?" He said, "Legion"; for many demons had entered him. They begged him not to order them to go back into the abyss. Now there on the hillside a large herd of swine was feeding; and the demons begged Jesus to let them enter these. So he gave them permission. Then the demons came out of the man and entered the swine, and the herd rushed down the steep bank into the lake and was drowned. When the swineherds saw what had happened, they ran off and told it in the city and in the country. Then people came out to see what had happened, and when they came to Jesus, they found the man from whom the demons had gone sitting at the feet of Jesus, clothed and in his right mind. And they were afraid. Those who had seen it told them how the one who had been possessed by demons had been healed. Then all the people of the surrounding country of the Gerasenes asked Jesus to leave them; for they were seized with great fear. So he got into the boat and returned. The man from whom the demons had gone begged that he might be with him; but Jesus sent him away, saying, "Return to your home, and declare how much God has done for you." So he went away, proclaiming throughout the city how much Jesus had done for him.

JAIRUS'S DAUGHTER AND THE WOMAN WITH A HEMORRHAGE

When Jesus had crossed again in the boat to the other side, a great crowd gathered around him; and he was by the sea. Then one of the leaders of the synagogue named Jairus came and, when he saw him, fell at his feet and begged him repeatedly, "My little daughter is at the point of death. Come and lay your hands on her, so that she may be made well, and live."

So he went with him. And a large crowd followed him and pressed in on him. Now there was a woman who had been suffering from hemorrhages for twelve years. She had endured much under many physicians, and had spent all that she had; and she was no better, but rather grew worse. She had heard about Jesus, and came up behind him in the crowd and touched his cloak, for she said, "If I but touch his clothes, I will be made well." Immediately her hemorrhage stopped; and she felt in her body that she was healed of her disease. Immediately aware that power had gone forth from him, Jesus turned about in the crowd and said, "Who touched my clothes?" And his disciples said to him, "You see the crowd pressing in on you; how can you say, 'Who touched me?'" He looked all around to see who had done it. But the woman, knowing what had happened to her, came in fear and trembling, fell down before him, and told him the whole truth. He said to her,

> ### SCENIC VIEW
> One of Mark's favorite strategies for telling stories is a sandwich narrative. He will start one story, move to a second story, then return to the original story. By pairing the stories together, they help explain each other. Check out Mark 7:1-30 and Mark 11:12-25. How do the stories that Mark paired together in these examples inform one another?

SCENIC VIEW

Miracles and belief function differently in the first three gospels than in the Gospel of John. In Matthew, Mark, and Luke, belief precedes the miracle. When people believe, Jesus is empowered to heal them. In John, the miracles are signs that lead to belief; people see the miracle, and then they believe. Can you spot which miracles in this chapter are from Matthew, Mark, or Luke and which are from John?

"Daughter, your faith has made you well; go in peace, and be healed of your disease."

While he was still speaking, some people came from the leader's house to say, "Your daughter is dead. Why trouble the teacher any further?" But overhearing what they said, Jesus said to the leader of the synagogue, "Do not fear, only believe." He allowed no one to follow him except Peter, James, and John, the brother of James. When they came to the house of the leader of the synagogue, he saw a commotion, people weeping and wailing loudly. When he had entered, he said to them, "Why do you make a commotion and weep? The child is not dead but sleeping." And they laughed at him. Then he put them all outside, and took the child's father and mother and those who were with him, and went in where the child was. He took her by the hand and said to her, "Talitha cum," which means, "Little girl, get up!" And immediately the girl got up and began to walk about (she was twelve years of age). At this they were overcome with amazement. He strictly ordered them that no one should know this, and told them to give her something to eat.

JESUS COMMISSIONS THE DISCIPLES

POINT OF INTEREST

The gospels all agree that there were twelve disciples who were closest to Jesus. Who the twelve were varies from list to list, with Peter, James, and John always occupying a primary place.

Then Jesus went about all the cities and villages, teaching in their synagogues, and proclaiming the good news of the kingdom, and curing every disease and every sickness. When he saw the crowds, he had compassion for them, because they were harassed and helpless, like sheep without a shepherd. Then he said to his disciples, "The harvest is plentiful, but the laborers are few; therefore ask the Lord of the harvest to send out laborers into his harvest."

Then Jesus summoned his twelve disciples and gave them authority over unclean spirits, to cast them out, and to cure every disease and every sickness. These are the names of the twelve apostles: first, Simon, also known as Peter, and his brother Andrew; James son of Zebedee, and his brother John; Philip and Bartholomew; Thomas and Matthew the tax collector; James son of Alphaeus, and Thaddaeus; Simon the Cananaean, and Judas Iscariot, the one who betrayed him.

Now when Jesus had finished instructing his twelve disciples, he went on from there to teach and proclaim his message in their cities.

JESUS FEEDS A LARGE CROWD

After this Jesus went to the other side of the Sea of Galilee, also called the Sea of Tiberias. A large crowd kept following him, because they saw the signs that he was doing for the sick. Jesus went up the mountain and sat down there with his disciples. Now the Passover, the festival of the Jews, was near. When he looked up and saw a large crowd coming toward him, Jesus said to Philip, "Where are we to buy bread for these people to eat?" He said this to test him, for he himself knew what he was going to do. Philip answered him, "Six months' wages would not buy enough bread for each of them to get a little." One of his disciples, Andrew, Simon Peter's brother, said to him, "There is a boy here who has five barley loaves and two fish. But what are they among so many people?" Jesus said, "Make the people sit down." Now there was a great deal of grass in the

> **POINT OF INTEREST**
> There are very few miracle stories that are narrated in all four gospels. The feeding of the 5,000 is one of them. Only John offers this detail about the boy and his lunch.

place; so they sat down, about five thousand in all. Then Jesus took the loaves, and when he had given thanks, he distributed them to those who were seated; so also the fish, as much as they wanted. When they were satisfied, he told his disciples, "Gather up the fragments left over, so that nothing may be lost." So they gathered them up, and from the fragments of the five barley loaves, left by those who had eaten, they filled twelve baskets. When the people saw the sign that he had done, they began to say, "This is indeed the prophet who is to come into the world."

JESUS EXPLAINS THE SIGNIFICANCE OF THE LOAVES AND FISHES

Jesus said to them, "I am the bread of life. Whoever comes to me will never be hungry, and whoever believes in me will never be thirsty. But I said to you that you have seen me and yet do not believe. Everything that the Father gives me will come to me, and anyone who comes to me I will never drive away; for I have come down from heaven, not to do my own will, but the will of him who sent me. And this is the will of him who sent me, that I should lose nothing of all that he has given me, but raise it up on the last day. This is indeed the will of my Father, that all who see the Son and believe in him may have eternal life; and I will raise them up on the last day." Then the Jews began to complain about him because he said, "I am the bread that came down from heaven." They were saying, "Is not this Jesus, the son of Joseph, whose father and mother we know? How can he now say, 'I have come down from heaven'?" Jesus answered them, "Do not complain among yourselves. No one can come to me unless drawn by the Father who sent me; and I will raise that person up on the last day. It

> **POINT OF INTEREST**
> The "I am" statements are only found in the Gospel of John. Sometimes they are metaphorical ("I am the bread of life," "I am the light of the world," "I am the good shepherd.") Sometimes they appear to underscore Jesus' divinity ("Before Abraham was, I am.") This statement also draws on the revelation of God to Moses in Exodus 3: "I Am Who I Am."

is written in the prophets, 'And they shall all be taught by God.' Everyone who has heard and learned from the Father comes to me. Not that anyone has seen the Father except the one who is from God; he has seen the Father. Very truly, I tell you, whoever believes has eternal life. I am the bread of life. Your ancestors ate the manna in the wilderness, and they died. This is the bread that comes down from heaven, so that one may eat of it and not die. I am the living bread that came down from heaven. Whoever eats of this bread will live forever; and the bread that I will give for the life of the world is my flesh. Very truly, I tell you, unless you eat the flesh of the Son of Man and drink his blood, you have no life in you. Those who eat my flesh and drink my blood have eternal life, and I will raise them up on the last day; for my flesh is true food and my blood is true drink. Those who eat my flesh and drink my blood abide in me, and I in them. Just as the living Father sent me, and I live because of the Father, so whoever eats me will live because of me. This is the bread that came down from heaven, not like that which your ancestors ate, and they died. But the one who eats this bread will live forever."

THE TRANSFIGURATION

Six days later, Jesus took with him Peter and James and John, and led them up a high mountain apart, by themselves. And he was transfigured before them, and his clothes became dazzling white, such as no one on earth could bleach them. And there appeared to them Elijah with Moses, who were talking with Jesus. Then Peter said to Jesus, "Rabbi, it is good for us to be here;

SCENIC VIEW
The Transfiguration is an incredibly important moment in the life and ministry of Jesus. The details of the Transfiguration are directly linked to God's revelation to Moses in Exodus 24 and 34. The presence of Moses and Elijah on either side of Jesus reminds us that Jesus does not destroy the law and the prophets of the Old Testament, he fulfills them. This moment of Transfiguration harkens back to Jesus' baptism at the beginning of his ministry (Matthew 3:13-17) and will also serve as a touchstone for the disciples who are present, when they later remember and proclaim the risen Jesus (2 Peter 1:16-18).

let us make three dwellings, one for you, one for Moses, and one for Elijah." He did not know what to say, for they were terrified. Then a cloud overshadowed them, and from the cloud there came a voice, "This is my Son, the Beloved; listen to him!" Suddenly when they looked around, they saw no one with them any more, but only Jesus.

As they were coming down the mountain, he ordered them to tell no one about what they had seen, until after the Son of Man had risen from the dead. So they kept the matter to themselves, questioning what this rising from the dead could mean.

THE WOMAN CAUGHT IN ADULTERY

Then each of them went home, while Jesus went to the Mount of Olives. Early in the morning he came again to the temple. All the people came to him and he sat down and began to teach them. The scribes and the Pharisees brought a woman who had been caught in adultery; and making her stand before all of them, they said to him, "Teacher, this woman was caught in the very act of committing adultery. Now in the law Moses commanded us to stone such women. Now what do you say?" They said this to test him, so that they might have some charge to bring against him. Jesus bent down and wrote with his finger on the ground. When they kept on questioning him, he straightened up and said to them, "Let anyone among you who is without sin be the first to throw a stone at her." And once again he bent down and wrote on the ground. When they heard it, they went away, one by one, beginning with the elders; and Jesus was left alone with the woman standing before him. Jesus straightened up and said to her, "Woman, where are they? Has no one condemned you?" She said, "No one, sir." And Jesus said, "Neither do I condemn you. Go your way, and from now on do not sin again."

THE CENTURION'S SERVANT

When he entered Capernaum, a centurion came to him, appealing to him and saying, "Lord, my servant is lying at home paralyzed, in terrible distress." And he said to him, "I will come and cure him." The centurion answered, "Lord, I am not worthy to have you come under my roof; but only speak the word, and my servant will be healed. For I also am a man under authority, with soldiers under me; and I say to one, 'Go,' and he goes, and to another, 'Come,' and he comes, and to my slave, 'Do this,' and the slave does it." When Jesus heard him, he was amazed and said to those who followed him, "Truly I tell you, in no one in Israel have I found such faith. I tell you, many will come from east and west and will eat with Abraham and Isaac and Jacob in the kingdom of heaven, while the heirs of the kingdom will be thrown into the outer darkness, where there will be weeping and gnashing of teeth." And to the centurion Jesus said, "Go; let it be done for you according to your faith." And the servant was healed in that hour.

JESUS HEALS THE MAN BORN BLIND

As he walked along, he saw a man blind from birth. His disciples asked him, "Rabbi, who sinned, this man or his parents, that he was born blind?" Jesus answered, "Neither this man nor his parents sinned; he was born blind so that God's works might be revealed in him. We must work the works of him who sent me while it is day; night is coming when no one can work. As long as I am in the world, I am the light of the world." When he had said this, he spat on the ground and made mud with the saliva and spread the mud on the man's eyes, saying to him, "Go, wash in the pool of Siloam" (which means Sent). Then he went and washed and came back able to see.

THE CANAANITE WOMAN

Jesus left that place and went away to the district of Tyre and Sidon. Just then a Canaanite woman from that region came out and started shouting, "Have mercy on me, Lord, Son of David; my daughter is tormented by a demon." But he did not answer her at all. And his disciples came and urged him, saying, "Send her away, for she keeps shouting after us." He answered, "I was sent only to the lost sheep of the house of Israel." But she came and knelt before him, saying, "Lord, help me." He answered, "It is not fair to take the children's food and throw it to the dogs." She said, "Yes, Lord, yet even the dogs eat the crumbs that fall from their masters' table." Then Jesus answered her, "Woman, great is your faith! Let it be done for you as you wish." And her daughter was healed instantly.

THE RICH YOUNG MAN

As he was setting out on a journey, a man ran up and knelt before him, and asked him, "Good Teacher, what must I do to inherit eternal life?" Jesus said to him, "Why do you call me good? No one is good but God alone. You know the commandments: 'You shall not murder; You shall not commit adultery; You shall not steal; You shall not bear false witness; You shall not defraud; Honor your father and mother.'" He said to him, "Teacher, I have kept all these since my youth." Jesus, looking at him, loved him and said, "You lack one thing; go, sell what you own, and give the money to the poor, and you will have treasure in heaven; then come, follow me." When he heard this, he was shocked and went away grieving, for he had many possessions.

Then Jesus looked around and said to his disciples, "How hard it will be for those who have wealth to enter the kingdom of God!" And the disciples were perplexed at these words. But Jesus said to them again, "Children, how hard it is to enter the kingdom of God! It is easier for a camel to go through the eye of a needle than for someone who is rich to enter the kingdom of God." They were greatly astounded and said to one another, "Then who can be saved?" Jesus looked at them and said, "For mortals it is impossible, but not for God; for God all things are possible."

ZACCHAEUS

He entered Jericho and was passing through it. A man was there named Zacchaeus; he was a chief tax collector and was rich. He was trying to see who Jesus was, but on account of the crowd he could not, because he was short in stature. So he ran ahead and climbed a sycamore tree to see him, because he was going to pass that way. When Jesus came to the place, he looked up and said to him, "Zacchaeus, hurry and come down; for I must stay at your house today." So he hurried down and was happy to welcome him. All who saw it began to grumble and said, "He has gone to be the guest of one who is a sinner." Zacchaeus stood there and said to the Lord, "Look, half of my possessions, Lord, I will give to the poor; and if I have defrauded anyone of anything, I will pay back four times as much." Then Jesus said to him, "Today salvation has come to this house, because he too is a son of Abraham. For the Son of Man came to seek out and to save the lost."

THE RAISING OF LAZARUS

Now a certain man was ill, Lazarus of Bethany, the village of Mary and her sister Martha. Mary was the one who anointed the Lord with perfume and wiped his feet with her hair; her brother Lazarus was ill. So the sisters sent a message to Jesus, "Lord, he whom you love is ill." But when Jesus heard it, he said, "This illness does not lead to death; rather it is for God's glory, so that the Son of God may be glorified through it." Accordingly, though Jesus loved Martha and her sister and Lazarus, after having heard that Lazarus was ill, he stayed two

SCENIC VIEW

Scholars commonly divide the Gospel of John into two books: the Book of Signs (John 1:19-12:50) and the Book of Glory (John 13:1-20:31). The Book of Signs describes seven miracles that are increasingly spectacular. The raising of Lazarus is the final and most spectacular of all the signs and ultimately what leads to the religious leaders plotting Jesus' death. The Book of Glory narrates Jesus' final week: his prayers for his followers, his trial, his crucifixion, and his resurrection.

days longer in the place where he was. Then after this he said to the disciples, "Let us go to Judea again." The disciples said to him, "Rabbi, the Jews were just now trying to stone you, and are you going there again?" Jesus answered, "Are there not twelve hours of daylight? Those who walk during the day do not stumble, because they see the light of this world. But those who walk at night stumble, because the light is not in them." After saying this, he told them, "Our friend Lazarus has fallen asleep, but I am going there to awaken him." The disciples said to him, "Lord, if he has fallen asleep, he will be all right." Jesus, however, had been speaking about his death, but they thought that he was referring merely to sleep. Then Jesus told them plainly, "Lazarus is dead. For your sake I am glad I was not there, so that you may believe. But let us go to him." Thomas, who was called the Twin, said to his fellow disciples, "Let us also go, that we may die with him."

When Jesus arrived, he found that Lazarus had already been in the tomb four days. Now Bethany was near Jerusalem, some two miles away, and many of the Jews had come to Martha and Mary to console them about their brother. When Martha heard that Jesus was coming, she went and met him, while Mary stayed at home. Martha said to Jesus, "Lord, if you had been here, my brother would not have died. But even now I know that God will give you whatever you ask of him." Jesus said to her, "Your brother will rise again." Martha said to him, "I know that he will rise again in the resurrection on the last day." Jesus said to her, "I am the resurrection and the life. Those who believe in me, even though they die, will live, and everyone who lives and believes in me will never die. Do you believe this?" She said to him, "Yes, Lord, I believe that you are the Messiah, the Son of God, the one coming into the world." When she had said this, she went back and called her sister Mary, and told her privately, "The Teacher is here and is calling for you." And when she heard it, she got up quickly and went to him. Now Jesus had not yet come to the village, but was still at the place where Martha had met him. The Jews who were with her in the house, consoling her, saw Mary get up quickly and go out. They followed her because they thought that she was going to the tomb to weep there. When Mary came where Jesus was and saw him, she knelt at his feet and said to him, "Lord, if you had been here, my brother would not have died."

> **YOU ARE HERE**
> Jesus knew that Lazarus would be raised, but he still experienced deep grief, weeping over the death of his beloved friend. Thus Jesus reminds us that our belief in resurrection does not mean that we can't, or shouldn't, grieve the death of those we love. Jesus wept over Lazarus's death, even as he raised him from death. How have you grieved your loved one's death? Pray for someone you have loved and lost.

When Jesus saw her weeping, and the Jews who came with her also weeping, he was greatly disturbed in spirit and deeply moved. He said, "Where have you laid him?" They said to him, "Lord, come and see." Jesus began to weep. So the Jews said, "See how he loved him!" But some of them said, "Could not he who opened the eyes of the blind man have kept this man from dying?" Then Jesus, again greatly disturbed, came to the tomb. It was a cave, and a stone was lying against it. Jesus said, "Take away the stone." Martha, the sister of the dead man, said to him, "Lord, already there is a stench because he has been dead four days." Jesus said to her, "Did I not tell you that if you believed, you would see the glory of God?" So they took away the stone. And Jesus looked upward and said, "Father, I thank you for having heard me. I knew that you always hear me, but I have said this for the sake of the crowd standing here, so that they may believe that you sent me." When he had said this, he cried with a loud voice, "Lazarus, come out!" The dead man came out, his hands and feet bound with strips of cloth, and his face wrapped in a cloth. Jesus said to them, "Unbind him, and let him go."

Many of the Jews therefore, who had come with Mary and had seen what Jesus did, believed in him. But some of them went to the Pharisees and told them what he had done. So the chief priests and the Pharisees called a meeting of the council, and said, "What are we to do? This man is performing many signs. If we let him go on like this, everyone will believe in him, and the Romans will come and destroy both our holy place and our nation." But one of them, Caiaphas, who was high priest that year, said to them, "You know nothing at all! You do not understand that it is better for you to have one man die for the people than to have the whole nation destroyed." He did not say this on his own, but being high priest that year he prophesied that Jesus was about to die for the nation, and not for the nation only, but to gather into one the dispersed children of God. So from that day on they planned to put him to death.

Scripture Citations
Luke 5:17-26 | 8:26-39 | 19:1-10
Mark 5:21-43 | 9:2-10 | 10:17-27
Matthew 9:35-10:4; 11:1 | 8:5-13 | 15:21-28
John 6:1-14 | 6:35-51, 53-58 | 7:53-8:11 | 9:1-7 | 11:1-53

QUESTIONS FOR THE JOURNEY

1. Is belief necessary for miracles or do miracles lead to belief? Are both somehow true at the same time?

2. Which miracle is most important to you for understanding who Jesus is?

3. Is there a miracle story not in this chapter that has been significant for you in your faith journey? What made it important for you?

4. Which story in this chapter is most difficult for you to accept? Why?

5. Why do you think the feeding of the 5,000 is one of the only stories to be included in all four gospels? Why do you think the evangelists considered this an important story about Jesus?

NEXT STEPS

- Read the Gospel of Mark. How is Jesus different in that gospel from how he has been presented in these chapters?

- Read John 1-12. How do miracles and belief interact? How are Jesus' discourses related to the miracles?

19
Crucify Him!

THE TRIUMPHANT ENTRY

Six days before the Passover Jesus came to Bethany, the home of Lazarus, whom he had raised from the dead. When the great crowd of the Jews learned that he was there, they came not only because of Jesus but also to see Lazarus, whom he had raised from the dead. So the chief priests planned to put Lazarus to death as well, since it was on account of him that many of the Jews were deserting and were believing in Jesus.

The next day the great crowd that had come to the festival heard that Jesus was coming to Jerusalem. When Jesus and his disciples were approaching Jerusalem, at Bethphage and Bethany, near the Mount of Olives, he sent two of his disciples and said to them, "Go into the village ahead of you, and immediately as you enter it, you will find tied there a colt that has never been ridden; untie it and bring it. If anyone says to you, 'Why are you doing this?' just say this, 'The Lord needs it and will send it back here immediately.'" They went away and found a colt tied near a door, outside in the street. As they were untying it, some of the bystanders said to them, "What are you doing, untying the colt?" They told them what Jesus had said; and they allowed them to take it. Then they brought the colt to Jesus and threw their cloaks on it; and he sat on it. Many people spread their cloaks on the road, and others spread leafy branches that they had cut in the fields. Then those who went ahead and those who followed were shouting,

"Hosanna!
Blessed is the one who comes in the
name of the Lord!
Blessed is the coming kingdom of our
ancestor David!
Hosanna in the highest heaven!"

Then he entered Jerusalem and went into the temple; and when he had looked around at everything, as it was already late, he went out to Bethany with the twelve.

CLEANSING OF THE TEMPLE

On the following day, when they came from Bethany, he was hungry. Seeing in the distance a fig tree in leaf, he went to see whether perhaps he would find anything on it. When he came to it, he found nothing but leaves, for it was not the season for figs. He said to it, "May no one ever eat fruit from you again." And his disciples heard it.

Then they came to Jerusalem. And he entered the temple and began to drive out those who were selling and those who were buying in the temple, and he overturned the tables of the money changers and the seats of those who sold doves; and he would not allow anyone to carry anything through the temple. He was teaching and saying, "Is it not written,

> 'My house shall be called a house of prayer for
> > all the nations'?
> But you have made it a den of robbers."

And when the chief priests and the scribes heard it, they kept looking for a way to kill him; for they were afraid of him, because the whole crowd was spellbound by his teaching. And when evening came, Jesus and his disciples went out of the city.

In the morning as they passed by, they saw the fig tree withered away to its roots. Then Peter remembered and said to him, "Rabbi, look! The fig tree that you cursed has withered."

JESUS TEACHES IN THE TEMPLE

The next day Jesus returned to the temple to teach. Religious leaders asked him what authority he had to speak and act on behalf of God. Jesus answered mostly by telling parables and other stories.

SCENIC VIEW

This event is described in all four gospels. Matthew, Mark, and Luke place it at the end of Jesus' ministry, John at the beginning. Scholars generally agree that it happened at the end of Jesus' ministry and was a catalyst for his crucifixion. The temple gathered tributes, some of which were sent on to Rome. The attack on the temple, then, was an attack on Rome. Crucifixion was reserved largely for seditionists. Jesus' activity in the temple could easily be understood as incitement of rebellion.

POINT OF INTEREST

Did you notice the sandwich storytelling technique? Mark brackets the cleansing of the temple with the cursing of the fig tree. The fig tree is used as a symbol for barrenness, to represent Israel's failure to bear the fruit of good works.

THE PARABLE OF THE WICKED TENANTS

There was a landowner who planted a vineyard, put a fence around it, dug a wine press in it, and built a watchtower. Then he leased it to tenants and went to another country. When the harvest time had come, he sent his slaves to the tenants to collect his produce. But the tenants seized his slaves and beat one, killed another, and stoned another. Again he sent other slaves, more than the first; and they treated them in the same way. Finally he sent his son to them, saying, 'They will respect my son.' But when the tenants saw the son, they said to themselves, 'This is the heir; come, let us kill him and get his inheritance." So they seized him, threw him out of the vineyard, and killed him. Now when the owner of the vineyard comes, what will he do to those tenants?" They said to him, "He will put those wretches to a miserable death, and lease the vineyard to other tenants who will give him the produce at the harvest time." Jesus said to them, "Have you never read in the scriptures: 'The stone that the builders rejected has become the cornerstone; this was the Lord's doing, and it is amazing in our eyes'? Therefore I tell you, the kingdom of God will be taken away from you and given to a people that produces the fruits of the kingdom. The one who falls on this stone will be broken to pieces; and it will crush anyone on whom it falls." When the chief priests and the Pharisees heard his parables, they realized that he was speaking about them. They wanted to arrest him, but they feared the crowds, because they regarded him as a prophet.

THE GREAT COMMANDMENT

One of the scribes came near and heard them disputing with one another, and seeing that he answered them well, he asked him, "Which commandment is the first of all?" Jesus answered, "The first is, 'Hear, O Israel: the Lord our God, the Lord is one; you shall love the Lord your God with all your heart, and with all your soul, and with all your mind, and with all your strength.' The second is this, 'You shall love your neighbor as yourself.'

> **SCENIC VIEW**
>
> When Jesus gives the great commandment, he is not saying something new. These two commandments come straight from the Hebrew scriptures: Deuteronomy 6:4-5 and Leviticus 19:8. Jesus is reminding people that they already know how they are called to live; they just have to actually do it. In John's Gospel, Jesus will go one step further and give his followers a new commandment: to love one another as he has loved them (John 13:31-35). How is loving others like Jesus loves different from loving our neighbors as ourselves?

There is no other commandment greater than these." Then the scribe said to him, "You are right, Teacher; you have truly said that 'he is one, and besides him there is no other'; and 'to love him with all the heart, and with all the understanding, and with all the strength,' and 'to love one's neighbor as oneself,' —this is much more important than all whole burnt offerings and sacrifices." When Jesus saw that he answered wisely, he said to him, "You are not far from the kingdom of God." After that no one dared to ask him any question.

A WARNING ABOUT THE SCRIBES

As he taught, he said, "Beware of the scribes, who like to walk around in long robes, and to be greeted with respect in the marketplaces, and to have the best seats in the synagogues and places of honor at banquets! They devour widows' houses and for the sake of appearance say long prayers. They will receive the greater condemnation."

WIDOW'S MITE

He looked up and saw rich people putting their gifts into the treasury; he also saw a poor widow put in two small copper coins. He said, "Truly I tell you, this poor widow has put in more than all of them; for all of them have contributed out of their abundance, but she out of her poverty has put in all she had to live on."

POINT OF INTEREST
The story of the Widow's Mite comes immediately after the denunciation of the scribes who devour widows' houses. Yes, the woman is a model of faith. She also is a witness to the corruption of the religious leaders.

THE MINI-APOCALYPSE

As he came out of the temple, one of his disciples said to him, "Look, Teacher, what large stones and what large buildings!" Then Jesus asked him, "Do you see these great buildings? Not one stone will be left here upon another; all will be thrown down."

When he was sitting on the Mount of Olives opposite the temple, Peter, James, John, and Andrew asked him privately, "Tell us, when will this be, and what will be the sign that all these things are about to be accomplished?" Then Jesus began to say to them, "Beware that no one leads you astray. Many will come in my name and say, 'I am he!' and they will lead many astray. When you hear of wars and rumors of wars, do not be alarmed; this must take place, but the end is still to come. For nation will rise against nation, and kingdom against kingdom; there will be earthquakes in various places; there will be famines. This is but the beginning of the birthpangs.

"As for yourselves, beware; for they will hand you over to councils; and you will be beaten in synagogues; and you will stand before governors and kings because of me, as a testimony to them. And the good news must first be proclaimed to all nations. When they bring you to trial and hand you over, do not worry beforehand about what you are to say; but say whatever is given you at that time, for it is not you who speak, but the Holy Spirit. Brother will betray brother to death, and a father his child, and children will rise against parents and have them put to death; and you will be hated by all because of my name. But the one who endures to the end will be saved."

JESUS IS ANOINTED

It was two days before the Passover and the festival of Unleavened Bread. The chief priests and the scribes were looking for a way to arrest Jesus by stealth and kill him; for they said, "Not during the festival, or there may be a riot among the people."

While he was at Bethany in the house of Simon the leper, as he sat at the table, a woman came with an alabaster jar of very costly ointment of nard, and she broke open the jar and poured the ointment on his head. But some were there who said to one another in anger, "Why was the ointment wasted in this way? For this ointment could have been sold for more than three hundred denarii, and the money given to the poor." And they scolded her. But Jesus said, "Let her alone; why do you trouble her? She has performed a good service for me. For you always have the poor with you, and you can show kindness to them whenever you wish; but you will not always have me. She has done what she could; she has anointed my body beforehand for its burial. Truly I tell you, wherever the good news is proclaimed in the whole world, what she has done will be told in remembrance of her."

> **POINT OF INTEREST**
> Nard or spikenard was a fragrant ointment or perfume that cost a year's wages. Fragrant perfumes were used to anoint kings, as in 1 Samuel 10.1 or 2 Kings 9:6; they were also used to anoint bodies for burial, as in Mark 16:1. This beautiful story occurs in all four gospels. Although the woman's act is praised, the story does not tell us her name.

Then Judas Iscariot, who was one of the twelve, went to the chief priests in order to betray him to them. When they heard it, they were greatly pleased, and promised to give him money. So he began to look for an opportunity to betray him.

JESUS' LAST MEAL WITH HIS FRIENDS

On the first day of Unleavened Bread the disciples came to Jesus, saying, "Where do you want us to make the preparations for you to eat the Passover?" He said, "Go into the city to a certain man, and say to him, 'The Teacher says, My time is near; I will keep the Passover at your house with my disciples.'" So the disciples did as Jesus had directed them, and they prepared the Passover meal.

When it was evening, he took his place with the twelve; and while they were eating, he said, "Truly I tell you, one of you will betray me." And they became greatly distressed and began to say to him one after another, "Surely not I, Lord?" He answered, "The one who has dipped his hand into the bowl with me will betray me. The Son of Man goes as it is written of him, but woe to that one by whom the Son of Man is betrayed! It would have been better for that one not to have been born." Judas, who betrayed him, said, "Surely not I, Rabbi?" He replied, "You have said so."

> **POINT OF INTEREST**
> Throughout his ministry, Jesus ate with all sorts of people. He ate with friends and enemies, people of status and people of ill repute. This practice communicated a radical acceptance that ruffled more than a few feathers. It is fitting that Jesus shares one final meal with his closest friends.

While they were eating, Jesus took a loaf of bread, and after blessing it he broke it, gave it to the disciples, and said, "Take, eat; this is my body." Then he took a cup, and after giving thanks he gave it to them, saying, "Drink from it, all of you; for this is my blood of the covenant, which is poured out for many for the forgiveness of sins. I tell you, I will never again drink of this fruit of the vine until that day when I drink it new with you in my Father's kingdom." When they had sung the hymn, they went out to the Mount of Olives.

Then Jesus said to them, "You will all become deserters because of me this night; for it is written, 'I will strike the shepherd, and the sheep of the flock will be scattered.' But after I am raised up, I will go ahead of you to Galilee." Peter said to him, "Though all become deserters because of you, I will never desert you." Jesus said to him, "Truly I tell you, this very night, before the cock crows, you will deny me three times." Peter said to him, "Even though I must die with you, I will not deny you." And so said all the disciples.

GETHSEMANE

[Jesus] came out and went, as was his custom, to the Mount of Olives; and the disciples followed him. When he reached the place, he said to them, "Pray that you may not come into the time of trial." Then he withdrew from them about a stone's throw, knelt down, and prayed, "Father, if you are willing, remove this cup from me; yet, not my will but yours be done." Then an angel from heaven appeared to him and gave him strength. In his anguish he prayed more earnestly, and his sweat became like great drops of blood falling down on the ground. When he got up from prayer, [Jesus] came to the disciples and found them sleeping because of grief, and he said to them, "Why are you sleeping? Get up and pray that you may not come into the time of trial."

JESUS IS ARRESTED

While he was still speaking, suddenly a crowd came, and the one called Judas, one of the twelve, was leading them. He approached Jesus to kiss him; but Jesus said to him, "Judas, is it with a kiss that you are betraying the Son of Man?" When those who were around him saw what was coming, they asked, "Lord, should we strike with the sword?" Then one of them struck the slave of the high priest and cut off his right ear. But Jesus said, "No more of this!" And he touched his ear and healed him. Then Jesus said to the chief priests, the officers of the temple police, and the elders who had come for him, "Have you come out with swords and clubs as if I were a bandit? When I was with you day after day in the temple, you did not lay hands on me. But this is your hour, and the power of darkness!"

PETER DENIES JESUS

Then they seized him and led him away, bringing him into the high priest's house. But Peter was following at a distance. When they had kindled a fire in the middle of the courtyard and sat down together, Peter sat among them. Then a servant-girl, seeing him in the firelight, stared at him and said, "This man also was with him." But he denied it, saying, "Woman, I do not know him." A little later someone else, on seeing him, said, "You also are one of them." But Peter said, "Man, I am not!" Then about an hour later still another kept insisting, "Surely this man also was with him; for he is a

Galilean." But Peter said, "Man, I do not know what you are talking about!" At that moment, while he was still speaking, the cock crowed. The Lord turned and looked at Peter. Then Peter remembered the word of the Lord, how he had said to him, "Before the cock crows today, you will deny me three times." And he went out and wept bitterly.

JESUS BEFORE THE SANHEDRIN

Now the chief priests and the whole council were looking for false testimony against Jesus so that they might put him to death, but they found none, though many false witnesses came forward. At last two came forward and said, "This fellow said, 'I am able to destroy the temple of God and to build it in three days.'" The high priest stood up and said, "Have you no answer? What is it that they testify against you?" But Jesus was silent. Then the high priest said to him, "I put you under oath before the living God, tell us if you are the Messiah, the Son of God." Jesus said to him, "You have said so. But I tell you, From now on you will see the Son of Man seated at the right hand of Power and coming on the clouds of heaven." Then the high priest tore his clothes and said, "He has blasphemed! Why do we still need witnesses? You have now heard his blasphemy. What is your verdict?" They answered, "He deserves death." Then they spat in his face and struck him; and some slapped him, saying, "Prophesy to us, you Messiah! Who is it that struck you?"

SCENIC VIEW

Pilate was an incredibly vicious ruler. Although he is depicted in the gospels (especially John, which you are reading here) as a reasonable man who only reluctantly condemned Jesus to death, Pilate was actually recalled to Rome for using excessive force.

JESUS DELIVERED TO PILATE

When morning came, all the chief priests and the elders of the people conferred together against Jesus in order to bring about his death. They bound him, led him away, and handed him over to Pilate the governor. It was early in the morning. They themselves did not enter the headquarters, so as to avoid ritual defilement and to be able to eat the Passover. So Pilate went out to them and said, "What accusation do you bring against this man?" They answered, "If this man were not a criminal, we would not have handed him over to you." Pilate said to them, "Take him yourselves and judge him according to your law." The Jews replied, "We are not permitted to put anyone to death." (This was to fulfill what Jesus had said when he indicated the kind of death he was to die.)

Then Pilate entered the headquarters again, summoned Jesus, and asked him, "Are you the King of the Jews?" Jesus answered, "Do you ask this on your own, or did others tell you about me?" Pilate replied, "I am not a Jew, am I? Your own nation and the chief priests have handed you over to me. What have you done?" Jesus answered, "My kingdom is not from this world. If my kingdom were from this world, my followers would be fighting to keep me from being handed over to the Jews. But as it is, my kingdom is not from here." Pilate asked him, "So you are a king?" Jesus answered, "You say that I am a king. For this I was born, and for this I came into the world, to testify to the truth. Everyone who belongs to the truth listens to my voice." Pilate asked him, "What is truth?"

After he had said this, he went out to the Jews again and told them, "I find no case against him. But you have a custom that I release someone for you at the Passover. Do you want me to release for you the King of the Jews?" They shouted in reply, "Not this man, but Barabbas!" Now Barabbas was a bandit.

Then Pilate took Jesus and had him flogged. And the soldiers wove a crown of thorns and put it on his head, and they dressed him in a purple robe. They kept coming up to him, saying, "Hail, King of the Jews!" and striking him on the face. Pilate went out again and said to them, "Look, I am bringing him out to you to let you know that I find no case against him." So Jesus came out, wearing the crown of thorns and the purple robe.

Pilate said to them, "Here is the man!" When the chief priests and the police saw him, they shouted, "Crucify him! Crucify him!" Pilate said to them, "Take him yourselves and crucify him; I find no case against him." The Jews answered him, "We have a law, and according to that law he ought to die because he has claimed to be the Son of God."

Now when Pilate heard this, he was more afraid than ever. He entered his headquarters again and asked Jesus, "Where are you from?" But Jesus gave him no answer. Pilate therefore said to him, "Do you refuse to speak to me? Do you not know that I have power to release you, and power to crucify you?" Jesus answered him, "You would have no power over me unless it had been given you from above; therefore the one who handed me over to you is guilty of a greater sin." From then on Pilate tried to release him, but the Jews cried out, "If you release this man, you are no friend of the emperor. Everyone who claims to be a king sets himself against the emperor."

When Pilate heard these words, he brought Jesus outside and sat on the judge's bench at a place called The Stone Pavement, or in Hebrew Gabbatha. Now it was the day of Preparation for the Passover; and it was about noon. He said to the Jews, "Here is your King!" They cried out, "Away with him! Away with him! Crucify him!" Pilate asked them, "Shall I crucify your King?" The chief priests answered, "We have no king but the emperor." Then he handed him over to them to be crucified.

SCENIC VIEW

Crucifixion was frequently used in Rome to kill people who had rebelled against the empire. This cruel punishment tormented the condemned for days. They were a public spectacle, a warning to anyone who might think to challenge the might of the empire. The punishment was so gruesome that very few ancient sources actually depict it. The gospels tell us more about crucifixion than many ancient authors were willing to divulge.

JESUS IS CRUCIFIED

They compelled a passer-by, who was coming in from the country, to carry his cross; it was Simon of Cyrene, the father of Alexander and Rufus. Then they brought Jesus to the place called Golgotha (which means the place of a skull). And they offered him wine mixed with myrrh; but he did not take it. And they crucified him, and divided his clothes among them, casting lots to decide what each should take.

It was nine o'clock in the morning when they crucified him. The inscription of the charge against him read, "The King of the Jews." And with him they crucified two bandits, one on his right and one on his left.

Those who passed by derided him, shaking their heads and saying, "Aha! You who would destroy the temple and build it in three days, save yourself, and come down from the cross!" In the same way the chief priests, along with the scribes, were also mocking him among themselves and saying, "He saved others; he cannot save himself. Let the Messiah, the King of Israel, come down from the cross now, so that we may see and believe."

THE TWO THIEVES

One of the criminals who were hanged there kept deriding him and saying, "Are you not the Messiah? Save yourself and us!" But the other rebuked him, saying, "Do you not fear God, since you are under the same sentence of condemnation? And we indeed have been condemned justly, for we are getting what we deserve for our deeds, but this man has done nothing wrong." Then he said, "Jesus, remember me when you come into your kingdom." He replied, "Truly I tell you, today you will be with me in Paradise."

YOU ARE HERE

All four gospels tell us that Jesus was crucified between two thieves, but only Luke tells us this detail about what the thieves say. One thief mocks Jesus, while simultaneously asking Jesus to save him. The other expresses belief and asks for Jesus to remember him. What might we learn about ourselves and about Jesus from this exchange?

THE DEATH OF JESUS

When it was noon, darkness came over the whole land until three in the afternoon. At three o'clock Jesus cried out with a loud voice, "Eloi, Eloi, lema sabachthani?" which means, "My God, my God, why have you forsaken me?" When some of the bystanders heard it, they said, "Listen, he is calling for Elijah." And someone ran, filled a sponge with sour wine, put it on a stick, and gave it to him to drink, saying, "Wait, let us see whether Elijah will come to take him down." Then Jesus gave a loud cry and breathed his last. And the curtain of the temple was torn in two, from top to bottom. Now when the centurion, who stood facing him, saw that in this way he breathed his last, he said, "Truly this man was God's Son!"

> **TRAIL CROSSING**
>
> In the Gospel of Mark, Jesus dies completely alone. All of his closest friends have abandoned him. Only a few faithful women watch from the distance. It is a very different scene than in the Gospel of John (John 19:16-30). Read that version and notice the differences.

There were also women looking on from a distance; among them were Mary Magdalene, and Mary the mother of James the younger and of Joses, and Salome. These used to follow him and provided for him when he was in Galilee; and there were many other women who had come up with him to Jerusalem.

JESUS IS BURIED

When evening had come, and since it was the day of Preparation, that is, the day before the sabbath, Joseph of Arimathea, a respected member of the council, who was also himself waiting expectantly for the kingdom of God, went boldly to Pilate and asked for the body of Jesus. Then Pilate wondered if he were already dead; and summoning the centurion, he asked him whether he had been dead for some time. When he learned from the centurion that he was dead, he granted the body to Joseph. Then Joseph bought a linen cloth, and taking down the body, wrapped it in the linen cloth, and laid it in a tomb that had been hewn out of the rock. He then rolled a stone against the door of the tomb. Mary Magdalene and Mary the mother of Joses saw where the body was laid.

Scripture Citations
JOHN 12:1, 9-12 | 18:28b-19:16a
MARK 11:1-21, 27 | 12:28-34 | 12:38-40 | 13:1-13
   14:1-11 | 15:21-32a | 15:33-47
MATTHEW 21:33b-46 | 26:17-35 | 26:59-68 | 27:1-2
LUKE 21:1-4 | 22:39-62 | 23:39-43

QUESTIONS FOR THE JOURNEY

1. Jesus accuses the scribes of devouring widows' houses but praises the woman who pours nard worth a year of wages on his feet. Do you see a contradiction here? Why do you think the woman receives praise?

2. This is the story of how Jesus spent his final days and hours on this earth. What do we learn about what he valued most from the story—what he did, where he went, and with whom he spent his time in these final moments? What might that teach us?

3. According to the text, why does Jesus have to die? What other explanations have you heard for why Jesus had to die?

4. In his final days, Jesus is denounced by religious leaders, betrayed and denied by two of his disciples, and abandoned by almost all of his followers. What might we learn from these difficult parts of Jesus' life?

5. The liturgies of Holy Week developed as a way of mystically transporting Christians to Jerusalem so that we could walk with Jesus through his final days. How does the liturgical journey

that we take during Holy Week connect to these stories? How has walking with Jesus through Holy Week impacted your faith journey?

6. In church, we share Holy Communion as a way to remember and connect to Jesus' Last Supper with his disciples. What connections do you hear between the stories we read and your church's celebration of Holy Communion? How do worship and communion nourish you for your journey with God?

NEXT STEPS

- Each of the gospels describes Jesus' death differently. Read Matthew 27:45-54; Mark 15:33-39; Luke 23:44-48; and John 19:28-30. Which scene do you find most compelling? Why?

- From the cross, Jesus cries out "My God, my God, why have you forsaken me?," which is the beginning of Psalm 22. Read this psalm. What do you notice about this prayer? When have you felt like the psalmist? What does it mean to you that Jesus prayed this prayer?

20
We Have Seen the Lord

Jesus had died and was buried, laid in a tomb with a stone rolled in front of it. The cross stood empty. The disciples had scattered, full of sadness and fear. It seemed like the end. Since Jesus had died on Friday afternoon, right as the Sabbath was beginning, he had to be buried quickly; the commandments prevented people from doing any work, even burying a body, on the Sabbath. So Jesus' followers rested according to the commandment and waited until the Sabbath was over to tend Jesus' body. Deep in grief, Mary Magdalene, Mary the mother of James, and Salome bought the spices needed for anointing the body, and they went with heavy hearts to the tomb that Joseph of Arimathea had given to Jesus. They were sure that the Lord that they had loved and followed was dead, and they went to mourn and to lovingly and carefully prepare his body for burial.

But on the first day of the week, at early dawn, [the women] came to the tomb, taking the spices that they had prepared. They found the stone rolled away from the tomb, but when they went in, they did not find the body.

While they were perplexed about this, suddenly two men in dazzling clothes stood beside them. The women were terrified and bowed their faces to the ground, but the men said to them, "Why do you look for the living among the dead? He is not here, but has risen. Remember how he told you, while he was still in Galilee, that the Son of Man must be handed over to sinners, and be crucified, and on the third day rise again." Then they remembered his words, and returning from the tomb, they told all this to the eleven and to all the rest. Now it was Mary Magdalene, Joanna, Mary the mother of James, and the other women with them who told this to the apostles. But these words seemed to them an idle tale, and they did not believe them. But Peter got up and ran to the tomb; stooping and looking in, he saw the linen cloths by themselves; then he went home, amazed at what had happened.

When it was evening on that day, the first day of the week, and the doors of the house where the disciples had met were locked for fear of the Jews, Jesus came and stood among them and said, "Peace be with you." After he said this, he showed them his hands and his side. Then the disciples rejoiced when they saw the Lord. Jesus said to them again, "Peace be with you. As the Father has sent me, so I send you." When he had said this, he breathed on them and said to them, "Receive the Holy Spirit. If you forgive the sins of any, they are forgiven them; if you retain the sins of any, they are retained."

POINT OF INTEREST
Because of this incident, Thomas is often called "Doubting Thomas." But Thomas gets a bad rap. All he wants is what the other disciples already had—the privilege of seeing and touching Jesus.

But Thomas (who was called the Twin), one of the twelve, was not with them when Jesus came. So the other disciples told him, "We have seen the Lord." But he said to them, "Unless I see the mark of the nails in his hands, and put my finger in the mark of the nails and my hand in his side, I will not believe."

A week later his disciples were again in the house, and Thomas was with them. Although the doors were shut, Jesus came and stood among them and said, "Peace be with you." Then he said to Thomas, "Put your finger here and see my hands. Reach out your hand and put it in my side. Do not doubt but believe." Thomas answered him, "My Lord and my God!" Jesus said to him, "Have you believed because you have seen me? Blessed are those who have not seen and yet have come to believe."

THE ROAD TO EMMAUS

Now on that same day two of them were going to a village called Emmaus, about seven miles from Jerusalem, and talking with each other about all these things that had happened. While they were talking and discussing, Jesus himself came near and went with them, but their eyes were kept from recognizing him. And he said to them, "What are you discussing with each other while you walk along?" They stood still, looking sad. Then one of them, whose name was Cleopas, answered him, "Are you the only stranger in Jerusalem who does not know the things that have taken place there in these days?" He asked them, "What things?" They replied, "The things about Jesus of Nazareth, who was a prophet mighty in deed and word before God and all the people, and how our chief priests and leaders handed him over to be condemned to death and crucified him. But we had hoped that he was the one to redeem Israel. Yes, and besides all this, it is now the third day since these things took place. Moreover, some women of our group astounded us. They were at the tomb early this morning, and when they did not find his body there, they came back and told us that they had indeed seen a vision of angels who said that he was alive. Some of those who were with us went to the tomb and found it just as the women had said; but they did not see him." Then he said to them, "Oh, how foolish you are, and how slow of heart to believe all that the prophets have declared! Was it not necessary that the Messiah should suffer these things and then enter into his glory?" Then beginning with Moses and all the prophets, he interpreted to them the things about himself in all the scriptures.

As they came near the village to which they were going, he walked ahead as if he were going on. But they urged him strongly, saying, "Stay with us, because it is almost evening and the day is now nearly over." So he went in to stay with them. When he was at the table with them, he took bread, blessed and broke it, and gave it to them. Then their eyes were opened, and they recognized him; and he vanished from their sight. They said to each other, "Were not our hearts burning within us while he was talking to us on the road, while he was opening the scriptures to us?" That same hour they got up and returned to Jerusalem; and they found the eleven and their companions gathered together. They were saying, "The Lord has risen indeed, and he has appeared to Simon!" Then they told what had happened on the road, and how he had been made known to them in the breaking of the bread.

POINT OF INTEREST

The gospels are emphatic that Jesus' resurrection was bodily. They are clear that Jesus is not a ghost or a vision. This is why Jesus eats food, and the disciples touch him: Ghosts can't eat or be touched! Even though the gospels are clear that the resurrection was physical, Jesus still does very surprising things like appear out of nowhere and enter into rooms that are locked and shuttered.

While they were talking about this, Jesus himself stood among them and said to them, "Peace be with you." They were startled and terrified, and thought that they were seeing a ghost. He said to them, "Why are you frightened, and why do doubts arise in your hearts? Look at my hands and my feet; see that it is I myself. Touch me and see; for a ghost does not have flesh and bones as you see that I have." And when he had said this, he showed them his hands and his feet. While in their joy they were disbelieving and still wondering, he said to them, "Have you anything here to eat?" They gave him a piece of broiled fish, and he took it and ate in their presence.

Then he said to them, "These are my words that I spoke to you while I was still with you—that everything written about me in the law of Moses, the prophets, and the psalms must be fulfilled." Then he opened their minds to understand the scriptures, and he said to them, "Thus it is written, that the Messiah is to suffer and to rise from the dead on the third day, and that repentance and forgiveness of sins is to be proclaimed in his name to all nations, beginning from Jerusalem. You are witnesses of these things. And see, I am sending upon you what my Father promised; so stay here in the city until you have been clothed with power from on high."

JESUS APPEARS IN GALILEE

Now the eleven disciples went to Galilee, to the mountain to which Jesus had directed them. When they saw him, they worshiped him; but some doubted. And Jesus came and said to them, "All authority in heaven and on earth has been given to me. Go therefore and make disciples of all nations, baptizing them in the name of the Father and of the Son and of the Holy Spirit, and teaching them to obey everything that I have commanded you. And remember, I am with you always, to the end of the age."

> **SCENIC VIEW**
>
> These instructions by Jesus are often called "The Great Commission" since they summarize what Jesus commissions his disciples to do to continue his work. Yet Jesus' disciples do not carry out this work alone. Jesus promises to be with them always, a reminder that he is the one prophesied in Isaiah, "Emmanuel," God is with us (Matthew 1:23).

After these things Jesus showed himself again to the disciples by the Sea of Tiberias; and he showed himself in this way. Gathered there together were Simon Peter, Thomas called the Twin, Nathanael of Cana in Galilee, the sons of Zebedee, and two others of his disciples. Simon Peter said to them, "I am going fishing." They said to him, "We will go with you." They went out and got into the boat, but that night they caught nothing. Just after daybreak, Jesus stood on the beach; but the disciples did not know that it was Jesus. Jesus said to them, "Children, you have no fish, have you?" They answered him, "No." He said to them, "Cast the net to the right side of the boat, and you will find some." So they cast it, and now they were not able to haul it in because there were so many fish. That disciple whom Jesus loved said to Peter, "It is the Lord!" When Simon Peter heard that it was the Lord, he put on some clothes, for he was naked, and jumped into the sea. But the other disciples came in the boat, dragging the net full of fish, for they were not far from the land, only about a hundred yards off.

When they had gone ashore, they saw a charcoal fire there, with fish on it, and bread. Jesus said to them, "Bring some of the fish that you have just caught." So Simon Peter went aboard and hauled the net ashore, full of large fish, a hundred fifty-three of them; and though there were so many, the net was not torn. Jesus said to them, "Come and have breakfast." Now none of the disciples dared to ask him, "Who are you?" because they knew it was the Lord. Jesus came and took the bread and gave it to them, and did the same with the fish. This was now the third time that Jesus appeared to the disciples after he was raised from the dead.

POINT OF INTEREST

Jesus asks Peter the same question three times. This recalls Peter's triple denial of Jesus before his death (John 18:17-27). Peter is given a chance to affirm Jesus three times, just as he had previously denied him three times.

When they had finished breakfast, Jesus said to Simon Peter, "Simon son of John, do you love me more than these?" He said to him, "Yes, Lord; you know that I love you." Jesus said to him, "Feed my lambs." A second time he said to him, "Simon son of John, do you love me?" He said to him, "Yes, Lord; you know that I love you." Jesus said to him, "Tend my sheep." He said to him the third time, "Simon son of John, do you love me?" Peter felt hurt because he said to him the third time, "Do you love me?" And he said to him, "Lord, you know everything; you know that I love you." Jesus said to him, "Feed my sheep. Very truly, I tell you, when you were younger, you used to fasten your own belt and to go wherever you wished. But when you grow old, you will stretch out your hands, and someone else will fasten a belt around you and take you where you do not wish to go." (He said this to indicate the kind of death by which he would glorify God.) After this he said to him, "Follow me."

Now Jesus did many other signs in the presence of his disciples, which are not written in this book. But these are written so that you may come to believe that Jesus is the Messiah, the Son of God, and that through believing you may have life in his name.

JESUS' ASCENSION

After his suffering [Jesus] presented himself alive to [the apostles] by many convincing proofs, appearing to them during forty days and speaking about the kingdom of God. While staying with them, he ordered them not to leave Jerusalem, but to wait there for the promise of the Father. "This," he said, "is what you have heard from me; for John baptized with water, but you will be baptized with the Holy Spirit not many days from now."

> **SCENIC VIEW**
> After Jesus' Ascension, the disciples just stand around, staring up at heaven. Two men in white robes, messengers from God, are there to remind them that standing and staring at heaven is a waste of time—they have work to do. The rest of the book of Acts will tell the story of what happens once the disciples get moving and follow through on Jesus' commission to them.

So when they had come together, they asked him, "Lord, is this the time when you will restore the kingdom to Israel?" He replied, "It is not for you to know the times or periods that the Father has set by his own authority. But you will receive power when the Holy Spirit has come upon you; and you will be my witnesses in Jerusalem, in all Judea and Samaria, and to the ends of the earth." When he had said this, as they were watching, he was lifted up, and a cloud took him out of their sight. While he was going and they were gazing up toward heaven, suddenly two men in white robes stood by them. They said, "Men of Galilee, why do you stand looking up toward heaven? This Jesus, who has been taken up from you into heaven, will come in the same way as you saw him go into heaven."

Jesus, who had died, was raised from the dead; death no longer had a hold on him. And even after his ascension, Jesus continued to appear in visions. One of his most famous appearances was to a man named Saul, who would later become Paul, one of the leaders in the early Church. Years later, Paul wrote a letter, describing his encounter with the risen Jesus.

PAUL'S ENCOUNTER WITH JESUS

Now I would remind you, brothers and sisters, of the good news that I proclaimed to you, which you in turn received, in which also you stand... For I handed on to you as of first importance what I in turn had received: that Christ died for our sins in accordance with the scriptures, and that he was buried, and that he was raised on the third day in accordance with the scriptures, and that he appeared to Cephas, then to the twelve. Then he appeared to more than five hundred brothers and sisters at one time, most of whom are still alive, though some have died. Then he appeared to James, then to all the apostles. Last of all, as to one untimely born, he appeared also to me.

The stories of Jesus' resurrection and appearances to the disciples marked the beginning of a new chapter in the understanding of God's relationship with humanity. In the coming months, years, and decades, the disciples and their followers would grapple with what Jesus' life, death, resurrection, and ascension meant for God's relationship with humanity. What the disciples had believed was the end—the death of Jesus on the cross—was only the beginning. As Jesus ascended into heaven, leaving his followers behind, staring at the sky, a new chapter was beginning; the Holy Spirit was being sent anew into the world, and the Church was being born.

Scripture Citations
LUKE 24:1-12 | 24:13-49
JOHN 20:19-31 | 21:1-19
MATTHEW 28:16-20
ACTS 1:3-11
1 CORINTHIANS 15:1, 3-8

QUESTIONS FOR THE JOURNEY

1. In this chapter, we hear the stories of a number of different people who experience the death and resurrection of Jesus: the women who visit the tomb, Peter, Thomas, the disciples on the road to Emmaus, and others. Who do you most identify with in this story, and why?

2. The women are the first to proclaim the good news of the resurrection. What might this mean for us today?

3. In many of Jesus' resurrection appearances, his disciples do not immediately recognize him. Why do you think this is? What might this say to us about God? What do you notice about how Jesus is made known to them?

4. Each time Jesus appears to the disciples after his resurrection, he gives them instructions and commissions them. Look back at each of Jesus' appearances. What are the specific things that Jesus tells his disciples to do each time? What might these instructions say to us about our job as Jesus' disciples?

5. Jesus appears on the road to Emmaus and walks alongside the disciples as a companion on their journey. When have you especially felt Jesus "walking with you" in your journey? What was that like? Did you recognize Jesus while you were walking, or did you notice his presence only in hindsight?

NEXT STEPS

- We have heard the story of the resurrection so many times that it is familiar and unsurprising to us, but when the disciples first hear the story of the women, it "seemed to them an idle tale;" it was astonishing and unbelievable. Close your eyes and try to imagine yourself in the place of the disciples, living this story for the first time. What would you feel? How would you respond?

- The story of Jesus' resurrection that you read in this chapter is from the Gospel of Luke. But each of the gospel writers tells the story of the resurrection in a different way. Read the four stories of the resurrection: Luke 24:1-12, Matthew 28:1-10, Mark 16:1-8, and John 20:1-18. What similarities do you notice? What differences stand out to you? Which version is your favorite, and why? Which version is your least favorite, and why? How does God speak to you through these different narratives?

21
Filled with the Holy Spirit

When Jesus ascended into the heavens, he promised that he would one day return. As he was departing, Jesus told the disciples that they would be filled with the Holy Spirit and would be witnesses to him in "Jerusalem, in all Judea and Samaria, and to the ends of the earth." The disciples were the ones who would pick up the story of Jesus and spread it into the whole world. So they left Olivet without Jesus physically among them, yet they were sent out with a mission and a promise of God's continual presence.

THE TWELVE RESTORED: MATTHIAS REPLACES JUDAS

Then they returned to Jerusalem from the mount called Olivet, which is near Jerusalem, a sabbath day's journey away. When they had entered the city, they went to the room upstairs where they were staying, Peter, and John, and James, and Andrew, Philip and Thomas, Bartholomew and Matthew, James son of Alphaeus, and Simon the Zealot, and Judas son of James. All these were constantly devoting themselves to prayer, together with certain women, including

Mary the mother of Jesus, as well as his brothers.

In those days Peter stood up among the believers (together the crowd numbered about one hundred twenty persons) and said, "Friends, the scripture had to be fulfilled, which the Holy Spirit through David foretold concerning Judas, who became a guide for those who arrested Jesus—for he was numbered among us and was allotted his share in this ministry."

"So one of the men who have accompanied us during all the time that the Lord Jesus went in and out among us, beginning from the baptism of John until the day when he was taken up from us—one of these must become a witness with us to his resurrection." So they proposed two, Joseph called Barsabbas, who was also known as Justus, and Matthias. Then they prayed and said, "Lord, you know everyone's heart. Show us which one of these two you have chosen to take the place in this ministry and apostleship from which Judas turned aside to go to his own place." And they cast lots for them, and the lot fell on Matthias; and he was added to the eleven apostles.

THE DAY OF PENTECOST

When the day of Pentecost had come, they were all together in one place. And suddenly from heaven there came a sound like the rush of a violent wind, and it filled the entire house where they were sitting. Divided tongues, as of fire, appeared among them, and a tongue rested on each of them. All of them were filled with the Holy Spirit and began to speak in other languages, as the Spirit gave them ability.

Now there were devout Jews from every nation under heaven living in Jerusalem. And at this sound the crowd gathered and was bewildered, because each one heard them speaking in the native language of each. Amazed and astonished, they asked, "Are not all these who are speaking Galileans? And how is it that we hear, each of us, in our own native language? Parthians, Medes, Elamites, and residents of Mesopotamia, Judea and Cappadocia, Pontus and Asia, Phrygia and Pamphylia, Egypt and the parts of Libya belonging to Cyrene, and visitors from Rome, both Jews and proselytes, Cretans and Arabs—in our own languages we hear them speaking about God's deeds of power." All were amazed and perplexed, saying to one another, "What does this mean?" But others sneered and said, "They are filled with new wine."

> **SCENIC VIEW**
> The Holy Spirit, the third person of the Trinity, has been around from the beginning of creation. The "sound like the rush of a violent wind" echoes "the wind from God that swept over the waters" in Genesis 1:2. That same Holy Spirit created people (Job 33:4), inspired leaders (Numbers 11:25-29, Judges 6:34) and spoke through the prophets (Nehemiah 9:30 and Zechariah 7:12). On the day of Pentecost, we hear about the continued outpouring of the Holy Spirit filling the apostles in a miraculous and powerful way, just as Jesus had promised.

But Peter, standing with the eleven, raised his voice and addressed them, "Men of Judea and all who live in Jerusalem, let this be known to you, and listen to what I say. Indeed, these are not drunk, as you suppose, for it is only nine o'clock in the morning. No, this is what was spoken through the prophet Joel:

'In the last days it will be, God declares,
    that I will pour out my Spirit upon all flesh,
        and your sons and your daughters shall prophesy,
    and your young men shall see visions,
        and your old men shall dream dreams.
Even upon my slaves, both men and women,
        in those days I will pour out my Spirit;
            and they shall prophesy.
And I will show portents in the heaven above

and signs on the earth below, blood, and fire,
    and smoky mist.
The sun shall be turned to darkness
    and the moon to blood,
        before the coming of the Lord's great and
        glorious day.
Then everyone who calls on the name of the Lord
        shall be saved.'

"You that are Israelites, listen to what I have to say: Jesus of Nazareth, a man attested to you by God with deeds of power, wonders, and signs that God did through him among you, as you yourselves know—this man, handed over to you according to the definite plan and foreknowledge of God, you crucified and killed by the hands of those outside the law. But God raised him up, having freed him from death, because it was impossible for him to be held in its power. For David says concerning him,

'I saw the Lord always before me,
    for he is at my right hand so that I will not be shaken;
therefore my heart was glad, and my tongue rejoiced;
    moreover my flesh will live in hope.
For you will not abandon my soul to Hades,
    or let your Holy One experience corruption.
You have made known to me the ways of life;
    you will make me full of gladness with your presence.'

"Fellow Israelites, I may say to you confidently of our ancestor David that he both died and was buried, and his tomb is with us to this day. Since he was a prophet, he knew that God had sworn with an oath to him that he would put one of his descendants on his throne. Foreseeing this, David spoke of the resurrection of the Messiah, saying, 'He was not abandoned to Hades, nor did his flesh experience corruption.' This Jesus God raised up, and of that all of us are witnesses. Being therefore exalted at the right hand of God, and having received from the Father the promise of the Holy Spirit, he has poured out this that you both see and hear. For David did not ascend into the heavens, but he himself says,

> 'The Lord said to my Lord,
> "Sit at my right hand,
>   until I make your enemies
>   your footstool.' "

Therefore let the entire house of Israel know with certainty that God has made him both Lord and Messiah, this Jesus whom you crucified."

Now when they heard this, they were cut to the heart and said to Peter and to the other apostles, "Brothers, what should we do?" Peter said to them, "Repent, and be baptized every one of you in the name of Jesus Christ so that your sins may be forgiven; and you will receive the gift of the Holy Spirit. For the promise is for you, for your children, and for all who are far away, everyone whom the Lord our God calls to him." And he testified with many other arguments and exhorted them, saying, "Save yourselves from this corrupt generation." So those who welcomed his message were baptized, and that day about three thousand persons were added.

POINT OF INTEREST
This is a summary of what the early Church looked like. Though it was not perfect and would endure its share of conflict, there was much that was hopeful and inspiring.

They devoted themselves to the apostles' teaching and fellowship, to the breaking of bread and the prayers. Awe came upon everyone, because many wonders and signs were being done by the apostles. All who believed were together and had all things in common; they would sell their possessions and goods and distribute the proceeds to all, as any had need. Day by day, as they spent much time together in the temple, they broke bread at home and ate their food with glad and generous hearts, praising God and having the goodwill of all the people. And day by day the Lord added to their number those who were being saved.

Peter and John were the leaders of the early Jesus movement, sometimes called "The Way." While witnessing in Jerusalem through both miracles and words, they ran into trouble with the religious authorities. After healing a crippled beggar preaching about the resurrection, they were arrested and brought before the Council, where they had to defend themselves.

PETER AND JOHN BEFORE THE COUNCIL

While Peter and John were speaking to the people, the priests, the captain of the temple, and the Sadducees came to them, much annoyed because they were teaching the people and proclaiming that in Jesus there is the resurrection of the dead. So they arrested them and put them in custody until the next day, for it was already evening. But many of those who heard the word believed; and they numbered about five thousand.

The next day their rulers, elders, and scribes assembled in Jerusalem, with Annas the high priest, Caiaphas, John, and Alexander, and all who were of the high-priestly family. When they had made the prisoners stand in their midst, they inquired, "By what power or by what name did you do this?" Then Peter, filled with the Holy Spirit, said to them, "Rulers of the people and elders, if we are questioned today because of a good deed done to someone who was sick and are asked how this man has been healed, let it be known to all of you, and to all the people of Israel, that this man is standing before you in good health by the name of Jesus Christ of Nazareth, whom you crucified, whom God raised from the dead. This Jesus is 'the stone that was rejected by you, the builders; it has become the cornerstone.' There is salvation in no one else, for there is no other name under heaven given among mortals by which we must be saved." Now when they saw the boldness of Peter and John and realized that they were uneducated and ordinary men, they were amazed and recognized them as companions of Jesus.

When they saw the man who had been cured standing beside them, they had nothing to say in opposition.

So they ordered them to leave the council while they discussed the matter with one another. They said, "What will we do with them? For it is obvious to all who live in Jerusalem that a notable sign has been done through them; we cannot deny it. But to keep it from spreading further among the people, let us warn them to speak no more to anyone in this name." So they called them and ordered them not to speak or teach at all in the name of Jesus. But Peter and John answered them, "Whether it is right in God's sight to listen to you rather than to God, you must judge; for we cannot keep from speaking about what we have seen and heard." After threatening them again, they let them go, finding no way to punish them because of the people, for all of them praised God for what had happened. For the man on whom this sign of healing had been performed was more than forty years old.

Peter and John were confident before the chief priests and elders, but the meeting shook them to the core. They returned to the other believers and prayed for boldness.

THE BELIEVERS SHARE THEIR POSSESSIONS

Now the whole group of those who believed were of one heart and soul, and no one claimed private ownership of any possessions, but everything they owned was held in common. With great power the apostles gave their testimony to the resurrection of the Lord Jesus, and great grace was upon them all. There was not a needy person among them, for as many as owned lands or houses sold them and brought the proceeds of what was sold. They laid it at the apostles' feet, and it was distributed to each as any had need. There was a Levite, a native of Cyprus, Joseph, to whom the apostles gave the name Barnabas (which means "son of encouragement"). He sold a field that belonged to him, then brought the money, and laid it at the apostles' feet.

ANANIAS AND SAPPHIRA

But a man named Ananias, with the consent of his wife Sapphira, sold a piece of property; with his wife's knowledge, he kept back some of the proceeds, and brought only a part and laid it at the apostles' feet. "Ananias," Peter asked, "why has Satan filled your heart to lie to the Holy Spirit and to keep back part of the proceeds of the land? While it remained unsold, did it not remain your own? And after it was sold, were not the proceeds at your disposal? How is it that you have contrived this deed in your heart? You did not lie to us but to God!" Now when Ananias heard these words, he fell down and died. And great fear seized all who heard of it. The young men came and wrapped up his body, then carried him out and buried him.

After an interval of about three hours his wife came in, not knowing what had happened. Peter said to her, "Tell me whether you and your husband sold the land for such and such a price." And she said, "Yes, that was the price." Then Peter said to her, "How is it that you have agreed together to put the Spirit of the Lord to the test? Look, the feet of those who have buried your husband are at the door, and they will carry you out." Immediately she fell down at his feet and died. When the young men came in they found her dead, so they carried her out and buried her beside her husband. And great fear seized the whole church and all who heard of these things.

The disciples continued to work wonders in Jerusalem and to proclaim the gospel. They incurred the wrath of the authorities and were persecuted. Within the Church, they struggled to meet the needs of all in the community, especially Jewish Christians who spoke Greek. They decided to set aside certain leaders as deacons, one of the first named orders of ministry in the church.

SEVEN DEACONS CHOSEN

 Now during those days, when the disciples were increasing in number, the Hellenists complained against the Hebrews because their widows were being neglected in the daily distribution of food. And the twelve called together the whole community of the disciples and said, "It is not right that we should neglect the word of God in order to wait on tables. Therefore, friends, select from among yourselves seven men of good standing, full of the Spirit and of wisdom, whom we may appoint to this task, while we, for our part, will devote ourselves to prayer and to serving the word." What they said pleased the whole community, and they chose Stephen, a man full of faith and the Holy Spirit, together with Philip, Prochorus, Nicanor, Timon, Parmenas, and Nicolaus, a proselyte of Antioch. They had these men stand before the apostles, who prayed and laid their hands on them.

SCENIC VIEW

Here we get a look at how the early church is beginning to develop and organize itself. The disciples are realizing that they are called to do many things: study, preach, and teach the word of God; spend time in prayer; care for widows and the needy; and serve and share food. They have been neglecting some of their duties in order to accomplish others. So they decide to divide the tasks and set aside some people as those especially dedicated to a ministry of service. In later centuries, a particular order of ministry, that of deacons, will be formed out of this understanding.

Stephen, one of the seven chosen to serve the community as deacons, was brought before the Council for creating a controversy in the synagogue. When it was his turn to speak, Stephen gave a careful defense that told the story of the prophets who were rejected throughout Israel's history. Stephen proclaimed that what was happening with this new community of Jesus' followers was a continuation of that activity of the Holy Spirit.

STEPHEN BEFORE THE COUNCIL

"You stiff-necked people, uncircumcised in heart and ears, you are forever opposing the Holy Spirit, just as your ancestors used to do. Which of the prophets did your ancestors not persecute? They killed those who foretold the coming of the Righteous One, and now you have become his betrayers and murderers. You are the ones that received the law as ordained by angels, and yet you have not kept it."

When they heard these things, they became enraged and ground their teeth at Stephen. But filled with the Holy Spirit, he gazed into heaven and saw the glory of God and Jesus standing at the right hand of God. "Look," he said, "I see the heavens opened and the Son of Man standing at the right hand of God!" But they covered their ears, and with a loud shout all rushed together against him. Then they dragged him out of the city and began to stone him; and the witnesses laid their coats at the feet of a young man named Saul. While they were stoning Stephen, he prayed, "Lord Jesus, receive my spirit." Then he knelt down and cried out in a loud voice, "Lord, do not hold this sin against them." When he had said this, he died.

POINT OF INTEREST
Saul is introduced here for the first time. He will later encounter the risen Christ and be renamed Paul. No other figure in early Christianity, other than Jesus himself, will have a greater impact on the Church.

And Saul approved of their killing him. That day a severe persecution began against the church in Jerusalem, and all except the apostles were scattered throughout the countryside of Judea and Samaria. Devout men buried Stephen and made loud lamentation over him. But Saul was ravaging the church by entering house after house; dragging off both men and women, he committed them to prison.

The persecution scattered the leaders of the young church throughout Judea and Samaria. Jesus' promise that they would be witnesses in Jerusalem, Judea, and Samaria began to come to fruition, though perhaps not in the way that people had expected. Philip, Peter, and John went to Samaria, and from there to other distant lands.

PHILIP AND THE ETHIOPIAN EUNUCH

Then an angel of the Lord said to Philip, "Get up and go toward the south to the road that goes down from Jerusalem to Gaza." (This is a wilderness road.) So he got up and went. Now there was an Ethiopian eunuch, a court official of the Candace, queen of the Ethiopians, in charge of her entire treasury. He had come to Jerusalem to worship and was returning home; seated in his chariot, he was reading the prophet Isaiah. Then the Spirit said to Philip, "Go over to this chariot and join it." So Philip ran up to it and heard him reading the prophet Isaiah. He asked, "Do you understand what you are reading?" He replied, "How can I, unless someone guides me?" And he invited Philip to get in and sit beside him. Now the passage of the scripture that he was reading was this: "Like a sheep he was led to the slaughter, and like a lamb silent before its shearer, so he does not open his mouth. In his humiliation justice was denied him. Who can describe his generation? For his life is taken away from the earth." The eunuch asked Philip, "About whom, may I ask you, does the prophet say this, about himself or about someone else?" Then Philip began to speak, and starting with this scripture, he proclaimed to him the good news about Jesus. As they were going along the road, they came to some water; and the eunuch said, "Look, here is water! What is to prevent me from being baptized?" He commanded the chariot to stop, and both of them, Philip and the eunuch, went down into the water, and Philip baptized him. When they came up

> **POINT OF INTEREST**
> The Ethiopian eunuch was an outsider in every way possible. As an Ethiopian, he had a different skin color and a different culture than Philip and many other Jews. As a eunuch, a servant who had been castrated, he was considered ritually unclean (Deuteronomy 23:1) and of low social status. Yet he hears and receives the good news about Jesus and is baptized. His story makes it clear that the gospel of Jesus Christ is for all people, everywhere.

> **SCENIC VIEW**
> The Old Testament scriptures are very important in the early Christian movement. At this time, they did not have a New Testament to read and study; they only had the Old Testament, also known as the Hebrew Bible, to try to make sense of Jesus' life and witness.

out of the water, the Spirit of the Lord snatched Philip away; the eunuch saw him no more, and went on his way rejoicing. But Philip found himself at Azotus, and as he was passing through the region, he proclaimed the good news to all the towns until he came to Caesarea.

SAUL IS CALLED

Meanwhile Saul, still breathing threats and murder against the disciples of the Lord, went to the high priest and asked him for letters to the synagogues at Damascus, so that if he found any who belonged to the Way, men or women, he might bring them bound to Jerusalem. Now as he was going along and approaching Damascus, suddenly a light from heaven flashed around him. He fell to the ground and heard a voice saying to him, "Saul, Saul, why do you persecute me?" He asked, "Who are you, Lord?" The reply came, "I am Jesus, whom you are persecuting. But get up and enter the city, and you will be told what you are to do." The men who were traveling with him stood speechless because they heard the voice but saw no one. Saul got up from the ground, and though his eyes were open, he could see nothing; so they led him by the hand and brought him into Damascus. For three days he was without sight, and neither ate nor drank.

> **POINT OF INTEREST**
> The early Christian movement was called "the Way" and early Christians were sometimes called "followers of the Way" or those "who belonged to the Way." This was both a reference to Jesus' identity as "the way, the truth, and the life," (John 14:6) and also served as a reminder that Christianity was a way of life, rather than simply a system of belief.

Now there was a disciple in Damascus named Ananias. The Lord said to him in a vision, "Ananias." He answered, "Here I am, Lord." The Lord said to him, "Get up and go to the street called Straight, and at the house of Judas look for a man of Tarsus named Saul. At this moment he is praying, and he has seen in a vision a man named Ananias come in and lay his hands on him so that he might regain his sight." But Ananias answered, "Lord, I have heard from many about this man, how much evil he has done to your saints in Jerusalem; and here he has authority from the chief priests to bind all who invoke your name." But the Lord said to him, "Go, for he is an instrument whom I have chosen to bring my name before Gentiles and kings and before the people of Israel; I myself will show him how much he must suffer for the sake of my name." So Ananias went and entered the house. He laid his hands on Saul and said, "Brother Saul, the Lord Jesus, who appeared to you on your way here, has sent me so that you may regain your sight and be filled with the Holy Spirit." And immediately something like scales fell from his eyes, and his sight was restored. Then he got up and was baptized, and after taking some food, he regained his strength.

Saul began to preach in Damascus and, like the other disciples, created conflict. He was forced to leave the city and went to Jerusalem. Out of fear, not one of the disciples was willing to receive him because he was known for persecuting followers of Jesus. Only Barnabas welcomed Saul and introduced him to the community. Meanwhile, the Holy Spirit was also active in Caesarea, with Peter.

PETER AND CORNELIUS

In Caesarea there was a man named Cornelius, a centurion of the Italian Cohort, as it was called. He was a devout man who feared God with all his household; he gave alms generously to the people and prayed constantly to God. One afternoon at about three o'clock he had a vision in which he clearly saw an angel of God coming in and saying to him, "Cornelius." He stared at him in terror and said, "What is it, Lord?" He answered, "Your prayers and your alms have ascended as a memorial before God. Now send men to Joppa for a certain Simon who is called Peter; he is lodging with Simon, a tanner, whose house is by

> **SCENIC VIEW**
> The role of the Jewish Law in early Christian communities was a big question. The early Church will spend a great deal of time and energy wrestling with what portions of Jewish law are required, and which are no longer necessary. This conversation continues today.

the seaside." When the angel who spoke to him had left, he called two of his slaves and a devout soldier from the ranks of those who served him, and after telling them everything, he sent them to Joppa.

About noon the next day, as they were on their journey and approaching the city, Peter went up on the roof to pray. He became hungry and wanted something to eat; and while it was being prepared, he fell into a trance. He saw the heaven opened and something like a large sheet coming down, being lowered to the ground by its four corners. In it were all kinds of four-footed creatures and reptiles and birds of the air. Then he heard a voice saying, "Get up, Peter; kill and eat." But Peter said, "By no means, Lord; for I have never eaten anything that is profane or unclean." The voice said to him again, a second time, "What God has made clean, you must not call profane." This happened three times, and the thing was suddenly taken up to heaven.

Now while Peter was greatly puzzled about what to make of the vision that he had seen, suddenly the men sent by Cornelius appeared. They were asking for Simon's house and were standing by the gate. They called out to ask whether Simon, who was called Peter, was staying there.

While Peter was still thinking about the vision, the Spirit said to him, "Look, three men are searching for you. Now get up, go down, and go with them without hesitation; for I have sent them." So Peter went down to the men and said, "I am the one you are looking for; what is the reason for your coming?" They answered, "Cornelius, a centurion, an upright and God-fearing man, who is well spoken of by the whole Jewish nation, was directed by a holy angel to send for you to come to his house and to hear what you have to say."

Peter witnessed to Cornelius, and as he was preaching, the Holy Spirit fell on Cornelius and his family. In this way, God clearly demonstrated that non-Jews are acceptable to God and were able to receive God's salvation. Cornelius and his family were baptized, and Peter reported this good news back to the Jerusalem church.

"If then God gave them the same gift that he gave us when we believed in the Lord Jesus Christ, who was I that I could hinder God?" When they heard this, they were silenced. And they praised God, saying, "Then God has given even to the Gentiles the repentance that leads to life."

So it was that the church in Antioch grew, and the Good News of Jesus Christ spread through many countries, extending its reach beyond those who are Jewish to welcome Gentiles and other converts as well. Peter's travels took him to Lydda, to Joppa, to Caesarea, and finally back to Jerusalem. And Paul, once the chief persecutor of Jesus' followers, became the church's most ardent advocate. Paul traveled to Rome, where he lived for two years, proclaiming the kingdom of God and teaching about the Lord Jesus Christ with boldness.

Scripture Citations
ACTS 1:12-17, 21-26 | 2:1-47 | 4:1-22 | 4:32-37 | 5:1-11 | 6:1-6 | 7:51-8:3 | 8:26-40 | 9:1-19a | 10:1-22, 11:17-18

QUESTIONS FOR THE JOURNEY

1. What do you think of Acts' description of the believers sharing everything? Is this a helpful model for us today? Why or why not?

2. Acts depicts a lot of conflict but always returns to positive summaries about the Church. Do you think the same could be true of the Church today? How so?

3. Saul had a radical encounter with the risen Christ, and his whole life changed. Have you ever had an encounter that changed you in a significant way? What was it like?

4. Acts calls followers of Jesus "those who belonged to the Way." What does it mean to you to be someone who "belongs to the Way"? What might that description teach us about what it means to be a Christian?

5. In this chapter, we hear two important stories of journeys: the Ethiopian eunuch is converted and baptized while traveling on the Wilderness Road and Jesus appears to Saul on the road to Damascus. How do these stories speak to you about your journey with God?

6. Both Peter and Paul changed their minds about certain religious beliefs or practices: They came to see that both Jews *and* Gentiles could follow Jesus, and they changed their understanding about religious practices surrounding which foods were unclean. Have you ever changed your mind about a religious belief or practice? What precipitated that change?

7. Peter and Paul engage in lively debate with one another about matters of faith and practice. Their debate and exchange of ideas helped to shape the belief of the Church. Who are some people who have challenged aspects of your faith? How has that debate and exchange helped shape your beliefs?

NEXT STEPS

• This chapter recounts the first half of the book of Acts. Read Acts 12-28 to see how the rest of the story unfolds.

• The Holy Spirit is very active in Acts, directing the believers and guiding the church. In what ways does the Holy Spirit work today? In what direction do you think the Holy Spirit may be guiding the Church?

22
Grace May Abound

After his conversion on the road to Damascus, Paul became filled with zeal for sharing the good news of Jesus Christ with the whole world. Paul took seriously Jesus' command to witness "to the ends of the earth." After his original stint preaching and teaching in Jerusalem, Paul set off on a series of missionary journeys that made up the remainder of his ministry.

Paul took four separate missionary trips, spanning nearly twenty years and traveling over 10,000 miles. First Paul traveled with Barnabas to Cyprus and Antioch (modern-day Syria and Turkey). His second journey, with companions Silas and Timothy, took him to Philippi, Thessalonica, Corinth, Ephesus, and Caesarea, among other destinations. Next Paul visited Galatia, Ephesus, Macedonia and Greece with Timothy, Luke, and others. Paul's final journey took him to Rome. As Paul traveled, he told the story of his conversion,

POINT OF INTEREST
It is hard to overestimate the importance of Paul in the development of Christianity. He is named as author of thirteen of the twenty-seven books in the New Testament, and over half of the book of Acts is devoted to his story. Paul's letters to various churches and stories about him comprise about a third of the New Testament.

preached the gospel, healed the sick, and drove out demons. His preaching and teaching helped found many churches and encouraged some that were started by others. But although Paul's words and actions were inspiring, they also got him into trouble on many occasions.

One day, as we were going to the place of prayer, we met a slave-girl who had a spirit of divination and brought her owners a great deal of money by fortune-telling. While she followed Paul and us, she would cry out, "These men are slaves of the Most High God, who proclaim to you a way of salvation." She kept doing this for many days. But Paul, very much annoyed, turned and said to the spirit, "I order you in the name of Jesus Christ to come out of her." And it came out that very hour.

But when her owners saw that their hope of making money was gone, they seized Paul and Silas and dragged them into the marketplace before the authorities. When they had brought them before the magistrates, they said, "These men are disturbing our city; they are Jews and are advocating customs that are not lawful for us as Romans to adopt or observe." The crowd joined in attacking them, and the magistrates had them stripped of their clothing and ordered them to be beaten with rods. After they had given them a severe flogging, they threw them into prison and ordered the jailer to keep them securely. Following these instructions, he put them in the innermost cell and fastened their feet in the stocks.

About midnight Paul and Silas were praying and singing hymns to God, and the prisoners were listening to them. Suddenly there was an earthquake, so violent that the foundations of the prison were shaken; and immediately all the doors were opened and everyone's chains were unfastened. When the jailer woke up and saw the prison doors wide open, he drew his sword and was about to kill himself, since he supposed that the prisoners had escaped. But Paul shouted in a loud voice, "Do not harm yourself, for we are all here."

The jailer called for lights, and rushing in, he fell down trembling before Paul and Silas. Then he brought them outside and said, "Sirs, what must I do to be saved?" They answered, "Believe on the Lord Jesus, and you will be saved, you and your household." They spoke the word of the Lord to him and to all who were in his house. At the same hour of the night he took them and washed their wounds; then he and his entire family were baptized without delay. He brought them up into the house and set food before them; and he and his entire household rejoiced that he had become a believer in God.

Paul and Silas were released from prison, having used even that circumstance as an opportunity to share the message of Jesus Christ. Yet that was by no means the last time that Paul would experience hardship. As Paul attested to again and again, following Jesus was not always, or often, easy. Paul's preaching and teaching drew criticism, not only from authorities who were threatened by the message of Jesus, but also by those within the Church who disagreed with Paul about his teachings. In response to his critics, Paul wrote about his qualifications: both his Jewish qualifications by virtue of his birth but also his willingness to follow Jesus even when it meant danger and suffering.

Are they Hebrews? So am I. Are they Israelites? So am I. Are they descendants of Abraham? So am I. Are they ministers of Christ? I am talking like a madman—I am a better one: with far greater labors, far more imprisonments, with countless floggings, and often near death. Five times I have received from the Jews the forty lashes minus one. Three times I was beaten with rods. Once I received a stoning. Three times I was shipwrecked; for a night and a day I was adrift at sea; on frequent journeys, in danger from rivers, danger from bandits, danger from my

TRAIL CROSSING
Many of the hardships Paul experiences because he is a follower of Jesus are described in Acts (see 16:22-40 and 27:9-44). Forty was the maximum number of lashes Jewish law allowed leaders to give as punishment (Deuteronomy 25:3). In strict observance of the law, they would stop at forty minus one, so as not to accidentally go over and violate God's command.

own people, danger from Gentiles, danger in the city, danger in the wilderness, danger at sea, danger from false brothers and sisters; in toil and hardship, through many a sleepless night, hungry and thirsty, often without food, cold and naked. And, besides other things, I am under daily pressure because of my anxiety for all the churches. Who is weak, and I am not weak? Who is made to stumble, and I am not indignant?

If anyone else has reason to be confident in the flesh, I have more: circumcised on the eighth day, a member of the people of Israel, of the tribe of Benjamin, a Hebrew born of Hebrews; as to the law, a Pharisee; as to zeal, a persecutor of the church; as to righteousness under the law, blameless.

Yet whatever gains I had, these I have come to regard as loss because of Christ. More than that, I regard everything as loss because of the surpassing value of knowing Christ Jesus my Lord. For his sake I have suffered the loss of all things, and I regard them as rubbish, in order that I may gain Christ and be found in him, not having a righteousness of my own that comes from the law, but one that comes through faith in Christ, the righteousness from God based on faith. I want to know Christ and the power of his resurrection and the sharing of his sufferings by becoming like him in his death, if somehow I may attain the resurrection from the dead.

> **SCENIC VIEW**
> Paul's letters are the earliest surviving writings about Jesus. The earliest Gospel (Mark) was written around 70 CE. Paul's letters were written as early as two decades earlier, in the early 50s through the early 60s CE.

Paul believed deeply and passionately in Jesus Christ and dedicated his life to witnessing to Jesus, no matter the cost. As he traveled, Paul wrote many letters, sending out words of instruction and encouragement to the churches that he founded and even to some that he had never visited.

Sometimes Paul wrote letters to clarify his teaching or to encourage communities that had become disheartened. His earliest letter (and the earliest writing in the entire New Testament) was to the community of believers in Jesus living in Thessalonica, a city in Greece. Many of the Thessalonians believed that Jesus would return in their lifetime. When members of the community began to die before Jesus had come again, they began to lose hope. Paul wrote to offer them assurance.

But we do not want you to be uninformed, brothers and sisters, about those who have died, so that you may not grieve as others do who have no hope. For since we believe that Jesus died and rose again, even so, through Jesus, God will bring with him those who have died. For this we declare to you by the word of the Lord, that we who are alive, who are left until the coming of the Lord, will by no means precede those who have died. For the Lord himself, with a cry of command, with the archangel's call and with the sound of God's trumpet, will descend from heaven, and the dead in Christ will rise first. Then we who are alive, who are left, will be caught up in the clouds together with them to meet the Lord in the air; and so we will be with the Lord forever. Therefore encourage one another with these words.

> **POINT OF INTEREST**
> Paul and many of the first believers in Christ thought that Jesus would return in their lifetimes. Notice how Paul includes himself with those "who are still alive" when Christ returns.

Now concerning the times and the seasons, brothers and sisters, you do not need to have anything written to you. For you yourselves know very well that the day of the Lord will come like a thief in the night. When they say, "There is peace and security," then sudden destruction will come upon them, as labor pains come upon a pregnant woman, and there will be no escape! But you, beloved, are not in darkness, for that day to surprise you like a thief; for you are all children of light and children of the day; we are not of the night or of darkness.

So then let us not fall asleep as others do, but let us keep awake and be sober; for those who sleep sleep at night, and those who are drunk get drunk at night. But since we belong to the day, let us be sober, and put on the breastplate of faith and love, and for a helmet the hope of salvation. For God has destined us not for wrath but for obtaining salvation through our Lord Jesus Christ, who died for us, so that whether we are awake or asleep we may live with him.

Sometimes Paul wrote letters of instruction, trying to bring back faithful communities who had strayed from his teaching or attempting to resolve disputes or disagreements. Such was the case when Paul wrote 1 Corinthians, his first letter to the community of believers in Jesus living in Corinth. A leader in the church reached out to Paul with questions, and Paul responded, offering advice on a host of issues. Some of the issues were very practical; others were theological. In all these things, Paul wrote as a pastor, instructing and encouraging, calling people to account but grounded in love.

ON FOOD OFFERED TO IDOLS

Now concerning food sacrificed to idols: we know that "all of us possess knowledge." Knowledge puffs up, but love builds up. Anyone who claims to know something does not yet have the necessary knowledge; but anyone who loves God is known by him.

Hence, as to the eating of food offered to idols, we know that "no idol in the world really exists," and that "there is no God but one." Indeed, even though there may be so-called gods in heaven or on earth—as in fact there are many gods and many lords— yet for us there is one God, the Father, from whom are all things and for whom we exist, and one Lord, Jesus Christ, through whom are all things and through whom we exist.

It is not everyone, however, who has this knowledge. Since some have become so accustomed to idols until now, they still think of the food they eat as food offered to an idol; and their conscience, being weak, is defiled. "Food will not bring us close to God." We are no worse off if we do not eat, and no better off if we do. But take care that this liberty of yours does not somehow become a stumbling block to the weak. For if others see you, who possess knowledge, eating in the temple of an idol, might they not, since their conscience is weak, be encouraged to the point of eating food sacrificed to idols? So by your knowledge those weak believers for whom Christ died are destroyed. But when you thus sin against members of your family, and wound their conscience when it is weak, you sin against Christ. Therefore, if food is a cause of their falling, I will never eat meat, so that I may not cause one of them to fall.

ON SPIRITUAL GIFTS

If I speak in the tongues of mortals and of angels, but do not have love, I am a noisy gong or a clanging cymbal. And if I have prophetic powers, and understand all mysteries and all knowledge, and if I have all faith, so as to remove mountains, but do not have love, I am nothing. If I give away all my possessions, and if I hand over my body so that I may boast, but do not have love, I gain nothing.

Love is patient; love is kind; love is not envious or boastful or arrogant or rude. It does not insist on its own way; it is not irritable or resentful; it does not rejoice in wrongdoing, but rejoices in the truth. It bears all things, believes all things, hopes all things, endures all things.

Love never ends. But as for prophecies, they will come to an end; as for tongues, they will cease; as for knowledge, it will come to an end. For we know only in part, and we prophesy only in part; but when the complete comes, the partial will come to an end. When I was a child, I spoke like a child, I thought like a child, I reasoned like a child; when I became an adult, I put an end to childish ways. For now we see in a mirror, dimly, but then we will see face to face. Now I know only in part; then I will know fully, even as I have been fully known. And now faith, hope, and love abide, these three; and the greatest of these is love.

When Paul wrote letters to attempt to resolve disputes, he urged his readers to seek unity in Christ, even in the midst of disagreements.

Now I appeal to you, brothers and sisters, by the name of our Lord Jesus Christ, that all of you be in agreement and that there be no divisions among you, but that you be united in the same mind and the same purpose. For it has been reported to me by Chloe's people that there are quarrels among you, my brothers and sisters. What I mean is that each of you says, "I belong to Paul," or "I belong to Apollos," or "I belong to Cephas," or "I belong to Christ." Has Christ been divided? Was Paul crucified for you? Or were you baptized in the name of Paul? I thank God that I baptized none of you except Crispus and Gaius, so that no one can say that you were baptized in my name. (I did baptize also the household of Stephanas; beyond that, I do not know whether I baptized anyone else.) For Christ did not send me to baptize but to proclaim the gospel, and not with eloquent wisdom, so that the cross of Christ might not be emptied of its power.

> **YOU ARE HERE**
> Paul was deeply distressed that Christians were putting their allegiance to the person who baptized them above their allegiance to Christ. Divisions between followers of Jesus grieved Paul, just as they grieve the heart of God. What divisions do you see between believers today? What might Paul say about them?

At other times, Paul's letters included specific instructions about worship, reminding the community of the practices that Paul had taught them when he was with them. These letters contain the earliest descriptions of the Lord's Supper.

Now in the following instructions I do not commend you, because when you come together it is not for the better but for the worse. For, to begin with, when you come together as a church, I hear that there are divisions among you; and to some extent I believe it. Indeed, there have to be factions among you, for only so will it become clear who among you are genuine.

When you come together, it is not really to eat the Lord's supper. For when the time comes to eat, each of you goes ahead with your own supper, and one goes hungry and another becomes drunk. What! Do you not have homes to eat and drink in? Or do you show contempt for the church of God and humiliate those who have nothing? What should I say to you? Should I commend you? In this matter I do not commend you!

For I received from the Lord what I also handed on to you, that the Lord Jesus on the night when he was betrayed took a loaf of bread, and when he had given thanks, he broke it and said, "This is my body that is for you. Do this in remembrance of me." In the same way he took the cup also, after supper, saying, "This cup is the new covenant in my blood. Do this, as often as you drink it, in remembrance of me." For as often as you eat this bread and drink the cup, you proclaim the Lord's death until he comes.

Whoever, therefore, eats the bread or drinks the cup of the Lord in an unworthy manner will be answerable for the body and blood of the Lord. Examine yourselves, and only then eat of the bread and drink of the cup. For all who eat and drink without discerning the body, eat and drink judgment against themselves. For this reason many of you are weak and ill, and some have died. But if we judged ourselves, we would not be judged. But when we are judged by the Lord, we are disciplined so that we may not be condemned along with the world. So then, my brothers and sisters, when you come together to eat, wait for one another. If you are hungry, eat at home, so that when

> **POINT OF INTEREST**
> The earliest practice of the Lord's Supper (also called Holy Communion or Holy Eucharist) was in the context of an actual meal. The ritual act of sharing the bread and wine in remembrance of Jesus was followed by a community meal, where food was shared among everyone.
> Paul seems concerned that poorer members were arriving late to the meal and finding the food already gone.
> He is instructing the community both to take care in how they observe the ritual act of consuming the bread and wine in remembrance of Jesus, and how they treat one another in the sharing of a common meal. The act of communion and the act of common eating are linked.

you come together, it will not be for your condemnation. About the other things I will give instructions when I come.

One of the hallmarks of Paul's preaching and teaching was his claim that Christ's message was open to all: Jews and Gentiles alike. Though Paul himself had an impeccable Jewish pedigree, he was given authority to preach to the Gentiles. This message of a law-free gospel was endorsed by the leaders of the Jerusalem church, but other leaders found his teaching problematic. Again and again in his letters, Paul was forced to articulate his belief that the gospel was open to both Jews and Greeks.

For I am not ashamed of the gospel; it is the power of God for salvation to everyone who has faith, to the Jew first and also to the Greek. For in it the righteousness of God is revealed through faith for faith; as it is written, "The one who is righteous will live by faith."

Now before faith came, we were imprisoned and guarded under the law until faith would be revealed. Therefore the law was our disciplinarian until Christ came, so that we might be justified by faith. But now that faith has come, we are no longer subject to a disciplinarian, for in Christ Jesus you are all children of God through faith. As many of you as were baptized into Christ have clothed yourselves with Christ. There is no longer Jew or Greek, there is no longer slave or free, there is no longer male and female; for all of you are one in Christ Jesus. And if you belong to Christ, then you are Abraham's offspring, heirs according to the promise.

Paul then goes on to explain how all, Jew and Greek, are bound to sin and justified by faith in Christ.

But now, apart from law, the righteousness of God has been disclosed, and is attested

YOU ARE HERE

Jew or Greek, slave or free, male or female: These are the most basic and important aspects of social identity in Paul's time. By declaring that these fundamental divisions no longer exist, Paul is making a radical statement about the inclusive nature of following Jesus and the way that being baptized in Christ completely reshapes our identity. What aspects of social identity divide us today? How might we strive to eliminate those divisions?

by the law and the prophets, the righteousness of God through faith in Jesus Christ for all who believe. For there is no distinction, since all have sinned and fall short of the glory of God; they are now justified by his grace as a gift, through the redemption that is in Christ Jesus, whom God put forward as a sacrifice of atonement by his blood, effective through faith. He did this to show his righteousness, because In his divine forbearance he had passed over the sins previously committed; it was to prove at the present time that he himself is righteous and that he justifies the one who has faith in Jesus.

This raised an important question: If one is justified by faith in Christ, what then did we to do with the law? In his letter to the community of believers in Jesus living in Galatia (a region in modern-day Turkey), Paul appeared to advocate for a law-free gospel. This led to chaos, with Christians believing that they could do whatever they wanted without any ethical considerations. Paul wrote to the church in Rome to clarify this point, articulating that the free gift of God's grace could and should have implications for how Christians live.

What then are we to say? Should we continue in sin in order that grace may abound? By no means! How can we who died to sin go on living in it? Do you not know that all of us who have been baptized into Christ Jesus were baptized into his death? Therefore we have been buried with him by baptism into death, so that, just as Christ was raised from the dead by the glory of the Father, so we too might walk in newness of life. For if we have been united with him in a death like his, we will certainly be united with him in a resurrection like his. We know that our old self was crucified with him so that the body of sin might be destroyed, and we might no longer be enslaved to sin. For whoever has died is freed from sin. But if we have died with Christ, we believe that we will also live with him. We know that Christ, being raised from the dead, will never die again; death no longer has dominion over him. The death he died, he died to sin, once for all; but the life he lives, he lives to God. So you also must consider yourselves dead to sin and alive to God in Christ Jesus.

There is therefore now no condemnation for those who are in Christ Jesus. For the law of the Spirit of life in Christ Jesus has set you free from the law of sin and of death.

What then are we to say about these things? If God is for us, who is against us? He who did not withhold his own Son, but gave him up for all of us, will he not with him also give us everything else? Who will bring any charge against God's elect? It is God who justifies. Who is to condemn? It is Christ Jesus, who died, yes, who was raised, who is at the right hand of God, who indeed intercedes for us.

> **SCENIC VIEW**
>
> Scholars widely agree that seven of the New Testament letters were, in fact, written by Paul himself: Romans, 1 and 2 Corinthians, Galatians, Philippians, 1 Thessalonians, and Philemon. Scholars disagree about the other letters attributed to Paul: Ephesians, Colossians, 2 Thessalonians, 1 and 2 Timothy, and Titus. Students or followers may have written those letters in Paul's name, in order to carry on his legacy after his death.

Who will separate us from the love of Christ? Will hardship, or distress, or persecution, or famine, or nakedness, or peril, or sword? As it is written, "For your sake we are being killed all day long; we are accounted as sheep to be slaughtered." No, in all these things we are more than conquerors through him who loved us. For I am convinced that neither death, nor life, nor angels, nor rulers, nor things present, nor things to come, nor powers, nor height, nor depth, nor anything else in all creation, will be able to separate us from the love of God in Christ Jesus our Lord.

Though Paul intended to travel to Spain, we do not know if he ever made it there. Tradition tells us that Paul traveled as far as Rome and died in the 60s during Nero's persecution of Christians and Jews. Peter is also reported to have been martyred in Rome during this same time. We know that Paul's letters traveled far and wide, spanning not only distance but also time, encouraging and challenging churches in his age and even to today. After Paul's death, others picked up the torch to carry the message of Jesus Christ to the ends of the earth.

Scripture Citations
ACTS 16:16-34
2 CORINTHIANS 11:22-29
PHILIPPIANS 3:4b-11
1 THESSALONIANS 4:13-5:10
1 CORINTHIANS 8:1-13 | 13:1-13 | 1:10-17 | 11:17-34
ROMANS 1:16-17 | 3:21-26 | 6:1-11 | 8:1-2, 31-39
GALATIANS 3:23-29

QUESTIONS FOR THE JOURNEY

1. Paul and Silas find themselves in jail, and they use that experience as an opportunity to sing hymns of praise to God and to share the good news of Jesus with their jailer. Would you have done the same in their situation? Why or why not?

2. This is only a small sample of Paul's writing. What important teachings are missing?

3. Paul often speaks of his gospel (literally, "good news"). Which passage was especially good news to you? Why?

4. Which text(s) do not represent good news to you? Why?

5. Paul has great confidence in his understanding of God's activity in his life and in the world around him. Is this inspiring or challenging for you? Why?

6. Paul's letters are very situational; they are written to specific people in specific communities to address specific concerns. Why might this be important for us to remember as we now read them as scripture?

7. Much has been made about the differences between the teaching of Jesus and of Paul. How are they similar? How are they different?

NEXT STEPS

- Some of the writings attributed to Paul, particularly those about marriage (Ephesians 5.21-33) and the role of women (1 Corinthians 14:33-35 and 1 Timothy 2:9-15) have caused conflict in the church. How do you wrestle with these texts?

- As Paul travels around, he tells and re-tells the story of his conversion, his encounter of Jesus. It is his personal story of meeting and coming to follow Jesus that is central to the spread of the early Church. Take some time to reflect this week on the story of how you met and came to follow Jesus. Consider writing out your story briefly. Pray about how you might share that story with others.

23
Be Doers of the Word

While Paul traveled around preaching and teaching, others were also spreading the good news of God in Jesus Christ, starting churches and encouraging other believers. Belief in Jesus spread to the Jews in the Diaspora, those living outside of Palestine, as well as to Gentiles in those wider areas. Many of those early Christian leaders also wrote letters, just as Paul did. One author, known as James, wrote passionately about what following Jesus looked like, lived out in real life, in ways both large and small.

James, a servant of God and of the Lord Jesus Christ, To the twelve tribes in the Dispersion: Greetings.

My brothers and sisters, whenever you face trials of any kind, consider it nothing but joy, because you know that the testing of your faith produces endurance; and let endurance have its full effect, so that you may be mature and complete, lacking in nothing.

POINT OF INTEREST
Some people believe that the author of James was James, the brother of Jesus, mentioned in Galatians 1:19 and Acts 15:13 and who became a leader in the church in Jerusalem. But it may have been written by a later student or follower of James who used James's name to give authority to his teaching.

If any of you is lacking in wisdom, ask God, who gives to all generously and ungrudgingly, and it will be given you. But ask in faith, never doubting, for the one who doubts is like a wave of the sea, driven and tossed by the wind; for the doubter, being double-minded and unstable in every way, must not expect to receive anything from the Lord.

Let the believer who is lowly boast in being raised up, and the rich in being brought low, because the rich will disappear like a flower in the field. For the sun rises with its scorching heat and withers the field; its flower falls, and its beauty perishes. It is the same way with the rich; in the midst of a busy life, they will wither away.

Blessed is anyone who endures temptation. Such a one has stood the test and will receive the crown of life that the Lord has promised to those who love him. No one, when tempted, should say, "I am being tempted by God"; for God cannot be tempted by evil and he himself tempts no one. But one is tempted by one's own desire, being lured and enticed by it; then, when that desire has conceived, it gives birth to sin, and that sin, when it is fully grown, gives birth to death. Do not be deceived, my beloved.

Every generous act of giving, with every perfect gift, is from above, coming down from the Father of lights, with whom there is no variation or shadow due to change. In fulfillment of his own purpose he gave us birth by the word of truth, so that we would become a kind of first fruits of his creatures.

You must understand this, my beloved: let everyone be quick to listen, slow to speak, slow to anger; for your anger does

> ### SCENIC VIEW
> The letters of the Bible are also called "epistles." Most of the epistles are named after the people who were credited with writing them: James, Peter, John, and Jude. Others are named after the people to whom they are addressed: Hebrews, Philemon, and Thessalonians. We often don't know much about the authors of these letters or the circumstances surrounding them, but they teach us about the issues early Christian communities were facing; they also speak to us about how God calls us to live and act today.

not produce God's righteousness. Therefore rid yourselves of all sordidness and rank growth of wickedness, and welcome with meekness the implanted word that has the power to save your souls.

But be doers of the word, and not merely hearers who deceive themselves. For if any are hearers of the word and not doers, they are like those who look at themselves in a mirror; for they look at themselves and, on going away, immediately forget what they were like. But those who look into the perfect law, the law of liberty, and persevere, being not hearers who forget but doers who act—they will be blessed in their doing.

If any think they are religious, and do not bridle their tongues but deceive their hearts, their religion is worthless. Religion that is pure and undefiled before God, the Father, is this: to care for orphans and widows in their distress, and to keep oneself unstained by the world.

My brothers and sisters, do you with your acts of favoritism really believe in our glorious Lord Jesus Christ? For if a person with gold rings and in fine clothes comes into your assembly, and if a poor person in dirty clothes also comes in, and if you take notice of the one wearing the fine clothes and say, "Have a seat here, please," while to the one who is poor you say, "Stand there," or, "Sit at my feet," have you not made distinctions among yourselves, and become judges with evil thoughts? Listen, my beloved brothers and sisters. Has not God chosen the poor in the world to be rich in faith and to be heirs of the kingdom that he has promised to those who love him? But you have dishonored the poor. Is it not the rich who oppress you? Is it not they who drag you into court? Is it not they who blaspheme the excellent name that was invoked over you?

You do well if you really fulfill the royal law according to the scripture, "You shall love your neighbor as yourself." But if you show partiality, you commit sin and are convicted by the law as transgressors. For whoever keeps the whole law but fails in one point has become accountable for all of it. For the one who said, "You shall not commit adultery," also said, "You shall not murder." Now if you do not commit adultery but if you murder, you have become a transgressor of the law. So speak and so act as those who are to be judged by the law of liberty. For judgment will be without mercy to anyone who has shown no mercy; mercy triumphs over judgment.

What good is it, my brothers and sisters, if you say you have faith but do not have works? Can faith save you? If a brother or sister is naked and lacks daily food, and one of you says to them, "Go in peace; keep warm and eat your fill," and yet you do not supply their bodily needs, what is the good of that? So faith by itself, if it has no works, is dead. But someone will say, "You have faith and I have works." Show me your faith apart from your works, and I by my works will show you my faith. You believe that God is one; you do well. Even the demons believe—and shudder. Do you want to be shown, you senseless person, that faith apart from works is barren? Was not our ancestor Abraham justified by works when he offered his son Isaac on the altar? You see that faith was active along with his works, and faith was brought to completion by the works. Thus the scripture was fulfilled that says, "Abraham believed God, and it was reckoned to him as righteousness," and he was called the friend of God. You see that a person is justified by works and not by faith alone. Likewise, was not Rahab the prostitute also justified by works when she welcomed the messengers and sent them out by another road? For just as the body without the spirit is dead, so faith without works is also dead.

> **SCENIC VIEW**
>
> James focuses on the need for our faith to be expressed in works, so that what we believe should be seen in what we do. Martin Luther, a theologian and reformer, did not like the book of James and called it the "Epistle of Straw." Luther preferred Paul's understanding that one is saved by faith alone, and no amount of work is needed to earn God's love and redemption. The tension between faith and works would be a key issue of the Protestant Reformation during the sixteenth century.

Not many of you should become teachers, my brothers and sisters, for you know that we who teach will be judged with greater strictness. For all of us make many mistakes. Anyone who makes no mistakes in speaking is perfect, able to keep the whole body in check with a bridle. If we put bits into the mouths of horses to make them obey us, we guide their whole bodies. Or look at ships: though they are so large that it takes strong winds to drive them, yet they are guided by a very small rudder wherever the will of the pilot directs. So also the tongue is a small member, yet it boasts of great exploits.

How great a forest is set ablaze by a small fire! And the tongue is a fire. The tongue is placed among our members as a world of iniquity; it stains the whole body, sets on fire the cycle of nature, and is itself set on fire by hell. For every species of beast and bird, of reptile and sea creature, can be tamed and has been tamed by the human species, but no one can tame the tongue—a restless evil, full of deadly poison. With it we bless the Lord and Father, and with it we curse those who are made in the likeness of God. From the same mouth come blessing and cursing. My brothers and sisters, this ought not to be so. Does a spring pour forth from the same opening both fresh and brackish water? Can a fig tree, my brothers and sisters, yield olives, or a grapevine figs? No more can salt water yield fresh.

> **YOU ARE HERE**
> James has a lot to say, not only about our works but also about our words. He urges Christians to show forth Christ's love in both action and in speech. How can you show forth God's love in words, as well as deeds?

Who is wise and understanding among you? Show by your good life that your works are done with gentleness born of wisdom. But if you have bitter envy and selfish ambition in your hearts, do not be boastful and false to the truth. Such wisdom does not come down from above, but is earthly, unspiritual, devilish. For where there is envy and selfish ambition, there will also be disorder and wickedness of every kind. But the wisdom from

308 | THE PATH: A JOURNEY THROUGH THE BIBLE

above is first pure, then peaceable, gentle, willing to yield, full of mercy and good fruits, without a trace of partiality or hypocrisy. And a harvest of righteousness is sown in peace for those who make peace.

Those conflicts and disputes among you, where do they come from? Do they not come from your cravings that are at war within you? You want something and do not have it; so you commit murder. And you covet something and cannot obtain it; so you engage in disputes and conflicts. You do not have, because you do not ask. You ask and do not receive, because you ask wrongly, in order to spend what you get on your pleasures. Adulterers! Do you not know that friendship with the world is enmity with God? Therefore whoever wishes to be a friend of the world becomes an enemy of God. Or do you suppose that it is for nothing that the scripture says, "God yearns jealously for the spirit that he has made to dwell in us"? But he gives all the more grace; therefore it says, "God opposes the proud, but gives grace to the humble." Submit yourselves therefore to God. Resist the devil, and he will flee from you. Draw near to God, and he will draw near to you. Cleanse your hands, you sinners, and purify your hearts, you double-minded. Lament and mourn and weep. Let your laughter be turned into mourning and your joy into dejection. Humble yourselves before the Lord, and he will exalt you.

Do not speak evil against one another, brothers and sisters. Whoever speaks evil against another or judges another, speaks evil against the law and judges the law; but if you judge the law, you are not a doer of the law but a judge. There is one lawgiver and judge who is able to save and to destroy. So who, then, are you to judge your neighbor?

Come now, you who say, "Today or tomorrow we will go to such and such a town and spend a year there, doing business and making money." Yet you do not even know what tomorrow will bring. What is your life? For you are a mist that appears for a little while and then vanishes. Instead you ought to say, "If the Lord wishes, we will live and do this or that." As it is, you boast in your arrogance; all such boasting is evil. Anyone, then, who knows the right thing to do and fails to do it, commits sin.

Come now, you rich people, weep and wail for the miseries that are coming to you. Your riches have rotted, and your clothes are moth-eaten. Your gold and silver have rusted, and their rust will be evidence against you, and it will eat your flesh like fire. You have laid up treasure for the last days. Listen! The wages of the laborers who mowed your fields, which you kept back by fraud, cry out, and the cries of the harvesters have reached the ears of the Lord of hosts. You have lived on the earth in luxury and in pleasure; you have fattened your hearts in a day of slaughter. You have condemned and murdered the righteous one, who does not resist you.

> **TRAIL CROSSING**
> These words may sound harsh, but this fiery condemnation echoes both the words of the prophets and the words of Jesus. Compare this to Amos 6:4-7, Luke 6:24, or Matthew 6:19-21.

Be patient, therefore, beloved, until the coming of the Lord. The farmer waits for the precious crop from the earth, being patient with it until it receives the early and the late rains. You also must be patient. Strengthen your hearts, for the coming of the Lord is near. Beloved, do not grumble against one another, so that you may not be judged. See, the Judge is standing at the doors! As an example of suffering and patience, beloved, take the prophets who spoke in the name of the Lord. Indeed we call blessed those who showed endurance. You have heard of the endurance of Job, and you have seen the purpose of the Lord, how the Lord is compassionate and merciful.

Above all, my beloved, do not swear, either by heaven or by earth or by any other oath, but let your "Yes" be yes and your "No" be no, so that you may not fall under condemnation. Are any among you suffering? They should pray. Are any cheerful? They should sing songs of praise. Are any among you sick? They should call for the elders of the church and have them pray over them, anointing them with oil in the name of the Lord. The prayer of faith will save the sick, and the Lord will raise them up; and anyone who has committed sins will be forgiven. Therefore confess your sins to one another, and pray for one another, so that you may be healed. The prayer of the righteous is powerful and effective. Elijah was a human being like us, and he prayed fervently that it might not rain, and for three years and six months it did not rain on the earth. Then he prayed again, and the heaven gave rain and the earth yielded its harvest.

My brothers and sisters, if anyone among you wanders from the truth and is brought back by another, you should know that whoever brings back a sinner from wandering will save the sinner's soul from death and will cover a multitude of sins.

While some Christian leaders, like the author of James, tended to focus on the everyday, nitty-gritty aspects of a lived Christian life, others wrestled with deeper theological issues: questions about how Jesus could be both God and man and ideas about how Jesus' death and resurrection accomplished salvation. One leader of the church wrote "a word of exhortation," a sermon, that beautifully and passionately explored some of those issues. The Letter to the Hebrews, as it came to be known, grappled with the idea of how Christ's sacrifice was related to the sacrifices described in the Hebrew Bible and how Christ's death on the cross saves us.

CHRIST'S SACRIFICE ONCE FOR ALL

And it is by God's will that we have been sanctified through the offering of the body of Jesus Christ once for all. And every priest stands day after day at his service, offering again and again the same sacrifices that can never take away sins. But when Christ had offered for all time a single sacrifice for sins, "he sat down at the right hand of God," and since then has been waiting "until his enemies would be made a footstool for his feet." For by a single offering he has perfected for all time those who are sanctified. And the Holy Spirit also testifies to us, for after saying,

> "This is the covenant that I will
> make with them
> after those days, says the Lord:
> I will put my laws in their hearts,
> and I will write them on
> their minds,"

he also adds,

> "I will remember their sins and
> their lawless deeds
> no more."
> Where there is forgiveness of these, there is no
> longer any offering for sin.

POINT OF INTEREST
The author of the letter to the Hebrews does a lot of what Jesus himself did. He quotes sections from the Hebrew Bible and explains or shows them in a new light. These are references to Jeremiah 31:33 and Isaiah 43:25.

A CALL TO PERSEVERE

Therefore, my friends, since we have confidence to enter the sanctuary by the blood of Jesus, by the new and living way that he opened for us through the curtain (that is, through his flesh), and since we have a great priest over the house of God, let us approach with a true heart in full assurance of faith, with our hearts sprinkled clean from an evil conscience and our bodies washed with pure water. Let us hold fast to the confession of our hope without wavering, for he who has promised is faithful. And let us consider how to provoke one another to love and good deeds, not neglecting to meet together, as is the habit of some, but encouraging one another, and all the more as you see the Day approaching.

Like Paul and James, the author of the letter to the Hebrews wrote about faith, recounting the stories of faithful people through the ages and using them to both instruct and encourage faithful people in the present time.

Now faith is the assurance of things hoped for, the conviction of things not seen. Indeed, by faith our ancestors received approval. By faith we understand that the worlds were prepared by the word of God, so that what is seen was made from things that are not visible.

THE EXAMPLES OF NOAH AND ABRAHAM

By faith Noah, warned by God about events as yet unseen, respected the warning and built an ark to save his household; by this he condemned the world and became an heir to the righteousness that is in accordance with faith.

By faith Abraham obeyed when he was called to set out for a place that he was to receive as an inheritance; and he set out, not knowing where he was going. By faith he stayed for a time in the land he had been promised, as in a foreign land, living in tents, as did Isaac and Jacob, who were heirs with him of the same promise. For he looked forward to the city that has foundations, whose architect and builder is God. By faith he received power of procreation, even though he was too old—and Sarah herself was barren—because he considered him faithful who had promised. Therefore from one person, and this one as good as dead, descendants were born, "as many as the stars of heaven and as the innumerable grains of sand by the seashore."

All of these died in faith without having received the promises, but from a distance they saw and greeted them. They confessed that they were strangers and foreigners on the earth, for people who speak in this way make it clear that they are seeking a homeland. If they had been thinking of the land that they had left behind, they would have had opportunity to return. But as it is, they desire a better country, that is, a heavenly one. Therefore God is not ashamed to be called their God; indeed, he has prepared a city for them.

By faith Abraham, when put to the test, offered up Isaac. He who had received the promises was ready to offer up his only son, of whom he had been told, "It is through Isaac that descendants shall be named for you." He considered the fact that God is able even to raise someone from the dead—and figuratively speaking, he did receive him back. By faith Isaac invoked blessings for the future on Jacob and Esau. By faith Jacob, when dying, blessed each of the sons of Joseph, "bowing in worship over the top of his staff." By faith Joseph, at the end of his life, made mention of the exodus of the Israelites and gave instructions about his burial.

THE FAITH OF MOSES

By faith Moses was hidden by his parents for three months after his birth, because they saw that the child was beautiful; and they were not afraid of the king's edict. By faith Moses, when he was grown up, refused to be called a son of Pharaoh's daughter, choosing rather to share ill-treatment with the people of God than to enjoy the fleeting pleasures of sin. He considered abuse suffered for the Christ to be greater wealth than the treasures of Egypt, for he was looking ahead to the reward. By faith he left Egypt, unafraid of the king's anger; for he persevered as though he saw him who is invisible. By faith he kept the Passover and the sprinkling of blood, so that the destroyer of the firstborn would not touch the firstborn of Israel.

THE FAITH OF OTHER ISRAELITE HEROES

By faith the people passed through the Red Sea as if it were dry land, but when the Egyptians attempted to do so they were drowned. By faith the walls of Jericho fell after they had been encircled for seven days. By faith Rahab the prostitute did not perish with those who were disobedient, because she had received the spies in peace.

And what more should I say? For time would fail me to tell of Gideon, Barak, Samson, Jephthah, of David and Samuel and the prophets— who through faith conquered kingdoms, administered justice, obtained promises, shut the mouths of lions, quenched raging fire, escaped the edge of the sword, won strength out of weakness, became mighty in war, put foreign armies to flight. Women received their dead by resurrection. Others were tortured, refusing to accept release, in order to obtain a better resurrection. Others suffered mocking and flogging, and even chains and imprisonment. They were stoned to death, they were sawn in two, they were killed by the sword; they went about in skins of sheep and goats, destitute, persecuted, tormented— of whom the world was not worthy. They wandered in deserts and mountains, and in caves and holes in the ground.

POINT OF INTEREST
The author of the letter to the Hebrews sees faithful people not only as an example but also as companions on the journey of faith. They are a cloud of witnesses who surround us, here and now.

THE EXAMPLE OF JESUS

Therefore, since we are surrounded by so great a cloud of witnesses, let us also lay aside every weight and the sin that clings so closely, and let us run with perseverance the race that is set before us, looking to Jesus the pioneer and perfecter of our faith, who for the sake of the joy that was set before him endured the cross, disregarding its shame, and has taken his seat at the right hand of the throne of God. Consider him who endured such hostility against himself from sinners, so that you may not grow weary or lose heart. Therefore lift your drooping hands and strengthen your weak knees, and make straight paths for your feet, so that what is lame may not be put out of joint, but rather be healed.

You have not come to something that can be touched, a blazing fire, and darkness, and gloom, and a tempest, and the sound of a trumpet, and a voice whose words made the hearers beg that not another word be spoken to them. (For they could not endure the order that was given, "If even an animal touches the mountain, it shall be stoned to death." Indeed, so terrifying was the sight that Moses said, "I tremble with fear.") But you have come to Mount Zion and to the city of the living God, the heavenly Jerusalem, and to innumerable angels in festal gathering, and to the assembly of the firstborn who are enrolled in heaven, and to God the judge of all, and to the spirits of the righteous made perfect, and to Jesus, the mediator of a new covenant, and to the sprinkled blood that speaks a better word than the blood of Abel.

Therefore, since we are receiving a kingdom that cannot be shaken, let us give thanks, by which we offer to God an acceptable worship with reverence and awe; for indeed our God is a consuming fire.

Let mutual love continue. Do not neglect to show hospitality to strangers, for by doing that some have entertained angels without knowing it. Remember those who are in prison, as though you were in prison with them; those who are being tortured, as though you yourselves were being tortured. Let marriage be held in honor by all, and let the marriage bed be kept undefiled; for God will judge fornicators and adulterers. Keep your lives free from the love of money, and be content with what you have; for he has said, "I will never leave you or forsake you." So we can say with confidence,

> "The Lord is my helper;
>   I will not be afraid.
> What can anyone do to me?"

FINAL BLESSING

Now may the God of peace, who brought back from the dead our Lord Jesus, the great shepherd of the sheep, by the blood of the eternal covenant, make you complete in everything good so that you may do his will, working among us that which is pleasing in his sight, through Jesus Christ, to whom be the glory forever and ever. Amen.

Other leaders wrote letters and preached sermons as well, building up the Church as it grew and spread. In the centuries to come, followers of Jesus would debate and discuss the implications of Jesus' life and the biblical narrative for what they believed about God and humanity and would wrestle with how to live faithfully in a changing world, as they waited for Jesus to come again to judge the living and the dead. As Paul, James, Peter, John, the author of the letter to the Hebrews, and other early leaders taught, what people believed and how followers of Jesus lived and acted in this world mattered very much; by word and example the people of God were called to proclaim Jesus until his return. But they also waited with eager longing for Jesus to come again, as he had promised he would. So the Church lived in the meantime, balanced between the now and the not yet, living faithfully on earth while hoping for heaven, being in this world while not quite of this world.

Scripture Citations
JAMES
HEBREWS 10:10-25 | 11:1-3, 7-38 | 12:1-3, 12-13, 18-24 | 12:28-29 | 13:1-6, 20-21

QUESTIONS FOR THE JOURNEY

1. Which part of James's letter is most meaningful to you? Which part is the most difficult?

2. How do you understand James's assertion that "Religion that is pure and undefiled before God, the Father, is this: to care for orphans and widows in their distress, and to keep oneself unstained by the world"?

3. Some people see James and Paul to be in conflict: James says that faith without works is "dead" (James 2:17), but Paul says that we are saved by faith alone, apart from works (Romans 3:28). How do you understand the relationship between faith, works

(good deeds), and salvation? How does that understanding impact your life and actions?

4. Hebrews gives a stirring account of people who showed us what living "by faith" looks like. Think back on what you have read so far. Which faithful people from our story does the author fail to mention? Which biblical example of faith is most important to you? Who are some people in your life whose faithfulness has inspired you?

5. Many of the epistles are either anonymous or attributed to an important figure in the early Church but not necessarily written by that person. Does their anonymity change the way you think about them? Why or why not?

NEXT STEPS

- A number of the epistles are only a few pages long and can be read in one sitting (in fact, you read the entire letter of James in this chapter). Sit down and read either Philemon or 2 John. What stands out to you about either letter? How do they relate to letters that you have read or written? How do those letters, written to a particular person in a particular time, speak to you today?

- These epistles in our Bible were simply letters written between Christians to offer insight and encouragement. Write a letter of encouragement to a friend or family member who is struggling. Consider including a verse from one of the epistles that you think might speak to them.

24
The Alpha and the Omega

Jesus came into the world, lived, died, and was resurrected. He taught his followers, by word and example, what it looked like to follow God in this world, and he had by his death and resurrection, broken the power of sin and death forever. Yet even as he called people to faithfulness and righteousness in this world, Jesus also spoke about the world to come, and promised that he would come again in power and great glory. As Jesus' followers lived out life in this world, they waited for Christ to come again, at any moment, and they hoped and wondered what that coming would look like.

As Christianity grew and spread, some civic leaders felt threatened by the idea that Christians worshiped and obeyed Jesus, and not earthly leaders. As a result, many early Christians were persecuted, tortured, martyred, or exiled. The Roman emperors, Nero (54-68) and Domitian (81-96), were particularly infamous for this kind of persecution. During times of persecution, Christians often looked to apocalyptic

POINT OF INTEREST
Jesus talked about the end of time (also called the apocalypse) a number of times in his ministry. Mark 13:14-37 is often called the "mini apocalypse," because it is the longest description in the gospels of the end times.

language and Jesus' promise to come again in order to find hope in the midst of their suffering.

During one such time of persecution, a man named John, who tradition says had been exiled to the isle of Patmos, had a series of apocalyptic visions, which he described as "the revelation of Jesus Christ." These visions were rich with imagery, metaphor, and mystery. Sometimes John wrote in allegory or code. Many of John's references were to contemporary places, people, or situations that were difficult to understand outside of their context, and he made allusions that were culturally conditioned. But the force and beauty of John's vision echoes through time, revealing a small glimpse of the glory of God.

INTRODUCTION AND GREETING

The revelation of Jesus Christ, which God gave him to show his servants what must soon take place; he made it known by sending his angel to his servant John, who testified to the word of God and to the testimony of Jesus Christ, even to all that he saw.

POINT OF INTEREST

There are many Johns in the New Testament. This John is not to be confused with John the Baptist, John who was Jesus' disciple, or John the evangelist. This John, sometimes called John of Patmos, is a prophetic seer.

Blessed is the one who reads aloud the words of the prophecy, and blessed are those who hear and who keep what is written in it; for the time is near. John to the seven churches that are in Asia: Grace to you and peace from him who is and who was and who is to come, and from the seven spirits who are before his throne, and from Jesus Christ, the faithful witness, the firstborn of the dead, and the ruler of the kings of the earth. To him who loves us and freed us from our sins by his blood, and made us to be a kingdom, priests serving his God and Father, to him be glory and dominion forever and ever. Amen. Look! He is coming with the clouds; every eye will see him, even those who pierced him; and on his account all the tribes of the earth will wail. So it is to be. Amen. "I am the Alpha and the Omega," says the Lord God, who is and who was and who is to come, the Almighty.

A VISION OF THE RISEN CHRIST

I, John, your brother who share with you in Jesus the persecution and the kingdom and the patient endurance, was on the island called Patmos because of the word of God and the testimony of Jesus. I was in the spirit on the Lord's day, and I heard behind me a loud voice like a trumpet saying, "Write in a book what you see and send it to the seven churches, to Ephesus, to Smyrna, to Pergamum, to Thyatira, to Sardis, to Philadelphia, and to Laodicea." Then I turned to see whose voice it was that spoke to me, and on turning I saw seven golden lampstands, and in the midst of the lampstands I saw one like the Son of Man, clothed with a long robe and with a golden sash across his chest. His head and his hair were white as white wool, white as snow; his eyes were like a flame of fire, his feet were like burnished bronze, refined as in a furnace, and his voice was like the sound of many waters. In his right hand he held seven stars, and from his mouth came a sharp, two-edged sword, and his face was like the sun shining with full force. When I saw him, I fell at his feet as though dead. But he placed his right hand on me, saying, "Do not be afraid; I am the first and the last, and the living one. I was dead, and see, I am alive forever and ever; and I have the keys of Death and of Hades. Now write what you have seen, what is, and what is to take place after this. As for the mystery of the seven stars that you saw in my right hand, and the seven golden lampstands: the

> **POINT OF INTEREST**
> The number seven is an important number in the Bible—and is mentioned more than 700 times. The number is usually used to signify completeness, wholeness, or even perfection. The number seven occurs fifty-four times in Revelation, more than in any other book of the Bible. There are seven churches, seven angels, seven lamp stands, and seven stars, among many other sevens. All the sevens in Revelation echo the original seven in Genesis: the seven days of creation.

seven stars are the angels of the seven churches, and the seven lampstands are the seven churches.

John continued his vision with seven letters written to seven churches: the churches in Ephesus, Smyrna, Pergamum, Thyatria, Sardis, Philadelphia, and Laodicea. Each letter had a unique focus, praising that particular church's strengths and calling out its faults and failures. After concluding each message with "Let anyone who has an ear listen to what the Spirit is saying to the churches," the visions continued with John's mystical experience of heaven.

After this I looked, and there in heaven a door stood open! And the first voice, which I had heard speaking to me like a trumpet, said, "Come up here, and I will show you what must take place after this." At once I was in the spirit, and there in heaven stood a throne, with one seated on the throne! And the one seated there looks like jasper and carnelian, and around the throne is a rainbow that looks like an emerald. Around the throne are twenty-four thrones, and seated on the thrones are twenty-four elders, dressed in white robes, with golden crowns on their heads. Coming from the throne are flashes of lightning, and rumblings and peals of thunder, and in front of the throne burn seven flaming torches, which are the seven spirits of God; and in front of the throne there is something like a sea of glass, like crystal.

> **TRAIL CROSSING**
> John's vision of heaven is both beautiful and terrifying. God is not safe or simple but instead fills people with awe and holy terror. This is how people often encountered God in the Hebrew Bible as well. Compare this description with Exodus 24:9-18.

Around the throne, and on each side of the throne, are four living creatures, full of eyes in front and behind: the first living creature like a lion, the second living creature like an ox, the third living creature with a face like a human face, and the fourth living creature like a flying eagle. And the four living creatures, each of them with six wings, are full of eyes all around and inside. Day and night without ceasing they sing,

"Holy, holy, holy,
the Lord God the Almighty,
who was and is and is to come."

And whenever the living creatures give glory and honor and thanks to the one who is seated on the throne, who lives forever and ever, the twenty-four elders fall before the one who is seated on the throne and worship the one who lives forever and ever; they cast their crowns before the throne, singing,

"You are worthy, our Lord and God,
to receive glory and honor and power,
for you created all things,
and by your will they existed and were created."

> **YOU ARE HERE**
> Popular depictions of heaven often imagine people playing games, talking with friends, or enjoying leisure. Here and elsewhere in the Bible, the primary activity in heaven is praising and worshiping God. Does this change the way you envision heaven?

THE SCROLL AND THE LAMB

Then I saw in the right hand of the one seated on the throne a scroll written on the inside and on the back, sealed with seven seals; and I saw a mighty angel proclaiming with a loud voice, "Who is worthy to open the scroll and break its seals?" And no one in heaven or on earth or under the earth was able to open the scroll or to look into it. And I began to weep bitterly because no one was found worthy to open the scroll or to look into it. Then one of the elders said to me, "Do not weep. See, the Lion of the tribe of Judah, the Root of David, has conquered, so that he can open the scroll and its seven seals."

Then I saw between the throne and the four living creatures and among the elders a Lamb standing as if it had been slaughtered, having seven horns and seven eyes, which are the seven spirits of God sent out into all the earth. He went and took the scroll from the right hand of the one who was seated on the throne. When he had taken the scroll, the four living creatures and the twenty-four elders fell before the Lamb, each holding a harp and golden bowls full of incense, which are the prayers of the saints. They sing a new song:

> "You are worthy to take the scroll
>   and to open its seals,
> for you were slaughtered and by your blood
>   you ransomed for God
>   saints from every tribe and language
>   and people and nation;
> you have made them to be a kingdom and priests
>   serving our God,
>   and they will reign on earth."

Then I looked, and I heard the voice of many angels surrounding the throne and the living creatures and the elders; they numbered myriads of myriads and thousands of thousands, singing with full voice,

> "Worthy is the Lamb that was slaughtered
> to receive power and wealth and wisdom and might
> and honor and glory and blessing!"

Then I heard every creature in heaven and on earth and under the earth and in the sea, and all that is in them, singing,

> "To the one seated on the throne and to the Lamb
> be blessing and honor and glory and might
> forever and ever!"

And the four living creatures said, "Amen!" And the elders fell down and worshiped.

John recounted how the Lamb opened the seven seals, and judgment and destruction followed. Death, pestilence, and earthquakes were part of this great ordeal. Even amidst the suffering and devastation that John described, there were glimpses of hope and glory.

After this I looked, and there was a great multitude that no one could count, from every nation, from all tribes and peoples and languages, standing before the throne and before the Lamb, robed in white, with palm branches in their hands. They cried out in a loud voice, saying, "Salvation belongs to our God who is seated on the throne, and to the Lamb!"

And all the angels stood around the throne and around the elders and the four living creatures, and they fell on their faces before the throne and worshiped God, singing,

> "Amen! Blessing and glory and wisdom
> and thanksgiving and honor
> and power and might
> be to our God forever and ever! Amen."

Then one of the elders addressed me, saying, "Who are these, robed in white, and where have they come from?" I said to him, "Sir, you are the one that knows." Then he said to me, "These are they who have come out of the great ordeal; they have washed their robes and made them white in the blood of the Lamb.

> For this reason they are before the throne of God,
>   and worship him day and night within his temple,
>   and the one who is seated on the throne will
>   shelter them.
> They will hunger no more, and thirst no more;
>   the sun will not strike them,
>   nor any scorching heat;
> for the Lamb at the center of the throne will be
>   their shepherd,
>   and he will guide them to springs of the water of life,
> and God will wipe away every tear from their eyes."

John's vision included yet more destruction, with seven trumpets that heralded a series of plagues, epic battles with dragons and beasts, and bowls of wrath poured out on the earth. But in the end, the beast and its armies were defeated by the armies of heaven, led by the one who is the King of Kings and Lord of Lords. All the dead were raised and stood before the throne of God's judgment.

SCENIC VIEW

Modern readers who live in safety and comfort can find the violence and judgment in Revelation disturbing. But throughout history, Christians who have been persecuted have found these descriptions both realistic and hopeful. In the midst of real suffering, not unlike that described in these revelations, Christians have clung to the promise that God will both judge and deliver the faithful.

THE NEW HEAVEN AND THE NEW EARTH

Then I saw a new heaven and a new earth; for the first heaven and the first earth had passed away, and the sea was no more. And I saw the holy city, the new Jerusalem, coming down out of heaven from God, prepared as a bride adorned for her husband. And I heard a loud voice from the throne saying, "See, the home of God is among mortals. He will dwell with them as their God; they will be his peoples, and God himself will be with them; he will wipe every tear from their eyes. Death will be no more; mourning and crying and pain will be no more, for the first things have passed away."

And the one who was seated on the throne said, "See, I am making all things new." Also he said, "Write this, for these words are trustworthy and true." Then he said to me, "It is done! I am the Alpha and the Omega, the beginning and the end. To the thirsty I will give water as a gift from the spring of the water of life. Those who conquer will inherit these things, and I will be their God and they will be my children. But as for the cowardly, the faithless, the polluted, the murderers, the fornicators, the sorcerers, the idolaters, and all liars, their place will be in the lake that burns with fire and sulfur, which is the second death."

THE NEW JERUSALEM

Then one of the seven angels who had the seven bowls full of the seven last plagues came and said to me, "Come, I will show you the bride, the wife of the Lamb." And in the spirit he carried me away to a great, high mountain and showed me the holy city Jerusalem coming down out of heaven from God. It has the glory of God and a radiance like a very rare jewel, like jasper, clear as crystal. It has a great, high wall with twelve gates, and at the gates twelve angels, and on the gates are inscribed the names of the twelve tribes of the Israelites; on the east three gates, on the north three gates, on the south three gates, and on the west three gates. And the wall of the city has twelve foundations, and on them are the twelve names of the twelve apostles of the Lamb.

The angel who talked to me had a measuring rod of gold to measure the city and its gates and walls. The city lies foursquare, its length the same as its width; and he measured the city with his rod, fifteen hundred miles; its length and width and height are equal. He also measured its wall, one hundred forty-four cubits by human measurement, which the angel was using. The wall is built of jasper, while the city is pure gold, clear as glass. The foundations of the wall of the city are adorned with every jewel; the first was jasper, the second sapphire, the third agate, the fourth emerald, the fifth onyx, the sixth carnelian, the seventh chrysolite, the eighth beryl, the ninth topaz, the tenth chrysoprase, the eleventh jacinth, the twelfth amethyst. And the twelve gates are twelve pearls, each of the gates is a single pearl, and the street of the city is pure gold, transparent as glass.

I saw no temple in the city, for its temple is the Lord God the Almighty and the Lamb. And the city has no need of sun or moon to shine on it, for the glory of God is its light, and its lamp is the Lamb. The nations will walk by its light, and the kings of the earth will bring their glory into it. Its gates will never be shut by day—and there will be no night there. People will bring into it the glory and the honor of the nations.

> **POINT OF INTEREST**
> Many people think that at the end of time, people will leave the earth and go to heaven. The vision in Revelation, however, is that the earth is redeemed. See how the New Jerusalem is established on earth? This ties the renewal of creation at the end of time back to the original creation we read about in Genesis 1 and 2.

But nothing unclean will enter it, nor anyone who practices abomination or falsehood, but only those who are written in the Lamb's book of life.

THE RIVER OF LIFE

Then the angel showed me the river of the water of life, bright as crystal, flowing from the throne of God and of the Lamb through the middle of the street of the city. On either side of the river is the tree of life with its twelve kinds of fruit, producing its fruit each month; and the leaves of the tree are for the healing of the nations. Nothing accursed will be found there any more. But the throne of God and of the Lamb will be in it, and his servants will worship him; they will see his face, and his name will be on their foreheads. And there will be no more night; they need no light of lamp or sun, for the Lord God will be their light, and they will reign forever and ever.

> **TRAIL CROSSING**
> Isn't this image of a tree spanning a river odd? The author is making a clear allusion to the original garden in Genesis 2-3 and the restoration of that pristine paradise.

And he said to me, "These words are trustworthy and true, for the Lord, the God of the spirits of the prophets, has sent his angel to show his servants what must soon take place." "See, I am coming soon! Blessed is the one who keeps the words of the prophecy of this book."

CONCLUDING BLESSINGS AND WARNINGS

I, John, am the one who heard and saw these things. And when I heard and saw them, I fell down to worship at the feet of the angel who showed them to me; but he said to me, "You must not do that! I am a fellow servant with you and your comrades the prophets, and with those who keep the words of this book. Worship God!"

And he said to me, "Do not seal up the words of the prophecy of this book, for the time is near. Let the evildoer still do evil, and the filthy still be filthy, and the righteous still do right, and the holy still be holy." "See, I am coming soon; my reward is with me, to repay according to everyone's work. I am the Alpha and the Omega, the first and the last, the beginning and the end."

Blessed are those who wash their robes, so that they will have the right to the tree of life and may enter the city by the gates. Outside are the dogs and sorcerers and fornicators and murderers and idolaters, and everyone who loves and practices falsehood. "It is I, Jesus, who sent my angel to you with this testimony for the churches. I am the root and the descendant of David, the bright morning star."

The Spirit and the bride say, "Come." And let everyone who hears say, "Come." And let everyone who is thirsty come. Let anyone who wishes take the water of life as a gift. I warn everyone who hears the words of the prophecy of this book: if anyone adds to them, God will add to that person the plagues described in this book; if anyone takes away from the words of the book of this prophecy, God will take away that person's share in the tree of life and in the holy city, which are described in this book.

The one who testifies to these things says, "Surely I am coming soon." Amen. Come, Lord Jesus! The grace of the Lord Jesus be with all the saints. Amen.

Scripture Citations

Revelation 1 | 4-5 | 7: 9-17 | 21-22

QUESTIONS FOR THE JOURNEY

1. Many early Christians believed that Jesus would return in their lifetime. Is it problematic to you that he did not? What expectation do you have for Christ's return?

2. Which images from Revelation are hardest for you to consider? Why?

3. Which images offer you the most hope? Why?

4. Revelation is often read in funerals, in large part because of the images of heaven. How does heaven as John describes it relate to your visions of heaven? What might you learn from the similarities and differences?

5. The Book of Revelation (and the Bible as a whole) concludes with an image of a renewed earth. In what ways is the earth in need of renewal? What might your role be in that renewal?

6. The final sentences of the Bible are: "The one who testifies to these things says, 'Surely I am coming soon.' Amen. Come, Lord Jesus! The grace of the Lord Jesus be with all the saints. Amen." What do you think about this ending? Is this how you would have ended the Bible? Why or why not?

NEXT STEPS

- Read the letters to the churches in Revelation 2-3. How might these letters speak to our churches today?

- The Bible looks different when you are comfortable than it does when you are struggling. The images of judgment found in Revelation, in particular, often sound scary and distasteful to people who are comfortable but hopeful to those who are suffering. Why do you think that is? How might you be called to listen carefully to those whose experience is different from yours?

Epilogue

The Story Lives On; the Journey Continues

That's the end. Of the Bible, that is. What began in Genesis with, "In the beginning, when God created the heavens and the earth," now comes to its conclusion in the Revelation to John with, "Amen. Come, Lord Jesus! The grace of the Lord Jesus be with all the saints. Amen." These two phrases bookend the holy scriptures, the text that Christians through the centuries have proclaimed as "the Word of the Lord."

Yet, although Revelation is the end of the Bible, it's not the end of the story, the end of the journey. Far from it. The Bible continued as it was told and retold, shared and passed down. Parents would recite these words to their children, at bedtime and at mealtime, when they arose in the morning and when they laid down at night. They would tell them of Moses and Miriam, Abraham and Sarah, of the judges and the prophets, of Jesus and the disciples, of the faithful followers of Jesus who proclaimed him after his death and resurrection. And people would gather, early groups of the believers, the very first churches. They did not have buildings, but they met together in homes and in graveyards and wherever they could. And they shared these stories, first telling them from memory, then reading them from precious bits of parchment. And then they went out. Compelled by the power of this story, inspired to follow in the footsteps of Jesus, people walked into the world in witness to God's love, telling the story of Jesus everywhere they went.

It wasn't always easy, sharing these stories. The powers of this world were threatened by people who proclaimed the power of Jesus Christ. Rulers were wary of believers who said God was their ultimate King and Judge. In the centuries following Jesus' death and resurrection, being a Christian, sharing the stories of the Bible, could easily get you killed: hung on a cross, thrown to the lions, beaten and beheaded. And yet, the story persisted. People believed so passionately in the Lord Jesus Christ that they continued to proclaim him, even in the face of death. The story of God's extraordinary love for ordinary people was unstoppable, and the journey of God's people didn't end in the pages of the Bible; it continued out into the world and in the lives of those who knew and proclaimed the Risen Lord.

And so this story of God's great love was passed down, from one generation to the next. What began as oral narratives, relayed from one person to another by word of mouth, was written down, laboriously copied by hand onto scrolls and then into bound books. At first, these holy books were infinitely precious and incredibly expensive, and only the rich and privileged few possessed them. Centuries later, with the invention of the printing press, Bibles could be mass produced, so that today it is the best-selling book of all time, and anyone can hold in their hands the Holy Word of God.

The story of God's love spread, not only through time but also around the world. What started as a small band of bedraggled followers in Jerusalem grew and spread and changed into a worldwide Jesus Movement, with millions of disciples in every nation and corner of the globe, ordinary people made extraordinary by God's Spirit working in and through them. Some have been prophets and priests and princesses; some have been scholars and scribes and saints. Men and women and children from every walk of life have encountered the risen Jesus in Word and Sacrament and have been transformed by the extraordinary story of God's relentless, unwavering, unstoppable love.

And now you number among them. Now you have read for yourself the incredible story of God's relentless pursuit of his people. Now you have heard what is the breadth and length and height and depth of God's great love for you. Now you have journeyed through the Bible—you have seen its glorious vistas, you have traveled through its dark valleys, you have walked in the footsteps of generations of faithful people who would go anywhere to follow Jesus.

But although this book is over, your journey with this story has only just begun. You can go back to the beginning and read it again, making the journey not as a new explorer, but a seasoned hiker. Walking the same path again gives you the chance to notice things you didn't see the first time, to learn each bend in the road until it is as familiar as your own backyard. And then, you can pick up a Bible and explore the rest of the mountain, the parts that we had to skip but that are just as breathtaking and beautiful and holy as what you have read here. There are dozens of other trails, filled with new landmarks and exciting vistas, and beautiful scenery, and you have a lifetime to explore and discover them all.

Then, of course, you can tell the story of your adventure. Tell your family and friends about all that you've seen. Describe these amazing vistas to neighbors and strangers. Talk about them in your home and work and city and even to the ends of the earth. And then, invite them to come explore with you. You've traveled this path, so you can show them the way. Because this story isn't just for you. It's for everyone. It is the greatest story ever told, and it's much too good to keep to yourself.

So congratulations, you've finished *The Path*. You have completed your journey; you have read the Bible. And now it's time. Take the journey off of the page and into your life. Let the story of God's extraordinary love for ordinary people change your life and change the world.

Resources

Next Steps

What you have read in *The Path* is the Bible; all of the regular text is directly from the Bible. But, of course, *The Path* is not the entire Bible. It has been excerpted to make it easier to read, to give you the sense of the sweeping narrative. If you have enjoyed *The Path* and would like to read more, the next step is to get a Bible of your own and read it!

To read the Bible, you first need a Bible you can read. If you already own a Bible that you love to read, then that is wonderful: Start reading! If you don't own a Bible, or if the one you have seems confusing or boring, then the first thing you need to do is find a Bible that works for you. The good news is that there are many Bibles to choose from: There are dozens of different translations and many different kinds of Bibles: study Bibles, devotional Bibles, journaling Bibles, and many more. The difficult news is that picking a Bible is very personal. Some people love the poetry of the King James Version; others find it difficult to read and understand. Some people want to read the same translation that is read aloud in their church; others want a fresh way of looking at things. Finding a Bible that you like, and that you will want to read, is incredibly important.

If you can, go to a store that sells a variety of different Bibles, and set aside time to look through and compare them. It can be helpful to select one passage and look at it in a variety of different Bibles (Psalm 121, Ephesians 3:14-21, and Luke 15:1-7 are good possibilities, or choose your favorite Bible story!) If you are unable to go to a store, many websites have a "look inside" function, where you can see a few pages to get an idea of what the Bible might be like. Or, your church library, your minister, or even your public library might have a selection of different Bibles that you can look at and compare.

HERE ARE A FEW BIBLES TO CONSIDER:

* *The New Revised Standard Version (NRSV)*. This is the translation that we used for the excerpts in *The Path*. There are lots of different NRSV Bibles. An NRSV study Bible, such as *The New Oxford Annotated Bible* or *The Access Bible*, is a great choice. These study Bibles contain introductions to each book of the Bible, as well as notes about the culture and background of the Bible.

* *The Message* by Eugene Peterson. This is a modern rendering of the Bible that can be easier to read than other translations. It can be a good place to start if you find the language of the Bible intimidating or difficult to understand.

* *The Common English Study Bible (CEB)*. This is a modern translation that gives a fresh perspective to the words of the Bible while remaining faithful to the original text. The notes, maps, and charts are easy to read and understand.

* *The New Jerusalem Bible*. If you like poetry, this translation does a wonderful job of rendering the beautiful poetry of the biblical texts while still being easy to read.

ADDITIONAL RESOURCES

All you need in order to read the Bible is a Bible. Nothing can replace reading God's Word for yourself, and that is the most important thing to do. However, if you are interested, there are lots of books that you can read in addition to the Bible that might help deepen your understanding of the text. Below are just a few possibilities of the many great books that can help enhance your understanding of scripture.

INTRODUCTIONS TO THE BIBLE

The Bible Makes Sense by Walter Brueggemann, published by St. Anthony Messenger Press, Cincinnati, Ohio, 1989.

Making Sense of the Bible: Rediscovering the Power of Scripture Today by Adam Hamilton, published by HarperOne, New York, 2014.

Bible Babel: Making Sense of the Most Talked About Book of All Time by Kristin Swenson, published by Harper Perennial, New York, 2010.

Opening the Bible: The New Church's Teaching Series, Volume 2 by Roger Ferlo, published by Cowley Publications, Cambridge, Massachusetts, 1997.

HarperCollins Bible Commentary by James L. Mays, published by HarperOne, New York, 2000.

HarperCollins Bible Dictionary by Mark Allan Powell, published by HarperOne, New York, 2011.

Bible Women: All Their Words and Why They Matter by Lindsay Hardin Freeman, published by Forward Movement, Cincinnati, Ohio, 2014.

HOW TO READ THE BIBLE

The Bible Challenge: Read the Bible in a Year, edited by Marek P. Zabriskie, published by Forward Movement, Cincinnati, Ohio, 2012.

Scripture and the Authority of God: How to Read the Bible Today by N.T. Wright, published by HarperCollins, New York, 2013.

Sensing God: Reading Scripture with All Our Senses by Roger Ferlo, published by Cowley Publications, Cambridge, Massachusetts, 2002.

Conversations with Scripture and with Each Other by M. Thomas Shaw, SSJE, published by Rowman & Littlefield Publishers, Lanham, Maryland, 2008.

Writing in the Margins: Connecting with God on the Pages of Your Bible by Lisa Nichols Hickman, published by Abingdon Press, Nashville, Tenessee, 2013.

NEW TESTAMENT

Introducing the New Testament: A Historical, Literary, and Theological Survey by Mark Allan Powell, published by Baker Academic, Grand Rapids, Michigan, 2009.

The New Testament: a Very Short Introduction by Luke Timothy Johnson, published by Oxford University Press, Oxford, 2010

An Introduction to the New Testament by Raymond E. Brown, published by Yale University Press, New Haven, 1997.

OLD TESTAMENT

Getting Involved with God: Rediscovering the Old Testament by Ellen Davis, published by Cowley Publications, Cambridge, Massachusetts, 2001.

An Introduction to the Old Testament: The Canon and Christian Imagination by Walter Brueggemann, published by Westminster John Knox Press, Louisville and London, 2003.

This Strange and Sacred Scripture: Wrestling with the Old Testament and Its Oddities by Matthew Schlimm, published by Baker Academic, Grand Rapids, Michigan, 2015.

The Old Testament: A Very Short Introduction by Michael Coogan, published by Oxford University Press, Oxford, 2008.

SPECIFIC BOOKS OF THE BIBLE

If you are interested in learning more about a certain book or facet of the Bible, it can be helpful to get a commentary that is focused specifically on that book. Below are a few good commentary series that have resources on many, if not all, of the books of the Bible.

- *The 50 Day Bible Challenge*: This series includes volumes on each of the four gospels: Matthew, Mark, Luke, and John. Edited by Marek P. Zabriskie and published by Forward Movement, these books include the full text of each gospel, with daily reflections, prayers, and questions.

- *Conversations with Scripture* is a good, easy to read and understand series that has volumes on many of the biblical books. These books are written specifically in the Anglican tradition.

- *Interpretation: A Bible Commentary for Teaching and Preaching* has volumes for almost every biblical book. These are a little more in-depth, but still easy to read and understand.

- *The New Testament for Everyone* series is written by
  N.T. Wright, a bishop in the Church of England. The
  commentary series has small, easy-to-read volumes on
  each of the books of the New Testament. There is also a
  companion series, *The N.T. Wright for Everyone Bible Study
  Guides*, that offers a chapter by chapter survey of each book
  with accompanying reflection questions.

About the Editors

Melody Wilson Shobe is an Episcopal priest who has served churches in Rhode Island and Texas. A passionate lover of the Bible, she hears God speaking in a new way every time she reads this extraordinary story. A graduate of Tufts University and Virginia Theological Seminary, Melody is currently working on curriculum development for Forward Movement. Melody, her husband, and their two daughters live in Dallas, Texas, where she spends her spare time reading stories, building forts, conquering playgrounds, baking cookies, and exploring nature.

David Creech is an assistant professor of religion at Concordia College in Moorhead, Minnesota. Prior to earning his Ph.D. in theology from Loyola University Chicago, David earned a B.A. in anthropology from the University of California at Santa Barbara and an M.Div. from Fuller Theological Seminary in Pasadena, California. He spends most of his days reading, thinking, teaching, and writing on early Christianity. In his free time, he works as a short-order cook for his three delightful kids.

About the Illustrator

Roger Speer is a lifelong servant of The Episcopal Church. He has served with mission, congregational, diocesan, national, and international formation initiatives during an exciting tenure as a youth minister. At heart, Roger is an artist and craftsman. He holds degrees in art education and graphic design, as well as various training certifications that he uses to produce new ways to express the gospel with as much innovation as possible. He is husband to Fran and father to Fynn.

The icons featured at the beginning of each chapter are part of larger illustrations created by Speer for each story of *The Path*. They are available in color in *The Path: Family Storybook* or as coloring pages in *Pathways of Faith*, an all-ages coloring book. Both are available at www.ForwardMovement.org.

About Forward Movement

Forward Movement is committed to inspiring disciples and empowering evangelists. While we produce great resources like this book, Forward Movement is not a publishing company. We are a ministry.

Our mission is to support you in your spiritual journey, to help you grow as a follower of Jesus Christ. Publishing books, daily reflections, studies for small groups, and online resources is an important way that we live out this ministry. More than a half million people read our daily devotions through *Forward Day by Day,* which is also available in Spanish (*Adelante Día a Día*) and Braille, online, as a podcast, and as an app for your smartphones or tablets. It is mailed to more than fifty countries, and we donate nearly 30,000 copies each quarter to prisons, hospitals, and nursing homes. We actively seek partners across the Church and look for ways to provide resources that inspire and challenge.

A ministry of The Episcopal Church for eighty years, Forward Movement is a nonprofit organization funded by sales of resources and gifts from generous donors.

To learn more about Forward Movement and our resources, please visit us at www.ForwardMovement.org (or www.VenAdelante.org).

We are delighted to be doing this work and invite your prayers and support.